D0120386

TALES OF A

Cross Country Skier

Guy Sheridan

The Oxford Illustrated Press

© Guy Sheridan, 1987

ISBN 0–946609–47–0

Published by:
The Oxford Illustrated Press Limited, Haynes
Publishing Group, Sparkford, Nr Yeovil, Somerset
BA22 7JJ, England.

Haynes Publications Inc., 861 Lawrence Drive,
Newbury Park, California 91320, USA.

Printed in England by:
J.H. Haynes and Co. Limited, Sparkford, Nr. Yeovil,
Somerset.

British Library Cataloguing in Publication Data: 87-83276

Library of Congress Catalog Card Number
Sheridan, Guy
  Tales of a cross-country skier.
  1. Cross-country skiing
  I. Title
  796.93'092'4   GV855.3

ISBN 0-946609-47-0

Contents

Acknowledgements

I would like to thank the following for their help;

Molly for maps, diagrams and drawings.
Hugh Sheridan for advice on the draft manuscript.
Joan Garnsworthy for typing the draft manuscript.
Morten Smith-Petersen for checking my Norwegian spelling.
Erik Boehlke and Odd Eliassen for those long and 'short' tours.
The Royal Marines for teaching me and for their support.

For Molly and Peta

Foreword

Any idea that cross-country, or Nordic, skiing is only for those wanting a gentle wander on skis, not too far from the resort, will be dispelled by reading Guy Sheridan's descriptions in this book of his splendidly demanding adventures, ranging from international racing to very long, fast, ski-journeys in big, remote mountains.

The use of skis for travelling goes back thousands of years in Scandinavia; and even today in Lapland it is possible to buy the long, wide skis traditionally used by Lapp hunters.

Cross-country skiing should be seen as a sport evolving naturally from these long traditions, with an emphasis on the practicality and efficiency of travelling through snow-covered terrain, made easier and faster by lightweight equipment such as the edged, waxless ski and improved boots and bindings.

Like Guy Sheridan, I first started skiing in the Royal Marine Commandos, and it is plain to see how their emphasis on living and travelling in winter mountains, in most conditions of snow or weather, has provided a sound and robust basis for his approach to ski-touring. My own journeys include Scandinavia from end to end on Nordic skis, and the Alps from end to end on Alpine skis; and I have long wanted to read about the major journeys, especially those in Iran, Kashmir and the Yukon, which Guy Sheridan was undertaking at the same time, and which in some ways set new standards for this type of adventure.

This book tells, in a most refreshing way, the story of these expeditions, and brings out the problems necessarily involved in travelling such long distances on such a light-weight basis, together with something of the joy of doing so. It shows also the great contribution made by the two brilliant Norwegian mountaineers and skiers, Odd Eliassen and Eric Boehlke, with their ability to ski fast over very long distances, and to live off the country where possible.

It is often said, wrongly in my view, that only Alpine skis are suitable for mountain ski-touring. In fact, the Alps were skied from end to end on Nordic skis by an Austrian party in 1970; and I hope that the present book will be a further demonstration that the use of modern Nordic mountain skis is a perfectly valid option, even on steep ground, with their greater lightness and simplicity, and the dynamic freedom this creates, offsetting their lesser degree of control.

Guy Sheridan's journeys also show that, for the cross-country skier, the traditional techniques of the stem-Christie and the parallel swing, as used in Alpine skiing, together with the Nordic skating turns, are perfectly satisfactory in a wide range of snow conditions, especially when carrying loads, delightful though the alternative Telemark technique undoubtedly is.

To many of those interested in cross-country skiing, this book will I hope be an encouragement and an inspiration.

First, to those aspiring to competitive skiing, who may see something of the fun, adventure and discipline involved.

And secondly to all those seeking true freedom and adventure with their Nordic mountain skis in the winter moorlands and hills, whether in Britain or abroad. Even in Britain, the scope is great, with plenty of opportunities in most winters on the high moorlands of the Pennines, the Peak or Dartmoor, or on many of the hills of Wales, the Lake District and Scotland. I have even done the South Downs Way (Eastbourne to near Petersfield) on Nordic skis one hard winter!

For myself, I will be re-reading it, in the hope that, perhaps, one day soon, I may try to follow one of Guy Sheridan's routes.

What better than that others should be inspired to do likewise?

A. Blackshaw
(Chairman, British Ski Federation Ski-touring Committee)

Early Years and The Uniformed Connection

It was on a brilliantly warm August day in 1961, high on the Jostedals glacier, in Norway, that I first tried to stand on skis.

'Get with the problem Sheridan!' growled Jim who was the latest officer recruit to the Cliff Assault Troop, a specialist organisation in the Royal Marines towards which I had aspirations. It must have been my tenth attempt to untangle myself from those cumbersome long things attached to my feet, and I muffled a curse as my efforts came to naught.

'Come on you wimp!' he shouted again, shattering any residual pride. I tried hard, but our summer excursion to the Jotunheim mountains was over before I got anywhere near mastering a snow-plough turn, and almost a year and a half passed before I had another opportunity to ski.

I had volunteered for the Cliff Leaders Branch of the Royal Marines which was responsible for maintaining the Corps' experience of operating in snow and cold weather. I badly wanted to go on their annual winter training course in Norway as an entrée to the Branch. Hearing nothing for several weeks, I worried. But early in January I was put out of my misery and told to join the Cold Weather Warfare Course at Lympstone in Devon prior to travelling to Norway. I'd been accepted!

I was 'over the moon' and after excitedly informing my mother of the forthcoming adventure (she did not exactly share my enthusiasm), I drove over to Lympstone in an ageing and misfiring Morris Minor Convertible. The snow lay nearly a metre deep on Woodbury Common, which is a 200-metre high area of scrubby heathland and woods near Exeter. As I topped the crest to drop the 8 kilometres down to the Marine camp on the estuary of the Exe, I could see the rolling hills of Dartmoor on the horizon to the west. They were enveloped in a blanket of snow and I hoped that all this snow here in Devon would not spoil our chances of going to Norway.

'These are cobbly-wobblies,' Sergeant Bill Morrow decreed holding aloft a pair of boots 'and you will be using these on your skis this afternoon.' They looked no more like a pair of ski boots than did a pair of flip-flops. The 35 of us on the course were bemused and wondered what was coming next.

'And this is how you fit them to your boards.' A 'board' appeared, held aloft by an assistant. It resembled a plank, was painted white, and in its middle there was a large, cumbersome-looking binding topped by a butterfly nut. So this was what we were going to ski on! Bewilderment spread on the faces of all of us sitting around the stage. In two quick movements, Bill Morrow demonstrated how to fit cobbly-wobbly to board.

'Tighten up the toe strap, adjust the heel strap and away you go', he said confidently.

Our first lesson over, we were dismissed for 'Stand Easy', the splendid naval tradition of a mid-morning tea-break, and were issued with our cobbly-wobblies, boards, skis (210 cm) and sticks (140 cm) for the use of 6 foot 2-inch Jock and shortie Geordie alike. We had an early lunch, which was more an extension of 'Stand Easy', before boarding two lorries and heading the 8 kilometres up to Woodbury Common where we had our first glimpse of how things should be done.

'Pay great attention,' quipped Bill Morrow in a way befitting his Irishness, 'because tomorrow we're doing something special and *kind!*' That baffled us!

Not many of us learned much that afternoon but we could rise after a fall and that was important, so Bill Morrow said. Who were we to argue? The uncertainty of the morning and what was being hatched up for us dominated our thoughts and chatter during the journey back to camp.

The next day, as dawn was breaking and with muscles stiff from unusual exertions, we each drew a carrier pack and clattered into the back of two lorries, skis and sticks and all. We drove off in temperatures of $-5\,°C$, over Haldon Hill through Bovey Tracey and up towards Haytor on the eastern edge of Dartmoor where we parked in a lay-by.

'Fall in over there, in front of those bales of hay,' shouted Colour Sergeant Pusser Hill, one of the stalwarts of the Cliff Assault Troop. 'This afternoon we're going to do our little bit for community relations,' he said. 'Out over there,' he went on, pointing his ski stick up and beyond Haytor, 'are a whole heap of sheep which haven't eaten for the best part of two weeks. Well, see those bales of hay over there? You're going up over the hill to deliver their rations to them. Any questions?'

Just sheer incredulity.

'Right then, here's some ski wax, apply it thick under the middle of your boards.' I remember it was coloured blue and looked like a thick candle.

'Sharpen it up, we haven't got all day.' Perhaps the Colour Sergeant's anxiety was justified. No doubt he had visions of 35 men in total disarray, attempting to get back to the lay-by well after dark. 'Ready? Okay. Secure a bale on your carrying frame and follow me.'

We did, quite orderly at first, trying to get some sort of style into awkward shuffling movements. The bale of hay was not particularly heavy and strapped high on the frame it settled nicely on the shoulders. The snow was crisp for it was about $-2\,°C$; there was little wind but a front was visibly approaching high up to the west.

'Ideal conditions', one of the leaders was heard to say. And I suppose they were but what did we know about it to warrant a challenge? The shuffle slowly developed into a short slide as confidence and balance emerged. The slope steepened slightly, for we were skirting round to the north of Haytor, following the line of an old mining tramway and we must have been a curious sight to anyone who had just finished his lunch-time pint at the Rock Inn.

'Put your weight on your arms—use your sticks and push', Bill Morrow urged, as one by one we struggled with a steep little bump. 'If you find yourselves slipping back, lift the ski up and bang it down onto the snow. It'll help you get better grip.' He demonstrated. So that was what the wax was really for! It did just that and to our great surprise we slid down the other side too. Clever stuff this wax; gives you grip up a hill yet lets you slide down the other side! My fading memory of school physics tried to grapple with the rationale of this phenomenon. It failed, so I concentrated body and soul on keeping up with the fellow in front and avoiding the back end of his skis.

It must have been an hour and a half before we ditched our bales of hay. About a hundred grateful sheep were soon tucking into the stuff, and, thus lightened of our loads, we almost took off. We were gathered into groups of twelve and we had some lessons shortly afterwards on a good slope of hard packed snow.

'This is the fun part.' Our instructors had no trouble convincing us. 'You have just had a taste of things to come. It's going to be hard graft in Norway.' We spent an hour or so on that slope watching and practising, responding if we could to the cries of 'Weight on the lower ski! Face down the fall line! Bend the knees! Tips together. Open the legs! Get those skis apart!' We fell and fell. We became soaking wet. Up and down, a herring-bone here, a sidestep there, a kick turn on the end of a traverse to gain the top of the slope and then down again. Seemingly no progress, but what a lot of fun, and certainly something Dartmoor had hardly witnessed before.

The cobbly-wobblies were quite comfy and did a fine job keeping our feet warm and dry. They were unusual boots which had been produced for the harsh winter conditions of Korea some ten years before, and they had a rather bulbous double toe cap, reminiscent of a clown's boot. They were never made for skiing though and they dearly needed a groove to take the heel strap of the ski binding. Attempts at some diagonal gait instruction on the return to the lay-by highlighted this and torpedoed the attempts of most at having a go. Nevertheless, the basic cross-country skiing technique had been demonstrated: it is a bewildering gait, a mixture of tuning into the Blue Danube waltz, conducting the arms with a back swing on the one-two-three and doing a sliding balancing act on one foot while the other kicks back to propel you forward.

By the end of that week, we had progressed in the art and had ploughed our way through the remotest parts of Woodbury Common. We had even blazed a trail around the 10 kilometres of the Royal Marines cross-country running course which had its exciting descents and laborious climbs. Years later when I ran the course I remember thinking how much more preferable and seemingly less effort it was to ski around it, well above all the water, mud and gravel.

We received our briefing for the journey to Norway from Captain Ted Goddard (Uncle Edward), who was to be the 'Boss' over there. He was a big man and his size, close-cropped hair and bullish shoulders were ample, unspeaking evidence that his nickname 'Punchy' was probably justified. Our course, he said, was to be held in the home of the 2nd Battalion of the Norwegian Brigade North in a small village called Överbygd, just 50 kilometres as the crow flies from the Swedish/Finnish frontier.

The crossing to Bergen in Norway was smooth although our arrival on board with rifles and equipment brought interested inquiries from our Norwegian hosts. In Bergen we transferred to a smaller ferry for the five-day steam up the coast of Norway to Finnsnes. The ferry was built in the early 1920s, and furnished in the rich characteristic style of boats between the world wars. It had large open reception areas and a great flowing panelled staircase, but its triple expansion reciprocating steam engines were not going to break any records on the route north up the coast. Over drinks in the evenings, the tales of derring-do were told and pictures of the many characters who had served in the Cliff Assault Troop over the years began to emerge. Names like Joe Barry, Tom Patey, Sam Bemrose, Happy Day, Zeke Deacon, Vivian Stevenson (Steve), Mike Banks and Tim Priest; characters all, and legendary climbing exploits associated with most.

As we idled up through the islands past Namsos into Sandnessjøen and on towards Bodø, the nights grew longer and the snow deeper. When we crossed the Arctic Circle we chugged below the sun's horizon into a world of grey-blue cold skies with only the summits of the towering mountains heralding the return of the sun in early February. We passed Narvik at night and with its lights twinkling in the clear air it was a scene right out of Hansel and Gretel.

Once round the head of Ofotfjord and out of the glare of Narvik's lights, we were treated to a dazzling display of the other lights, the northern ones, the premier act of many we were to see from the stage of north Norway.

> And the sky of night was alive with light, with a throbbing, thrilling flame;
> Amber and rose and violet, opal and gold it came.
> It swept the sky like a giant scythe, it quivered back to a wedge.
> Argently bright, it cleft the night with a wavy golden edge.

Robert W. Service had captured the scene in those words he wrote over half a century before when he was in the Klondike far away in the Yukon Territory of Canada, and now, at the same latitude but on the other side of the Pole, the scene was the same, and how evocative those words were.

We arrived in Finnsnes the next afternoon. It had taken us a week to get there and for each one of us it was an extravagant experience. Steve met us on the quay-side and we were brought back to military reality. The course had begun. Överbygd and the camp called Skjøld were a good $1^1/2$ hours' drive by bus from Finnsnes. There was an awesome amount of snow and for those of us in Norway for the first time it was impressive. For a twenty-year-old with little memory of travel from the shores of Britain, this was all very exciting, and however much 'hard graft' was to be imposed upon us, just finding out how to go about our daily lives was going to be adventure enough!

We were issued with Norwegian Army ski boots and a variety of other bits and pieces and we met our Norwegian ski instructors, Sven Svendsen and Gerhard Grøtland. These two hardy men of the north were also to be our liaison officers with the 2nd Battalion from which all our numerous requirements would be met. The memories of that first week are of graceful demonstrations of the diagonal gait and how it should be done; of double-sticking, of three-phasing, of ascending and descending, and we learned a good deal more about waxing and the part it plays in cross-country skiing. Gerhard explained how important it was to select the correct wax to grip the snow when kicking off and going up a hill yet which would allow you to slide easily over the snow and down the hills. There were different types of wax for the different types of snow and temperatures that we would come across. He described how the snow crystals could be of many shapes and sizes and how they adhered to the wax when the ski was stationary, however momentary that was, yet when it was moving the pressure of the ski passing over the snow caused the crystals to thaw sufficiently to lose their grip and so allow the ski to slide forward. We were baffled by the science and Gerhard could see this: 'Do not worry we'll tell you what to put on every morning when we start—it's green today.'

Reassured, we applied and polished Swix green wax on to the whole sole and snaked off onto the football field to practise some more diagonal gait. Behind the camp there was a road which zig-zagged up the hillside to the Mauk, the name of the mountain looming over Skjøld. In the winter this road became a compacted rutted ski run used by the 2nd Battalion horses, sledges and oversnow vehicles (called Weasels) to reach the firing range at the top.

It was in the beginning of our second week that we donned rucksacks and, shuffling under their weight, set off up the track to dig snow holes. We were given a pulk, a Norwegian word for a shallow, boat-shaped sledge to carry our equipment. It was graft, hard, hard graft going up that hill, as we pulled and grunted on the traces of the pulk, sweat pouring beneath long johns and vests. So this was what Uncle Edward had gloated about back in Devon! He was right again but thanks to the wax I had liberally applied, the purgatory was at least reduced a little. Coporal Dave Pendleton was the brake man and he pushed with the tip of his ski stick from the back end as we both herring-boned up the steeper parts. It was a struggle. The unloved pulk is still with us today and another generation can tell the same tale of sweat and tears.

Military skiers, heavily loaded with rucksacks and rifles.

Snow holes were fun and warm but we became wet digging them and on the firing range the next day we were shown that there were other uses for our skis. We used them for crawling: lying on top of them and with butterfly movements with the arms, furrowing through deep snow. We bundled them up and pulled them behind us. We used our sticks to support our rifles when we fired them. We attacked unseen enemy on them; hilarity itself—the battle of the Mauk was fought and refought. Night patrols under the spectacle of the northern lights passed the long hours of darkness quicker than we could imagine. All the time, I suppose, we improved. It was cold too. While we were up there the temperature dropped to −43 °C down in the valley at Skjøld.

We had been up on the Mauk for the best part of a week and it was time to go down that rutted track. Uncle Edward and the instructors departed ahead. No doubt experience told them to keep clear of two-week-old novices on a five-kilometre downhill run—especially when one of them was bringing down a pulk (my brake man had scuttled over the edge and disappeared with a cry of 'Yippie!').

No-one heard the warning shout of the first man. What he had seen was 100 horses and men on their way *up* the track, about to meet 35 of us in the 'bomb' position on our way down! The retreat from Moscow could not have been a patch on the devastation that followed. Some horses bolted to either side, their handlers unable to restrain them. For my own part, I did the only thing possible when a laden pulk is attached to the waist—I sat down hoping to retain my place ahead of the sledge. There was no hope and the thing whizzed passed me spinning me around as it went by. Fortunately we spun off the track and came to a halt in deep snow. The second battle of the Mauk ended as abruptly as it began with the Brits the clear losers. The cost—many bruises, at least a dozen broken skis and a desire to get to the bar to inflate the experience!

The final act of the four-week course was the 10-kilometre race. Steve and Bill Morrow were the favourites to win, but it was the clock that most of us were against—65 minutes was the target for the award of the Norwegian bronze badge. The course was the usual one used by the 2nd Battalion and it weaved its way up, down and through the birch and pine forests surrounding Överbygd. 'Nothing difficult about it', postulated Steve. But that did not stop the adrenalin. Gerhard announced the wax of the day. Green it was to be. There was to be no secrecy between us on this race, no spying to see what wax our opponent was using. If Gerhard got it wrong, we all got it wrong. Some may think that 65 minutes is rather generous for a mere 10 kilometres. This may be so, but a pair of Norwegian Army skis with their bindings weighs in at 11 lb (5 kg) and the pundits will tell you every pound on the feet is equivalent to five on your back. No matter, that race was a personal little challenge for each of us.

My performance was far from brilliant but I scraped in two or three seconds under the hour and finished about half way up the field. Gerhard covered the course in $38^1/_2$ minutes.

Our journey home in an RAF Britannia bore none of the comforts of the outward leg. Many of us were impatient to get home, and away from *lapskaus,* a traditional Norwegian stew that seemed to be the staple diet for the military, but for me my love affair with Norway was just beginning, and I wanted to stay.

That summer Steve and Bill Morrow taught me how to climb—mostly in Cornwall where the sun shone on the red granite nearly all the time. Their love for climbing and excellence on the rock was impossible for me to match and I was never any good beyond Hard Severe, but I enjoyed it immensely and got to know every cliff in West Penwith while Steve produced the draft for the first guide book of the peninsula. They were heady days and I won my ticket into the Cliff Assault Troop and with it a guarantee of returning to the snow.

Snow was not to feature in my life for another eighteen months, during which time I enjoyed a very different sort of soldiering in the jungles of Sarawak and Sabah. With more experience under my belt, I returned home in January 1965 and by the end of the month found myself back at Skjøld. The place had not changed but Uncle Edward had long departed to roast in the heat of Aden. Steve had almost written himself off in a car smash in the Cairngorms, and was recovering from a broken neck. Pusser was in the jungles of the Far East but another Hill had appeared. Jan Hill. Now he was a king of a character. He came from Liskeard in Cornwall and, although I had not met him before, his reputation in the Branch was well ahead of him. He and I were despatched down the road to a large village called Saetermoen, there to teach 'Percy' the art of skiing.

'Percy' comprised a battery of 80 artillerymen on their first trip to Norway. I did not relish the idea one little bit—after all, I'd only just learned to ski myself.

Then along came Reidar Kjellstrup. He was a tall lieutenant from the Norwegian 1st Battalion whose home was on one of the outlying islands near Tromsø. He had seen the German battleship Tirpitz bombed and sunk near Tromsø during the war and had the scars on his legs of gunshot wounds inflicted by the Germans when he was fifteen. Reidar was a man of phenomenal patience and during the ten days that we were at Saetermoen before 'Percy' arrived, he worked Jan and me to the bone on the nearby ski track.

Reidar demonstrated and cajoled. He explained the mechanism of three

14

and four-phase alternating steps, of double poling, single and together with a kick, the faster tempo of climbing, and he hammered home the importance the sticks played in every movement. He drove us morning and afternoon until we were exhausted and weak from the effort, but encouraged us by saying it would all click into place so long as we gave it all we had. We did skating turns, snow ploughs, stems, and practised the crouch of the straight downhill run. We had never worked at anything with such ferocity and while progress seemed slow to begin with, it clicked in the end, just as Reidar said it would. We were better men for it and we were undoubtedly in better physical shape.

'Why don't you buy some skis?' Reidar asked one evening after we had been round the 10-kilometre track. 'You'll find it so much easier than using the Army ones.'

Reidar guided me to some Bonna skis. They were not racing ones but something in between, slightly wider and marginally heavier. Reidar got the shop to fit the bindings and I measured up for a pair of boots and a set of cane sticks. Like a dog with two tails I ventured out on my first pair of skis onto the floodlit ski track that evening. And wow, what an amazing difference!

Jan was a master of hoax, a practical joker of unequalled ability with a persuasion that fifteen years in the Climbing Branch had generated. I constantly fell victim to the 'bites' (a service term for falling for something hook, line and sinker), one of which was perpetrated by Jan.

In March 1965, Jan and I were 'umpires' for a company on the final exercise of that winter's training. We were to arbitrate the battles between opposing forces and that could mean anything from accompanying ski patrols day or night to following the company into the attack. On a final exercise umpires are very busy but are probably more comfortable and warm than their charges as they usually operate from vehicles. For this exercise we were joined by a Norwegian officer, Kjell Haavaldsen.

For the five-day exercise we shared the tasks, until the final attack, which I told Jan and Kjell I would do: it was a night ski of about 20 kilometres, climbing most of the way, with some activity at the end and an assault on the 'enemy' at dawn. Jan and Kjell would try and go forward by Weasel and hopefully we would all meet up at the end. I packed my kit and asked Jan to move it for me on the Weasel, declaring that I would be on the move all night and should not need it.

'Come on, Sir,' he quipped. 'Don't let me down, you know you should never get separated from your kit!'

'But . . .' my reply tailed off.

Of course he was correct and being still very much a learner, I donned my heavy rucksack and set off into the murk.

15

We skied all night. It was a long way and mostly uphill and 'spent' would not have described my condition the next morning. A dawn attack heralded the end of the exercise and I skied back to pick up my rucksack at the top of that hill. The Weasel was there.

'You b------!' I said with an acknowledging smile. I knew I had fallen for another bite!

'If you can't take a joke, you shouldn't have joined!'

Bites or otherwise, jokes or no jokes, the winter of '65 was magic. I thought, rather arrogantly perhaps, that I could now ski and felt that my love affair with Norway was beginning to blossom.

'You're going to Finland!' Terry Wills, the boss, had called me into his office in Evjemoen, just north of Kristiansand in southern Norway. Gerhard Grøtland was there and the gap between us in the 10-kilometre ski race had reduced. I was elated by that but even more by this surprise announcement. The visit was for a month and with a bit of luck, if I could take my Easter leave over there, I could accrue a total of $3^1/2$ months on snow that winter.

The Finns never do things by half measures. They had given the numerically superior Russians exceedingly bloody noses during their winter war in 1939–40, and were respected by the Germans too, against whom they also turned later in the war. They are masters of the sauna and smile at birch twig flagellation in the searing heat of 100 °C before an icy cold plunge. (It is not the depraved activity some may think—try it one day and you'll see what I mean!) Sausages fry on the stones while beer is kept cold in the snow outside the door, and you feel sparkling at the end of it all.

They can ski too. They ski over the sea ice, using their sticks to spread their long flowing greatcoats like sails so that the wind pushes them along at 10 kilometres an hour. One night we went almost 50 kilometres like that through the archipelago off the southern coast.

Luutenanti Charlie Palosarri, whom I had met at Lympstone the previous summer, took me to see the World Military Nordic Skiing Championships being run in Hämeenlinna, a small town some 100 kilometres north of Helsinki. I watched several competitions including the 30-kilometre individual and the 20-kilometre 4-man patrol races. It was exciting stuff and if ever I could pick a point in time when my interest towards racing began, I think it was during those few days.

Jarvinen, the Finnish ski manufacturers, had provided a sales tent at the competition and Charlie talked them into giving me a pair of skis, complete with bindings. They were proper racing skis and a lot lighter than the Bonnas I had brought with me from Norway. I was a proud man

16

and had a marvellous time trying them out. My enjoyment of Finland was made complete when I was told I could go up to Finnish Lapland for my two weeks' Easter leave.

The Coastal Jaeger Battalion had organised a military flight for me and Markhu Holte, another Luutenanti. This would take us up to Rovaniemi where we planned to take a bus to Kilpisjärvi where there is a large, remote and expensive hotel in the middle of some wonderful skiing terrain. Unfortunately for me, however, the month in the environs of Helsinki had been a drain on my pocket and hence I had a dilemma. I had enough cash for either food or the hotel but not for both. Thus, in the bus up from Rovaniemi, I told Markhu of my plan. 'I'm going to build an igloo outside the hotel', I declared, wondering what his reaction would be.

'Okay I'll help you.'

'No, no,' realising that he did not know why. 'I'm going to live in it!'

'Oh, I see. Well you can use my room for a bath', he said calmly.

The igloo was built and Markhu helped me. I never knew what he thought of me but I joined him for meals every day at the hotel. My liquid stocks from the Embassy dwindled slowly and I made friends with a couple of Lapps who gave me two reindeer skins and a pair of 'Finesko', the traditional Lapp boots, all for several generous tots. I now had a fine carpet to sleep upon!

The weather was cold and sunny every day and early in the holiday we skied many times the several kilometres to the Lapp camp where we were warmly received and invited into their wigwam-style tents; they too had layer upon layer of reindeer skins on their floor. A fire was burning in the middle and the smoke that didn't escape through the top smarted our eyes. We joined them for freshly barbecued reindeer meat and enjoyed their company until it was time to return.

We skied up Saanatunturi, the steep mountain overlooking Kilpisjärvi, and made a glorious descent towards the *tregrensespunkt*, the point where Finnish, Swedish and Norwegian frontiers meet. Skiing at these latitudes is delightful in mid-April: the sun is high and warm and the days are long but the snow remains cold—that well-favoured 'spring snow'. As an added bonus, Markhu and I met two sisters, so now we had good company wherever we went and danced into the small hours at the hotel, despite being satisfyingly fatigued after each day's skiing. The holiday was over too quickly and we departed by bus to Rovaniemi where we connected with an old Beaver aeroplane of the Finnish Air Force for the flight back to Helsinki.

My cousin, Cinders, was an air hostess on the flight from Helsinki to London and I was fêted with solitary attention in the first-class compartment of the plane. The Attaché had taken me to the airport, and when Cinders saw me in the terminal and ran over and gave me a kiss, I heard him remark to his wife 'Good God, I didn't know these Marines were so well organised!'

Yet another winter passed. Then 1967 and 1968. Norway was becoming routine but more alluring with every visit. Although I had a gap of two years while I was working in Oman, my embrace with Norway continued through my racing years and into 1972 when I was given command of the Mountain and Arctic Warfare Cadre.

The Cadre, a new name for the old Cliff Assault Troop, had moved up to Arbroath on the east coast of Scotland. Its home was now alongside 45 Commando, then commanded by Lieutenant Colonel Steuart Pringle (later to be the Commandant General and to lose a leg in an IRA bomb explosion in London). Concurrent with the British withdrawal from the Far East, there emerged a renewed interest in north Norway and Royal Marines began their first complete commando winter deployment in January 1973. I based myself with a company at Drevya, a Norwegian Army camp in the middle of a forest about 20 kilometres from Mosjøen.

I toured the civilian race circuit every weekend, competition still in my blood after the disappointment of the Olympic year (more about that in a following chapter), and attempted, sometimes successfully, to interest others. Jonathan Thomson, the Commander of the company (and a member of the British Orienteering Team that year), was a skiing enthusiast who was making such good progress that he was posing a threat to my hope of dominating the 20-kilometre military biathlon race which everyone had to complete! This race is physically demanding and has to be done on military skis, with an 11-kilogram rucksack and rifle. The results of the shooting are crucial: for every shot missed a two-minute penalty is accrued with no possibility of making up time by skiing fast.

The result of that race is of no consequence but Jonathan has never forgiven me for yelling 'track' to him on a long, narrow and particularly fast downhill stretch. Now, it is an unwritten law that if you hear 'track' yelled from behind, you have to get off it to allow the faster man to pass. But skiing ethics demand that you don't do this on a downhill stretch. You can imagine the result on a narrow fast track and this incident was no exception. I could hear the sound of trees being demolished behind me. Later I felt ashamed at my inconsiderate behaviour.

Shortly after that disgraceful breach of ski ethics, we travelled north and broke away from the main exercise with 45 Commando to go and do some winter climbing in the Lyngen Alps. The Cadre had received special clearance to go up there for some military mountaineering, but I needed to get up there for a good look before declaring our intentions to the Norwegians. We were loaned a jeep by the 2nd Battalion at Skjøld (nothing had changed there in ten years) and, together with Mike McMullen and Sergeant Don McLeod, we drove up to the tiny hamlet of Storeng, on the side of Lyngenfjord. The transport disappeared with a rendezvous arranged for the following evening.

We began skiing up Steindalen at midday. The snow was deep, it was an effort and not long after leaving the road we were forced by steep ground either side to weave to and fro upon fragile snow bridges on the river itself. Once past that narrow defile, the valley opened to reveal the Steindalen glacier snout and an ice fall a little higher up. Cloud obscured the remainder. We traversed up on the north side to reach a lateral moraine and found a spot to camp on the ice and below a high moraine ridge. Beyond the ridge there was a large dip before the ground rose quite steeply up into the cloud.

Three in a two-man tent is cosy but when I tell you that Mike was an extremely large man, and Don McLeod was no dwarf either, the scene was set for a fairly lousy night. Which indeed it was. Sandwiched between them, head up near the entrance, I chose to do the cooking. I thought I had been smart getting the best place but was rudely reminded that it was not by the clumsy midnight excursions of both my companions. It became extremely cold in the early hours, and the dawn broke at $-18\,°C$, red and clear.

We clambered out of the chaos of the tent and skied off up the glacier, roped up for safety. The scene was staggering. On either side two giants overhung the glacier, Gaskacakka (1,516 metres) to the north and Steindalstind (1,504 metres) to the south. Subsidiary ridges stretched down to the west from each, and then curved to meet each other like the claws of a pincer. It was through the gap that the glacier tumbled. Beyond was revealed a fairy-tale glacier basin about 700 metres above sea level, some 5 kilometres long and 3 kilometres wide, shaped like an inverted heart; a mini Koncordia. Rimming it to the north-west sat Nallangaisi, at 1,600 metres a magnificent sight, and Anntind (1,504 metres) with its cap of ice to the south. Between the two a pyramid of rock rose like a needle—Sfinxen—appropriately named.

Once above the ice fall, we unroped and skied the length and breadth of the basin, catching a veiw of Jiekkevarri from the narrow col to the north-east. The Lyngen Alps are real little alps, and we could easily have been on the Koncordia Platz in the Bernese Oberland. There were hanging glaciers, blue-green ice falls, and violent snow-plastered precipices in every direction—cold, portentous, and at that moment, silent. My mind was made up; it was to this glacier basin that we would come and base ourselves for 2¹/2 weeks in the middle of March.

We tried to descend the glacier roped up but our effort at synchronised changes of direction turned rope into spaghetti.

'To hell with the rope', roared Mike as Don and I added to the pile, tripped up by some unseen and unavoidable bight of white nylon. After that we 'bombed' it to the tent. At the end of our stay, we left behind the tent and a few bits of climbing gear to await our return.

Back in Skjøld, we joined some members of the 2nd Battalion in their cellar mess. Mike grabbed his guitar and the ingredients of a late night were upon us. He had a character as large as his frame, was a marvel on his guitar which was never far from him, and an irrepressible fount of songs, bawdy and otherwise. I had been with him to the summit of the Matterhorn and a couple of other peaks the summer before and knew him well. He was due to leave the Corps shortly after our return to the UK to follow his passion for sailing and make a living out of it. His disappearance at sea during the Single-Handed Trans-Atlantic race in 1976 is a mystery and a colossal tragedy. We talk of him still today; a character and what a chum.

The low pressures weaving in from the Norwegian Sea during the first fortnight of March hardly abated and they deposited huge snowfalls all over the north. Lyngen would be dangerous in those conditions so we waited for a clear spell and for the sun to do its work. Even this far north, the sun had residual warmth in mid-March. Because the wireless had been pumping out avalanche warnings, my $2^1/_2$-week plan had to be slashed to 2 weeks before we received the okay from the Norwegians to go.

There were 32 of us. Sergeants Don McLeod and Chris Chrystal were soon organising everyone into ferry parties, loading pulks with tents and food, and masses of climbing gear. With an intermediate camp halfway up and in the middle of the glacier, we thought we would be able to get everything up into the glacier basin in four days which would give us eight days for winter mountaineering before having to return to the road. Once the trail had been blazed, the ski track was almost a motorway of compacted snow. Easy going for some, but the pulk pullers had a hard time of it. Sweat gushed all the way up to the halfway camp and although the return run dried it off somewhat, the downhill was relished by everyone, oblivious of another round of pain ahead of them.

The cloud base was low when I set off from the camp on the glacier with Don McLeod to retrieve the tent left a fortnight before. As we skied the 4–500 metres over to the lateral moraine, there was a mighty roar and crash coming from dead ahead. We stopped in our tracks and after a few seconds were engulfed in a fine deluge of powder snow which slowly settled. In the ghostly silence that followed Don and I looked at each other. The chatter of the boys back at the camp had also stopped. We waited a few minutes and then skied gingerly over towards the edge of the moraine. As we dipped slightly we skied into the chaos of avalanche debris. Its size was soon apparent. The avalanche had been colossal and it had thundered down a steep couloir between the two peaks of Gaskacakka and Nallancakka. The cloud obscured its origin but all the snow of the previous two weeks must have come down because there was no sign of the high moraine ridge, and the dip behind it was also filled. Our tent was below it all. We tried to probe for it the next day but without success, so we abandoned the idea after an hour. It had been a close call and the tent wasn't that important.

Alerted to the danger of further avalanches, we pressed on up through the ice fall, our tracks zig-zagging through lines of crevasses and snow bridges, and into the middle of the basin. Here it would be safe to establish our camp. We had a wonderful time up there, skiing to the routes we wanted to do, depositing skis and sticks, and then completing a variety of them in magnificent surroundings. Each day's effort was rewarded with a 'banzai' ski descent back to the tents. We felt we were pioneering; indeed Sigurd Frisvold, our Norwegian Liaison Officer and boss of the Jaeger troop in the 2nd Battalion, reckoned most of our mixed routes were probably firsts. We cared little about that because it was just satisfying to be there and enjoy ski mountaineering at its best.

The last five days were spent in idyllic spring conditions. The sun was hot, and we achieved much before it was time to pack up and go. Pulks were given to the better skiers for the descent through the ice fall to the snout of the glacier. While the snow in the basin was good and cold, as we descended so it became progressively more slushy. Below the glacier in the valley, the river had opened and patches of heather and rocks had broken through the old track.

As we gathered together at the snout of the glacier, we heard the drone of a small aircraft. It flew betwen Sfinxen and Anntind and was soon skimming down the glacier towards and over us. It turned tightly and flew back, quite low. It was as though they were trying to see how we were going to negotiate ourselves and the pulks over the heather, rocks and open river further below. But then a packet was heaved out of the co-pilot's door and the aircraft climbed back into the sky and disappeared the way it had come. It was the mail!

We have come a long way since the days of a small course on the cobbly-wobblies of the late fifties and early sixties. Norway has paled for many, but for a few who share the same affinity with Norway as myself, it matters not whether it is the ninth or fifteenth winter over there. For us the appeal remains and we have the Royal Marines to thank for making it all possible. As I write, my eighteenth winter lies ahead and I cannot think of anything to better that prospect.

Competition

Gerhard Grøtland started the itch at Evjemoen, south Norway in 1966 and Charlie Palosarri compounded it by convincing the Jarvinen ski agent in Hämeenlinna, Finland, to release a pair of skis to a plodder. It is these two people who can be held responsible for my obsession with cross–country skiing. Whether on Pusser's planks (the name given to anything issued by the navy), or lightweight racing skis, I revelled in feeling the technique of kick and glide working, the wax giving the correct amount of grip and slip and arriving at the finish of a race in a satisfyingly tired condition knowing I had mustered everything for it. Anyone who has tested himself in competition will know that feeling and know how unquantifiable it is.

In the mid sixties there seemed to be no science to the way we did things in the Royal Marines. Every single thing was attacked with ferocity. PT in the mornings before we went climbing effectively reduced us to shivering, wheezing wrecks in obvious oxygen debt and with muscles denuded of glycogen. It was the same when we went 'ashore' in the evening. No half measures, just eight to twelve pints and the midnight oil burned to catch up on things wanting. Slowly, however, I began to realise that if I wanted to improve my individual results, I would have to make some sacrifices and impose some self discipline—especially once I decided to get into serious competition and perhaps into the national squad.

The winter of 1968 was my fifth in Norway and I decided to try my hand in a couple of races organised by the 3rd Battalion of Norway's Brigade North, on one of the northernmost islands in the Lofoten. I worked hard on the floodlit ski track every evening until two days before the first event, when I was cast into the sick bay with a high temperature. I had glandular fever and was moved to hospital where I stayed for two weeks. Upset at having missed the races, further disappointment was to come my way when I received notice that I had been drafted to a secondment with the Sultan of Oman's Armed Forces (SAF). I had asked for the job, but the reality of its divorcing me from pursuing skiing for two years was that much harder to accept while already feeling very sorry for myself.

An Arabic language course seemed utterly incongruous in Beaconsfield in April, but I attended it along with seven other officers, and twelve weeks later emerged with a pass and a cheque for £150, courtesy of the Civil Service. We all passed and thought we deserved the money although Mr Nasser, our Jordanian teacher, did not. He was glad to see the back of us for we were a stroppy lot and the course officer told us so.

What little Arabic I learned was lost in the next two weeks of leave when I joined my old friend Douglas Keelan in Chamonix to do some ski mountaineering. Douglas had just returned from the Falkland Islands where he was commanding Naval Party 8901 in Port Stanley, and had been to the Alps before a few times. We drove down in a battered old Mini Traveller, following the way of many impecunious climbers before us, and camped in a field in Argentière. We used the téléphérique to gain the Grand Montet and although it was late May, there was plenty of snow so we skied up to the Argentière hut. The glacier and hut were utterly deserted and we had an exciting week up there entirely on our own. But what amateurs we were on our Pusser's planks! This was serious country and on reflection we were lucky not to have an accident.

I flew out to Bahrain with Ranulph Twistleton-Wykeham-Fiennes and Patrick Brooke in mid-June. We had all been on the course at Beaconsfield together and now we were to join the Muscat Regiment in the SAF. Ranulph inherited his baronetcy at the age of a few months. A handsome member of the aristocracy and belonging to an expensive regiment, he is an unequalled extrovert. Visiting him in his room at Beaconsfield was akin to participating in a game of Russian roulette. After knocking on his door and listening for the yell to 'come in!', you soon learned to stand back, for more often than not, a knife would slice through the air and quiver into the plasterboard wall opposite. The perforations in the wall were evidence that this was a well-practised routine. 'Practising for my trip down the Nile', he'd said the first time I witnessed it.

Ranulph had taken his ski team from the Royal Scots Greys down to Bavaria the previous winter and on the plane we discussed Nordic skiing and racing. He described how the Army had its own Nordic races every year and that the Ski Federation of Great Britain had linked into these to call them the British and Army Championships. They were run for about three weeks in late January every year at a place called Oberjoch. Ranulph sensed I was more than just inquisitive.

'You wouldn't even bring up the rear, anyway, what do you know about it?' he baited. Since we had met in the Arabic classroom, a healthy rivalry had sprung up between us.

I had to get to Oberjoch if I wanted to fulfil this desire for competition and I decided that as soon as I reached Muscat I would try to lobby the commanding officer for my mid-tour leave to be in December and January.

When the Gulf Air Fokker Friendship landed in Muscat we disembarked into a humid boiler, simmering at 44 °C and 99% humidity. I had hardly clambered down the steps from the plane and reached mother earth when the CO strolled over and introduced himself.

'Hello Guy, I'm Peter Thwaites, your Colonel.'

'Good morning, Colonel, nice to be here', I lied.

'Don't get off the aeroplane, you're going on to Salalah to join 'C' Company.' Perhaps Salalah in Dhofar was less humid than Muscat! I tried to shout goodbye to Ran and Patrick, but they had disappeared into an airport building. As I turned to reascend the steps the Colonel passed me an envelope—

'You're not to open this until you have taken off!'

'Very good Sir!' Spice of life I thought! As soon as we had taken off I opened the envelope. The letter went something like this:

Dear Guy
I am sorry it was a rush at Bait al Falaj and time precluded me from giving you more of a welcome to Muscat and the Regiment. You are to join 'C' Company of the Regiment currently on operations in the Jebel* near Salalah. The Company is half Baluch half Arab and is commanded temporarily by Mike Peel, who will arrange for you to be issued all your equipment.

You are strongly advised to learn by heart the following commands in Arabic as you will most certainly need them in the coming weeks: take cover, covering fire, left flanking, right flanking. There are more which common-sense will tell you.

You should also ensure you know how to direct artillery fire. Good luck and I look forward to seeing you in about six weeks.
Yours ever
Peter.
*Jebel—Arabic for mountains.

Wow! There's nothing like being thrown in the deep end to concentrate the mind. I wished I had paid more attention to Mr Nasser in Beaconsfield, but I tried not to flap and reckoned that Mike Peel could get me out of any scrapes.

Any thoughts of a mid-tour skiing leave were put to one side whilst I completed an exciting six weeks with 'C' Company in the Jebel. After that we moved on to the north to Rostaq, an old fortified village nestling under the eastern side of the mountains of Jebel Akhdar. Mike Peel left us and Simon Sloane arrived to take command of the Company.

Having earned my baptism in the Regiment, I thought it reasonable to ask for my mid-tour leave and I explained to the Colonel what my plans were. He listened attentively.

'But you've only just arrived!'

'I know, but I'll be back for the work-up for the Battalion's tour in Salalah in March!' I said quickly, having anticipated his objection. 'Okay, let the Adjutant know and he'll fix your flights.'

What a relief! Now I was committed to the races in Oberjoch in January, I had to find out how to enter them and where, meanwhile, to train on snow. In early September I began some physical preparation. This progressed smoothly until one day Ranulph made a passing comment that I should do some shooting. 'Good practice for the biathlon races', he emphasised. Biathlon? I had no idea what it was, but I had my MK5 Pusser's Lee Enfield, so it wouldn't be difficult to arrange some shooting.

The real priority, however, was to work out a progressive running programme up to the end of November. I knew so little about the sport I was committing myself to that there was no scientific approach to what I should do, so I just worked instinctively, measuring and marking distances on the local jeep tracks, and wherever possible avoiding villages. Simon, who was nearing the end of his second year in the SAF, had warned me off running near the villages, pointing out that there was still a certain amount of resentment towards foreigners and that to bare one's legs and run in shorts would be offensive to Arabs—a pity since it was infernally hot and humid.

> Heat like the mouth of a hell, and deluge of cataract skies
> Stench of old offal decaying, and infinite torment of flies

Someone had written those lines over a century before during the troubled times of British rule in India. Rostaq was no different. To make matters worse, every time I ran out of the small camp that was 'C' Company's home, I had no choice but to pass the company abbatoir. It was no sterile tiled room with running water, efficient drainage and white-coated men, but just a spot in the desert where a wooden frame stood, and from which the slaughtered beasts were hung to be skinned, while a number of goats' heads, the remainder of that day's lunch, lay on the ground staring grotesquely into the sky, the offal being gobbled up by the flies.

That I have no record of my training is ample evidence that my efforts had no magic to them—I used my watch and simply attempted to better my previous time on each run. One thing I do recall however, is the heat. Daily temperatures were in the region of 45 °C until November when they cooled to a more tolerable 32 °C. With the drop in temperature, humidity fell as well. Nevertheless, it always took about an hour to cool down after a run, and only then when encouraged by the draught from an overworked air conditioner. The Omani and Baluchi soldiers must have thought I was mad, as indeed did Simon, my boss. An Argyll and Sutherland Highlander and a fine soldier, he favoured the good life and was actually finalising his order for a Fortnum and Mason Christmas hamper when I left Rostaq in early December for the three-hour bumpy drive to Bait al Falaj to catch the plane for home. By then, I believed I had done all I could do to prepare myself for the competition ahead.

Jim Goldsworthy, that person who had bellowed to me on the Jostedals glacier all those years ago, announced his engagement in December to a Norwegian lass from Harstad. I saw him briefly in London and he asked me to be his best man at the wedding which was to be in Harstad on Saturday, 1st February, 1969. The timing would be just right; it would come after the races in Germany so I could relax and enjoy the party, and I could just get it all in before having to return to Muscat. I agreed, caught the bus out to Heathrow and flew to Oslo.

On the flight over, I found myself sitting next to a lean, fit-looking fellow.

'I'm Spud Leaning', he said. 'What brings you to Norway then?'

Friendly fellow this, I thought, and unusually direct!

I explained that I was going to find a place to ski before going on to Germany and the Championships.

'Why don't you come and join me and my people?' he suggested.

'But who are you?' I asked.

Spud told his story. He had been in the British Ski Team himself and had raced in the Olympics in Grenoble the previous year. He was a major in 94 Locating Regiment Royal Artillery, and was flying over to train his regimental ski team for the very same championships in Bavaria.

'Are you serious about your offer?' I asked, at the same time questioning whether I would be better off on my own or among people who knew what the game was all about.

'We can fit you in Guy, you're very welcome.' I couldn't believe my good fortune.

His team were at Skramstadsaeter, about 15 kilometres up in the hills from Rena in the east of Norway. They had rented a warm, comfortable hut in just the right sort of environment for good, hard ski training. Spud turned out to be a mean task master and the disciplines of an Olympic skier were quickly imposed on his team of eight young men, including myself. The routine was fierce and I was under no illusions that my technique left much to be desired. My Mitty-like confidence from north Norway the previous winter was quickly shattered as I realised this, and wondered whether it was worth all the effort. Occasionally despair loomed, usually due to exhaustion, and then I thought I would have been better languishing with a bird on a beach in Tenerife and not pumping my heart out in –15 °C.

My Jarvinen skis were all I had. They had seen better days and were hopeless for racing, according to Spud. He had negotiated a good deal with Blå Skia and he encouraged me to take advantage of it and buy two pairs for 260 kroner (£13 at that time)—one with hickory soles and lignostone edges and the other with birch soles and hickory edges. I thought my Jarvinens were light but these, with the bindings, weighed in at just 1.7 kilos.

We made our own tracks for training and the more we used them, the better they became. Today there are machines that make tracks, but Spud was sure that the physical effort of wading through deep snow could only be beneficial. I am sure he was right because when it was time to go down to Germany at the end of December, we were all feeling extremely fit and ready for a race or two.

The first race was on 12th January 1969 at Mittenwald in Bavaria. It was 15 kilometres long, and run in brilliant sunshine on firm snow. Spud had told us which wax to use and it had worked well. There were 222 starters, mostly from the 1st Division of the British Army of the Rhine, and I had a good race, coming in 2nd to Phil Hoyland. Spud broke a ski stick and was not pleased with his 22nd place. Phil's time was 57 minutes and I was exactly 2 minutes behind him, but pleased to be one of the two to get in under the hour. With only one other race to do, the 4 x 10-kilometre relay, before departing for the main championships in Oberjoch, I harboured the unspoken confidence that if I could produce the same results there, I could possibly break into the echelons of the élite.

The Nationals at Oberjoch were a different affair and the confidence gained at Mittenwald was soon shaken. In the 15-kilometre race held on a crisp sunny morning on 25th January I pulled in at 16th. Disappointing— but I gained a little compensating satisfaction by finishing a minute closer to Phil Hoyland and getting in ahead of three members of the national team. The track was well made, in places very steep, and it was extremely fast and icy. No advice was available for waxing and if I were to recall what particular lessons I had learned in those first efforts of serious competition, I could narrow them down to two: I had to become more competent and confident going downhill, so I needed to practise using racing skis on downhill pistes, and I had to take a keener interest in waxing so I should keep a waxing diary to learn the peculiar qualities of each and how they performed in varying temperatures.

Before I left Germany I watched the biathlon race. This event was run over 20 kilometres carrying a rifle and 20 rounds of ammunition. This particular day there were three loops to be run each of about 4-kilometres after the first visit to the range. I had never seen a biathlon competition before and my attention was drawn particularly to the routines of each competitor on the range.

From the start line there was a 4-kilometre lead into the range where five shots in the lying down position were fired at one of two targets 150 metres away. Skiers then raced off one end of the range onto a 4-kilometre loop, to come into the range again but this time for five shots in the standing position at the other target. Off again they went to complete another 4-kilometre loop, returning for five more shots lying down, before disappearing on yet another 4-kilometre loop to return to the range for a final standing shoot. After that it was a race for the last 4 kilometres to the finish.

BIATHLON TARGET

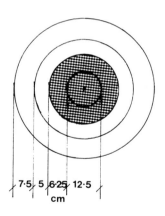

7·5 5 6·25 12·5
cm

The scoring areas for both lying and standing positions on the biathlon target. Scoring time penalties – lying: 12.5cm (nil), 6.25cm (1 min), outside (2 mins). Standing: 5cm (nil), 7.5cm (1 min), outside (2 mins).

The rules for the sport had been changed after the 1964 Olympics. At that time the first shoot was at 250 metres, then on down to 200, 150 and finally 100 metres. The adjustment of the rifle sight to suit each range was all important and one more thing to think about during a race. Biathlons were undoubtedly a lot more demanding for those who raced then but now the scoring areas for the two positions were different sizes and at 150 metres they looked dismally small and far away.

Penalty minutes for each shot missed were added to actual running time and it was obvious that fast running could not make up for bad shooting.

I felt exhausted watching that race but, before I left to catch my train, I managed to rush over to the race office to sneak away with a copy of the race rules and a spare cardboard target grudgingly provided by the armourers' shop. I said a grateful goodbye to Spud and clutching skis and happy memories, disappeared down the hill to Sonthofen for the long journey to Kiel and Oslo. I read the rules from cover to cover and before reaching Oslo had made up my mind to buy a biathlon rifle. How, what, when, and where, I would try to resolve after Jim's wedding in Harstad.

Jim's 'nuptials' were more enervating than a dozen ski marathons and were based on the Viking Hotel in the centre of the pretty little town where five of us lodged in a double room. Douglas Keelan, John Barry, Ed Means, Oliver Spankie and I drew lots for the three beds in the one room booked for us. Douglas and I lost out although with little caring as we were sure we were destined not to spend too much time in the horizontal!

Jim, Douglas and John were working in Skjøld and had driven over with a bunch of the Climbing Branch instructors—familiar faces all but grumpy that they had to bring their No 1 blue uniforms to Norway. For this was to be a military wedding, the like of which the modern triangular-shaped church in the centre of the town had never witnessed before. Oliver had driven up from our Embassy in Helsinki and Ed, a Marine Corps officer, had flown in from the States.

Ghastly hangovers blurred the wedding rehearsal and it was snowing heavily when the service began. The 'Jas' of the vows over, I walked over from my seat beside the best lady, to present the ring box to the priest. When I sat down again, I became conscious of being the centre of attention. The priest was revealing an empty box. I hurriedly searched the two large patch pockets of my jacket to see whether the ring had fallen out of the box. There was nothing there. Wondering what to do next, I looked down the aisle and happened to catch a guilty twinkle in Douglas' eye and a snigger of a smile from John, who was sitting beside him. This was a mean 'bite' I thought, but I had to do something quickly so I got up and, trying to appear calm and deliberate, slowly walked down the aisle to where Douglas sat. I recovered the ring and returned to the altar. The whole incident lasted less than a minute but I was embarrassed and feared the ensuing confrontation with parents, bride and groom.

Back at my seat and trying to appear as though nothing had happened, I caught Douglas' eye, and winked, partly to acknowledge the joke but also to say 'Just you wait!' Douglas, however, took the wink to be the signal for the guard of honour to leave and prepare themselves for an archway of ski sticks and ice axes outside. The second embarrassment in as many minutes began and caused the bride and groom to turn their heads and join the

29

remainder of the surprised congregation in watching all twelve Royals march out of the church.

But I had the last laugh!

The service far from over, the guard with their archway of winter implements had to stand outside for half an hour, the snow lying over an inch deep on their caps and uniforms, before Jim and his bride emerged. Perhaps divine justice was dispensed after all!

The reception and subsequent revelry are a tale too long to tell, but I did have a chat to an interesting character from the 3rd Battalion called Harald Hartvigsen. He asked me whether I would like to race in a 20-kilometre biathlon race the next morning.

'After this party? You must be joking!'

'*Nei,* it's a late start so it should be okay' Harald replied.

'Let me think about it.'

I then relied on the party to create diversions and a discreet lapse in memory, and avoided Harald for the best part of the evening. It was no good, Harald had perceived my ploy, and I was successfully ambushed with no avenue for retreat. My start time and number were in the hotel room when I clambered unsteadily and hiccupping into my sleeping bag on the floor. *Fait accompli!*

I raced not feeling 100 per cent and having borrowed a rifle from Kurt-Arne Olsen, a good shottist serving in the same Battalion as Harald. To my surprise I only achieved an eight-minute penalty by missing four shots out of the twenty and this brought me up to 7th place. I returned the rifle to Kurt-Arne and got from him the address of the manufacturers. That afternoon Douglas and John dropped me off at Bardufoss airfield to catch the evening SAS flight to Oslo. As the plane lifted into the air a sigh of relief confirmed that my mid-tour leave was over.

Within twenty-four hours I was on a BOAC flight to Bahrain, leaving skis and winter clothes behind with my mother in London. In Muscat I was met by Parshambe, my faithful orderly, who had brought my landrover from Rostaq. Back in another world, the reality of it was reinforced by the warmth of the Muscat winter: 29 °C. The bumpy three-hour ride back to Rostaq was spent catching up on the news in Arabic, rusty from eight weeks' absence.

The Battalion's work-up programme for a year's tour on operations in Dhofar, where a Communist-inspired revolt against Sultan Said bin Taimur had become quite a nasty menace, gave little time to do much else than get the Company ready for what lay ahead. We were earnest in our endeavours and we needed to be. The weekly situation reports from the Northern Frontier Regiment, whom we were to relieve in March, had revealed an increased proficiency and boldness amongst the rebels *(adoo)* and contacts with them, often bloody, were becoming more frequent. We roamed the high plateaux of Jebel Akhdar doing our infantry things and 2,000 metres above sea level in February, it was cold work. After one overnight storm, we awoke to 20 centimetres of snow around us and Jebel Shams, at 3,018 metres the loftiest summit of the Akhdar massif, shimmered white in the early morning sunlight—a sight rarely seen. Although the snow had been burnt off within two hours by the warm winter sun, I regretted not having a pair of skis to hand.

A month later in March 1969, I wrote to Spud asking for advice on summer training with an eye for a break at Oberjoch the following winter. Back came a small booklet in Norwegian entitled *Trennigs program, Langrenn menn.* Printed and distributed by the Norwegian Ski Federation, it had been devised by Kristen Kvello and Oddmund Jensen, both highly respected experts in cross-country ski racing. If I could stick to the book, Spud wrote, then I could be in with a chance. He had underlined the word 'could'.

Before we left Rostaq for the four-day drive down to Dhofar, I sat down and composed a letter direct to the Commandant General of the Royal Marines in London. My eighteen-month secondment was due to end in January 1970 and I asked him for support in my request to be relieved three months early. This would enable me to train and attempt to break into the British team at the National Championships in January 1970. I told him also that I felt confident that I could then aim for the 1972 Olympics. The letter was posted and I shuddered at the thought of how it might be received. Anxiety accompanied the wait for the reply.

'Nothing ventured, nothing gained, if you don't ask you don't get', said Simon, trying to bolster my flagging confidence.

A month passed before I received a reply. The Commandant General said that all would be done to try to find a fully-qualified relief as he believed in principle that it would be beneficial to the Corps for me to compete. I was overjoyed and although the Regiment would undoubtedly question who was to be the beneficiary, I cared not one jot. The vital thing for me was that I now had a target to aim for, and barring an *adoo* bullet, nothing was going to stop me.

A letter ordering a biathlon rifle from Kongsberg Vapenfabrikk in Norway lay sealed and ready to post, and when that long-awaited letter from London arrived, off it went with a cheque for £105 which included the cost of air freighting the weapon to Muscat. When it arrived we unwrapped the parcel and assembled the bits the same evening in the mess. I was like a dog with two tails!

It was June before I was able to begin any form of training.

Operations on the Jebel, mostly at night, and spanning in some cases several days, took rightful priority. It was physical work anyway, and personal aspirations had to be put to one side. Apart from the occasional daydream when mind and body got a chance to rest from the tempo of active service and its attending pressures, life was interestingly and demandingly schemed with trying to outwit the bandidos. They clobbered us and we reciprocated harder in hit-and-run affairs; it was absorbing, exciting and dangerous stuff. In June, at the beginning of the southwest monsoon, and as the mist and rain rolled in from the sea, we moved off the Jebel and down to the flat Salalah plains to a tin-roofed comp at Umm al Gwarif, some 5 kilometres from the town itself.

Although in the middle of the Arabian summer, when temperatures beyond the Jebel would be over 50 °C, a wet blanket of cloud and mist now smothered the plains and Jebel and the temperature dropped to around 30 °C. The fog dampened the tempo of operations and time was available for other things. The little green book from Norway became more comprehensible following the arrival in the post of a dictionary sent by my mother in Kent, who lovingly wondered why I wanted such a thing in Arabia! It was time to start training for the winter and soon my dedication to that little green book probably matched that of the *adoo* to their little red one by Mao Tse Tung. So the monsoon rolled its way through the mid-summer months of June, July and August 1969.

Four days' training a week in June and July built up to five in August; initially two days' distance (or endurance) work, 1 hour and $1^1/2$ hours on each, interval work using ski sticks for short hard bursts uphill, doing a special ski stride incorporating a springy kick with each foot (interval is a series of intense sprints with rests or jogging in between when the heart will reduce from about 180 beats to about 110 a minute), and strength and stretching exercises for stomach, arms and legs on the third day, and more distance on the fourth.

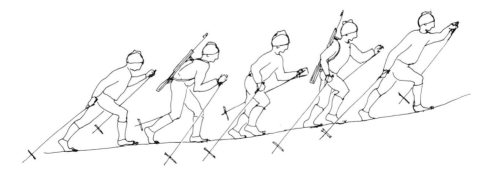

Skigang training: striding uphill using sticks and carrying a rifle.

I had found an ingenious set of weights in an oasis on the drive down from Muscat where the rusty remains of an oil camp scarred the skyline. It was a scaffolding bar with a drilling bit welded into each end. It had probably been invented by an American oilman, inspired to maintain square shoulders in the monotony of desert life. The Transport Department provided some tyre inner tubes which, when cut up into long strips 5 centimetres wide, were secured to a supporting post on the verandah outside my room in the mess. These were useful for imitating the front to rear arm movement of skiing. The tighter the rubber was drawn before the exercise, the harder it was for the arms, thus improvement, albeit slow and arduous, was possible. There was however one proviso made by the Colonel. He insisted that any training I did outside the camp wire had to be escorted. Parshambe and my driver Pir Mohammed were very happy to do this so long, they said, as I didn't make them run with me.

Four miles across the plains and across a shallow dry river bed was a set of four steep little hills. These were about 3 kilometres from the foot of the Jebel and all interval training with ski sticks was done over there. The battalion chippy had made up a set of targets and painted the bulls-eyes to the same measurements as the example I had got hold of in Oberjoch. Shooting was possible almost anywhere and I measured 150 metres out into the plains from a small bank of sand, a spitting distance from the sentries on the camp gate. I could maintain a circuit round the barbed wire security fence of the camp and thus do some running and shooting, more often referred to in the discipline as combination training. The battalion abbatoir was nearby and each session on the range became a game of dodgems with swarms of bloated bluebottles. I had always wondered why abbatoirs in the Sultan's Army were always outside the main gate of the camp!

By August, the effort of sticking to the little green book was beginning to have results: my resting pulse was down and much more was possible than I could ever have accomplished two months before. Actual training was recorded as shown in the table (page 34).

Operations contined apace and my diary records that on my tabulated training schedule for August, the Company was on operations from 1st to 4th; I lay in an ambush from 5th to 8th; was out on patrol for the night of 11th and 12th, the night of 14th, the morning of 16th, 25th, 26th and 29th.

My relief arrived on Monday 8th September 1969 and I flew to Bahrain the next day and home to the United Kingdom the day after that. I was saddened to leave the Regiment four months before schedule. The fifteen-month tour had passed by too quickly and I flew out with memories of the wonderful soldiers of 'C' Company. All were known to

Skigang — a summer training activity using
sticks and carrying a rifle

	Distance Running	Time (mins)	Skigang	Arms with elastic	Interval	Strength Squats 100lb	Pulse	Combination Shooting 4 x 1000m standing st = standing ly = lying
1	9 miles	58.30						
2			6 x 1 min	5 x 1½ mins	40 mins	2 x 30 sqts 2 x 30 situps		
3								st 1 ly 9 10 mins
4						2 x 30 sqts 2 x 30 situps		
5								
6								
7								
8								
9	10 miles	70.00		3 x 2½ mins		2 x 30 sqts 2 x 30 situps		
10			6 x 1 min		52 mins			st 3 ly 5 8 mins
11	10 miles	66.00		3 x 2½ mins		2 x 30 sqts 2 x 30 situps		
12								
13			5 x 45 secs		58 mins			st 5 ly 4 9 mins
14	10 miles	65.30						
15							56	st 5 ly 3 8 mins
16	10 miles	65.30		5 x 1½ mins		2 x 35 sqts 2 x 35 situps		
17			8 x 45 secs		48 mins			st 0 ly 7 13 mins
18	7 miles	44.30		3 x 2½ mins		2 x 35 sqts 2 x 35 situps		
19								
20	10 miles	64.30						st 5 ly 7 12 mins
21			5 x 1 min		61 mins			
22								st 2 ly 7 9 mins
23	10 miles	64.30		5 x 1½ mins		2 x 35 sqts 2 x 35 situps		
24	8 miles	55.00						st 1 ly 5 6 mins
25				3 x 2½ mins		2 x 35 sqts 2 x 35 situps		
26								
27	10 miles	67.00						st 8 ly 8 16 mins
28			5 x 45 secs		65 mins			
29							48	st 6 ly 6 12 mins
30	8 miles	51.00		5 x 1½ mins		2 x 35 sqts 2 x 35 situps		
31			8 x 1 min					st 0 ly 11 11 mins

me by name: dozens of Alis, a few Husseins, Salims, Suleimans, Ghulams and a hundred others and we had been through thick and thin together. But now I had to look ahead and begin the punishing programme that the green book suggested for September and October and the lead into the first winter snow.

The national team was scheduled to start training in mid-November at Nordsaeter near Lillehammer. At 800 metres above sea level, snow usually arrived in late October, and the Ski Federation had booked its team into a Norwegian Home Guard hut up there. The team would undoubtedly build a 150-metre shooting range somewhere and make a good track system to train upon, so I thought I ought to start my season up there as well. It would provide the opportunity to watch them use their tracks and their range, and more importantly, it would give me the chance to see how I rated. I reckoned also that I might not be popular but I cared little for what anybody thought; it was results that mattered.

I drove up to Newcastle and boarded the ferry for Bergen on 11th October. My car was stocked to the gunwales with paraphernalia to last me the best part of six months. It was the symbol of my independence and would enable me, over the following few months, to pursue my 'secret' strategy of meeting the national élite in its back garden.

Snow covered only the highest peaks of western Norway when I drove into Voss where, as the guest of a Norwegian Army officer, Per Lødøen, I stayed for three weeks. The tempo of the training programme increased dramatically under Per's direction. He was a brilliant skier himself and knew the routine of summer training better than most, but his real strength lay in good shooting. His was patient daily coaching, on the range at Bømoen, a few kilometres out of Voss. He introduced me to Odd Bakketun, then knocking on the door of the Norwegian junior squad, and together we charged around Hangur and the slopes of Lønahorgi (1,412 metres) which were waiting for winter snows and the arrival of the downhill skiing fraternity. In the last half of October distance training had doubled the figure for August, interval and skigang were increased in the same ratio and more pleasing than anything, shooting results reached a more consistent 4 to 8 minutes' penalty, even though we knew this had to be reduced even more.

In mid-November I drove over to Nordsaeter and found myself a small room in the Sportell and Fjellkro. It didn't take long to discover where the team was living nor to find the tracks that it had prepared. The manager of the team, Martin Bray, came over one evening to the Sportell. I remembered that he had been around the previous winter in Oberjoch, when he was racing with the team, but now he explained that he had opted for the managerial post to take things through to Sapporo in 1972. He warmly supported my crusade and promised to give me a list of the competitions that were planned for the team before they travelled down to Germany in January. With that list, and the guidance of the little green book, I was able to plan training appropriately to lead up to the first competition at Skytterkollen outside Oslo on Boxing Day.

The adjustment from running on foot to the kick and push of skiing is dramatic and for the first few days muscles unused for about seven months were tight and sore. For the first couple of weeks a lot of slow, gentle distance training up to 25–30 kilometres on each trip is necessary maintaining interval training on foot once or twice each week. Once over this period however, the pace of ski training increases and distances are pushed up to 40–50 kilometres for each session. Interval training on skis began to become more significant as the first competition towards the end of December approached. My training log reminds me that between 15th November and 16th December, the date of the first competition, total distance covered was a little over 800 kilometres. A waxing diary kept perfunctorily throughout that time had provided a greater in-depth knowledge of the idiosyncrasies of the various waxes, and with that knowledge came confidence. Shooting, alas, could not be overlooked and visits to the range were an almost daily necessity. Training scores for the combination work varied from a 2-minute penalty, which would evoke a delighted 'Yippie' to pierce the silence and still cold air, to a disappointing 9 or 10 minutes.

The national squad left Nordsaeter just before Christmas. I sensed that many of them resented my being present—perhaps I was a threat to some of them and their rather protected positions in the team. In retrospect, I now think that I should have done my training somewhere else and travelled down to Germany and the Championships as an unknown entity. It was not difficult to notice that the team was living three or four to a room in the Home Guard hut and that such circumstances generated a tense atmosphere where silence more often than not dominated the evenings and the 'off duty' times of the day. It seemed to me that they were on a military exercise and that their regimentation in the close confines of a stuffy hut was not the most conducive environment in which to enjoy the skiing and the efforts demanded of them by their trainer. To my mind, a relaxed and friendly atmosphere was as essential a foundation as the dedication and single mindedness required of each individual. Those six weeks looking in from the sidelines made me wonder whether I really wanted to join them, especially if I was going to be made to live in the same circumstances in the two winters leading up to the Olympics. Perhaps there was no choice but I did register the notion that if I did join them, I would try and continue to train the way I had in the past.

A good shoot with a 4-minute penalty and a fast run got me into 9th position in the Norwegian Home Guard race on Boxing Day ahead of the five from the team who raced. Three more competitions during the following week confirmed a fairly consistent placing in the middle of the team with more accuracy on the range. It could have been better. So I went off back to Nordsaeter for a week and concentrated on range work and more downhilling before heading south for the ferry to Kiel and the long drive down to Oberjoch.

The open biathlon race was on 22nd January. It was −5 °C and the conditions were good and fast. The track was much as I remembered it from the previous year and on the walk around the course the previous day the fast downhill stretches were not the awe–inspiring runs of yesteryear, and I was content that the extra bit of downhilling practice had improved confidence and balance at speed.

Alan Notley won the race by a margin of 4 minutes. He was a veteran of the 1964 Olympics and of 1968 in Grenoble, where he came 44th out of a field of 59. He was an excellent shot and endowed with experience from Bisley. His dominance of the ski track in those championships was clear to all. I was 5th, ahead of half the team, and was inwardly very gratified.

The biathlon relay was run the next day in almost the same conditions. The relay is much more of a spectator event, run over a course of 7.5 kilometres with a lying and standing shoot, one of each. However, instead of having the usual sized targets, this time five small bakelite types were inserted into a target frame. Using a maximum of eight bullets the task was to hit the five targets which shattered on impact. For every target missed, a penalty loop of 2–300 metres to one side of the range had to be run before proceeding back onto the main race track. The relay called for calm steady shooting, the possibility of running the extra 1–1^1/$_2$ kilometres compelling one to slow down and concentrate. It was a marvellously exciting race with a mass start. It was my first experience of the event, and I was asked to join an 'Hors concours' team with Alan Notley and Jeremy MacKenzie. Alan was our lead man, and I was the last to run. We all shot a satisfying clear round with no penalty loops, scoring a clear margin of 14 minutes over the second team and it was a bunch of fun.

During the evening of the prize-giving, Martin Bray as Team Manager trotted over and told me that the Chairman of the Biathlon Nordic Committee in the British Ski Federation wanted to see me. The Chairman was a retired brigadier of the Footguards called Vincent Budge. He was a tall, upright person, with a small moustache and a 'no nonsense' air about him which gave me a sense of apprehension as I approached his table. He introduced himself in a most military fashion.

'How old are you?' he asked with an accusing directness.

'28, Sir.' I wondered what my age had to do with this interview.

'You're a bit old, you know.'

If he thought 28 was old, then he must be a centenarian! I tried unsuccessfully to reason why he had begun in this way.

'What do you mean, Brigadier?' I asked rather cheekily.

'Well, you'll be 34 in '76.' He was right. I couldn't disagree with his mathematics.

'So?'

''76 Olympics. You'll be over the top; it takes 4–6 years to make a biathlete.'

My intuition was to address him openly.

'But I'm interested in the '72 Olympics, Sir', I said with a touch of impudence.

'You've done well down here.' He was thawing. 'I am inviting you to join the team for the remainder of the season. Are you able to and do you want to?'

'Yes to both questions', I blurted out, hardly believing what I had heard. I had a large glass of beer to celebrate, the first for over seven months although none of my friends would believe that! I was as happy as the proverbial porker and very pleased that the efforts and personal expense had paid off.

The next day I drove up to Kiel with Malcolm Hirst and he went through the race programme for the rest of the season. It was pretty full. The World Biathlon Championships were to be held at Östersund, Sweden, and naturally they dominated the fixture list. There were also the Lowlanders Cross-Country Championships in Hurdal, Norway, the Scandinavian Biathlon Championships in Finland, the Swedish Biathlon Championships at Falun and several biathlon and cross-country races of a more local character. We regarded each event as another rung in the ladder of experience at international-level competition and between each Henry Hermansen, the team trainer and himself a veteran of the Squaw Valley Olympics in 1960 when he raced for Norway in the biathlon, cajoled and coerced us to the finer points of technique. The pace was hot, but these were happy times.

Östersund and the World Championships were not for such a newcomer to the sport as myself but the chance to race in Finland, where the World Championships were scheduled for 1971, was a welcome opportunity to try out the course over which those races would be run. It was hard and the profile for it was very much up and down. The relay was just as fierce, the effort being rewarded by a clear round.

While I was there, some old friends from my days with the Finnish Army came to Hämeenlinna for a few days—Charlie Palosarri and one of the sisters I had met in Kilpisjärvi four years before. They watched the competitions and we caught up on each other's news afterwards.

Of the other races we entered that season which held vivid, and painful, memories were the 86-kilometre Vasaloppet in Sweden on 1st March, and the 56-kilometre Bjerkebenar in Norway on 22nd March. Terry Palliser and I were the only ones from the team to choose to do the Vasaloppet as we both thought that the longer distance racing would be beneficial for our endurance experience for subsequent years. We drove up to Salen and stayed with a friendly Swedish family who lived about 8 kilometres from the start. Our start numbers, drawn from the race registration housed in a large school, were 9,394 and 9,393. There were 9,397 starters, we were told, so if we wanted a good position in the line-up, we were advised to go down to the start at least three hours early. We remonstrated with the organisers that because we had been entered by the Ski Federation we ought to be at the head of the line-up, but to no avail.

Several layers of wax were polished into the skis for hour after patient hour. Green to begin with and then cold Blue Rode wax in the middle—the all important weather forecast cruelly placing a question mark over our decision. We could easily add waxes for warmer conditions so, secure in that knowledge we retired early to catch whatever shut-eye the tension would allow.

Our hosts woke us up at three o'clock in the morning and drove us to the start in my car which was then very kindly delivered to the finish in Mora.

Even at four o'clock it seemed that all 9,397 starters had been given the same message as us. Convinced that they had, we elbowed and barged our way through the lattice of skiers, sticks and skis until we got into the 2,000 line-up. We seemed a long way back and it was with despair that we thought of the last words said by our host when we were dropped off: 'You have to go as fast as you can for the first 2 kilometres; get to the bottleneck in the first 1,000 or else.' He was speaking from experience and, looking at the sea of backs ahead of us, it was going to be more than a problem to do that. Terry and I discussed the tactical subterfuge we would need to adopt and concluded that the human wall ahead could only be circumvented by moving on to the sidelines where it might just be possible to get round the hundreds of officials shepherding people hither and thither. We barged, pushed, heaved, tripped and worked our way over and took up station on the side about half an hour before the start. Inch by inch we shuffled forward, sometimes going into the deep snow to one side of the beaten track, and probably improved our line-up by 500, but we were still an awesome way back from the head of the field.

The minutes dragged on. At $-3\,°C$ it was cold standing there; our wax was right, at least for that moment although the temperature was expected to rise in the middle part of the day. To either side of the flat river bed which formed the first 2 kilometres of the race, there was a loudspeaker system which announced the countdown from minus five minutes at 6.55 am. We took our warming-up tops off and draped them over shoulders and joined the other 9,395 slapping their skis up and down, back and forth to remove any clogged snow from the soles. The crescendo of a winning try at a Twickenham final could not compare with the noise that now broke the peace of a remote Swedish valley.

At minus 2 minutes, the human wall jumped the gun; we were taken by surprise and hurriedly cast off our warming-up tops and joined the army of skiers, torsos bent with heads down, arms and legs giving all they could. The adrenalin was released and just as well too. It was a fight for that first 2 kilometres with collisions, broken skis, and falling competitors all having to be avoided with split-second timing. Somehow Terry and I made it within the first 1,000 and had an unrestricted run through the bottleneck. I remember looking back before the four-lane track disappeared into the forest at the start of an 8-kilometre climb, and the human jam in the bottleneck had already formed. Some unfortunates would find themselves there for $1^1/2$ hours before gaining that point. 'Poor sods', I remember thinking. It was time to switch off and get into the rhythm that would provide the best economy of effort for the 84 kilometres ahead.

It was rather a dreary race after 40 kilometres. The track had no downhill excitement with the accompanying rest and momentary regaining of breath. As we neared the end so the sprinkling of well-wishers shouting 'Heia! Heia!' thickened until it became a crowd on the finishing straight. Terry came in at 169th in 5 hours 58 minutes and I followed him 40 minutes later but well within 25 per cent of the winner's time to claim a medal. I wasn't pleased and was very dehydrated. Hindsight told me that I should have stopped at more of the drink stations on the course, and that was what I did religiously during the Bjerkebenar three weeks later.

Like the Vasaloppet, the Bjerkebenar commemorated an historical event. But unlike the Vasaloppet which recreated the epic escape of Gustav Vasa (later the King of Sweden) from the occupying Danes, the Bjerkebenar commemorated the flight of an infant prince in the arms of his escort over the mountains near Lillehammer. The prince weighed 6 kilos and to preserve this factor within the rules of the competition each man has to carry 6 kilos on his back. This was a significant burden on a course which climbed from 200 metres to almost 900 metres above sea level and then descended back to 200 metres over its 56 kilometre length. The race is run between Rena and Lillehammer with the start alternating between the two places year by year. In 1970 it was to Rena that I went with the team trainer, Henry Hermansen. He was in the 42–50 age class and knew the form—he had raced the course several times before and his advice was welcome.

There was not a mass start for everyone so there wasn't the same rush to get to the bottleneck as there was on the Vasaloppet. This time the starts were staggered by age groups, the eldest group being away first. There were over 500 starters in my 21–35 age group but plenty of room to get into a good stride before a gentle narrowing of the field to the neck where the two exit tracks emerged.

From the start it was uphill for 15 kilometres and so when the whistle blew, unlike the flat-out sprint at the Vasaloppet, it was a cautionary speed that the field adopted—such a distance uphill is a long way and calls for conservation of effort. Midway from start line to bottleneck, the Norwegian skiing on my right and slightly astern got his ski tip lodged into the rubber basket of my ski stick. It happened at that moment when my right arm was at the maximum thrust to the rear and his left ski was moving forward after a kick off with the other. The result was my ski stick wedged up into his ski binding, the elasticity of the rubber basket gripping it like a vice. I cursed him in English and he replied with the Norwegian equivalent, and no amount of wrestling with it would free the two. We had to stop and sort ourselves out which involved his taking his ski off and levering the two apart; all we could do was watch the back of the field disappearing out of the bottleneck, up and out of sight.

It took a long time to catch the back of the field and slowly ease past the rearguard, one by one. The first drinking station was at Skramstadsæter 15 kilometres out but there was no time to look about to identify where I had stayed with Spud's team two years before. My wax was perfect and the track was mostly in two lanes, but occasionally expanded to four. Six kilos of sand in the rucksack was packed up high and apart from some chafing at the hips by the light frame it was no trouble—I was used to the similar weight of a rifle and ammunition and it did not seem to be that much of a burden. It was hard work nevertheless, right up to the high undulating country between Hornsjøen and Sjusjøen, where the gentle downhill runs gave the legs a rest while arms pushed and pushed to the extreme.

At the drink station I was over half way up the field and feeling good—far better than I had at the corresponding distance on the Vasaloppet. From that final drink it was virtually all downhill for 16 kilometres to Lillehammer. It was a thrilling and demanding descent of nearly 700 metres and called for extra concentration in the narrowest parts through the forest. The final kilometre weaved down through the outer upper suburbs of the town, swinging into a football field for the last circuit into the finish. Crowds were yelling *'Heia! Heia!'* to everyone as they came into the stadium and I was conscious of a loudspeaker blaring my name.

'Her kommer mannen fra England', and it was all over. Four hours and one minute was on the clock; 30 minutes behind the leader. It was a big gap but I was elated to have got past about three quarters of the field and 15 minutes inside the maximum time to earn a small pewter cup and a medal, upon which were embossed images of the baby prince and his two viking escorts. Bjerkebenar marked the end of the season and it was time to think about going home. Time also to reminisce, evaluate the training I'd done, and more favourably, time to relax and pursue the more normal pastimes of a bachelor approaching his 30s.

The summer of '70, like a good vintage wine, was very fine and I found myself running Royal Marines climbing courses in Cornwall, Wales and Scotland. The Ski Federation had hired a new team trainer, Anders Besseberg, who was a young Army officer studying in the Norges Idrettshogskole in Olso, a kind of national sports university. His scientific summer training programme arrived in July attached to an invitation from the Brigadier to join the team for the 70/71 season. I couldn't say 'no' and the Marines said 'yes'. Almost at the same time an old friend arrived from Singapore for a short visit. Sam Bemrose was on the scrounge for climbing equipment and stores for an expedition he was about to mount to the Himalayas to attempt to scale Menthosa, a 6,400-metre peak in India. He invited me to go along and I couldn't say 'no' to that either. The Brigadier wasn't happy but after some white lies about continuing Anders' programme out in India I eventually received his blessing.

Before flying out to Singapore and India, I drove the car and a small caravan out to Norway. The caravan was on temporary loan from Jim Goldsworthy and was destined to be my home and my way of avoiding having to live in the tense and unwelcome atmosphere of the small hut with the rest of the team. Summer leave could just be scraped up before the flight to the Far East so I took off for the snowfields of the Jostedals glacier in the Norwegian mountains in the company of a girlfriend. It was akin to a pilgrimage to Mecca.

We whiled away ten days in scorching weather with a backdrop to our lonely tent of Lodalskåpå to the north and the Jotunheim and Hurrungene to the east and south. It was idyllic, and skiing with next to nothing on one day, rucksacks deposited not far away containing clothes in case the wind sprang up, our privacy was shattered by the arrival of an aircraft 2,000 metres overhead. Out popped five parachutists which sent us skittling 2 kilometres back to the rucksacks to cover any embarrassment; in the nick of time too. They landed nearby and we were skiing over to see who they were when a voice from behind said 'Hello Guy!'

Someone here who knew me?

'Great God, Ranulph, trust you to disturb the peace!'

'Thought we'd come out and look you up!' The healthy rivalry between us in the Muscat Regiment was still evident after a ten months' break.

Adhering to Anders' heavy training programme was not easy in the following two months in Singapore and India. Sam's expedition was a wonderful experience and Menthosa was scaled for the first time. Lasting friendships were forged and I discovered, rather painfully, that I was not good at altitude. The physical effort of a Himalayan expedition was good for maintaining a level plateau of fitness but it knocked the stuffing out of me and it took a few weeks to get back to normal weight and strength. This didn't go unnoticed and on my return the Brigadier reminded me that I was struggling for a place in the team and that, in short, a few stops had to be pulled out. This upset me at the time, but I had to admit that the remainder of the team was demonstrably in better form. But by adhering to Anders' programme through September and October things got better and by the time we travelled over to Norway in mid-November par had been achieved.

SEPTEMBER AND OCTOBER *Weekly Programme*
6 days a week

1st Day (Sunday)
Distance training: 'Skigang' and running in hill-country.
Heart rate about 140–150
Duration: 3–4 hours

2nd Day (Monday)
A. *Combination training: About 5 x 12 mins, running before shooting. Heart rate about 175.*
B. *Use strengthening apparatus for the arms: 4 series of 4 mins, 3 mins pause between each series.*
C. *Strengthening programme: 4 series of 25 reps. 1 min pause between each station. Stations:*

> *Situps with 15kg.*
> *Neck and back stretches with 10kg.*
> *Explosive jumps with 40kg.*
> *Torso and back strengthening with 10kg.*

3rd Day (Wednesday)
Distance training: 'Skigang' and running in hill-country.
Heart rate about 150.
Duration: 2 hours

4th Day (Thursday)
Same programme as 2nd day (Monday).

5th Day (Friday)
Distance training: 'Skigang' and running in hill-country.
Heart rate about 150.
Duration: $1^1/2$ hours.

6th Day (Saturday)
Interval training: 4 mins running up not too steep a hill, jogging back to the start in about 5 mins, and then start up again; 5 repetitions. At the end of the 4 mins running the heart rate ought to be about 175–180, and after jogging back, just before you start up again the heart rate ought to have fallen to about 100–120.

The World Biathlon Championships in February in Hämeenlinna, Finland, were the focus of the 1970–71 season and Anders geared our training accordingly. I bought a 6.5-mm barrel for my rifle and with it came a bullet with better ballistic qualities, higher muzzle velocity than the 7.62-mm round, and a hope for better shooting. We entered three competitions before going down to Oberjoch and the last of these was one of the Norwegian team selection races at Jonsvatnet near Trondheim. All the great men were there including Magnar Solberg, the 1968 Olympic Gold Medallist, and it was an opportunity to test our rating. The weather was foul and it rained throughout the race—ideal for red Klister wax! A good running time was no compensation for giving away 5 shots to some lucky person by shooting on the wrong target. I cursed a momentary lapse in concentration on the range, and to my fury, I did the same again a week later at Pellestova at another Norwegian team selection race. Trying to analyse the reason for two such lapses, I concluded that I must slow down on the range and take a little longer, perhaps an extra 25–30 seconds.

The Nationals in Oberjoch were run in mixed weather. New falling wet snow played havoc with the field in the Open Biathlon, and I joined another dozen who retired halfway through with seemingly half of all the snow in Oberjoch clogged under their skis. It did nothing to lessen my frustration over the results of those last three important competitions. However, a small gain was made in the relay where a clear round boosted downturned confidence. Better results were beyond reach until the team's return to Norway in early February where a series of races became the catalyst to prove that the poor results in Germany were not our true form. Teamed up with Alan Notley and Geoffrey Stevens, we came 2nd out of 10 teams in the east of Norway Relay Championships. The day before, reaffirmation that a good position in the team was possible was made in the 20-kilometre biathlon with a 3rd place, a shade behind Alan Notley and Peter Strong.

Had there been selection races then these two competitions, and perhaps the nationals, would have decided who was to go to Hameenlinna and the World Biathlon Championships. However, there weren't and it was only two days before the flight to Finland that we were told who was to travel. To my great relief I was amongst them. We flew to Helsinki together with the Norwegian team on 3rd March 1971.

Thirteen nations gathered their teams in the silence of the central square of Hämeenlinna for the opening ceremony. It was −8 °C and snowing very slightly. A pretty girl in a fur hat carried the Union Jack ahead of us and we lined up with the East Germans on our left and the Poles the other side. A magnificent bronze statue of Sibelius, the composer, towered over the square, and on his head was a thick cap of snow. The formality of the occasion was magnified by the colossal bronze and so dominant was it that I recall humming the closing bars of his 5th symphony while welcoming speeches were made in several languages. I felt proud to be there and to have been chosen to race.

The individual 20-kilometre race was won by a Russian, Alexander Tichonov, and Malcolm Hirst came in 16th with a magnificent run and no penalties. He had beaten all the Swedish team. Alan Notley, Keith Oliver and Jeffrey Stevens were a little lower down in the field but without exception, we were all thrilled with Malcolm's fantastic performance. The relay was run on 7th March and I was selected for the anchor leg. It was an unenviable leg to run as a lot could depend on it and it would have been preferable to pitch in as number 2 or 3 when there was considerable other activity going on, but I felt reasonably confident as I knew the course from the previous year and waxing was not critical.

A good supporting crowd shouting 'Hyvaa! Hyvaa!' spurred competitors to dig into their reserves just that little bit more, and the 'Aahh' of disappointment could be heard as the lead Finn dropped two shots on his standing shoot and belted round the penalty loop. Malcolm ran the start leg for us and incurred one penalty; Alan Notley was the second away and got a clear round, Keith Oliver was next with a 1-minute penalty and when he handed over to me we were 11 seconds ahead of the American team.

Disaster struck on the first steep downhill at the 1^1/2-kilometre point. I crossed my skis at speed and tumbled into the deep snow to one side, finishing up spreadeagled against a small fir tree. No damage was done outwardly, the skis were still intact, but my cartwheel through the snow couldn't have done my rifle any good. While I was sorting myself out the American flashed by. Words cannot describe my anger and disappointment at letting down my team mates. But there was still a chance that the Yank would have to run a penalty loop, so with blood up, I went after him at a tempo that I had hardly experienced before. He was just taking up his position for the first lying shot when I entered the range, so I reckoned he was about 15–20 seconds ahead. Tantalising!

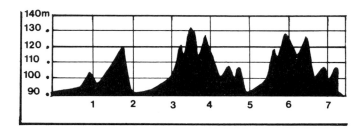

Profile of the men's 7.5-km relay in the World Biathlon Championships, Hämeenlinna, Finland 1971, showing 230m of climbing.

Eight shots and two targets still standing clinched the results. The Yank had gone out with only one penalty loop and I followed him onto it for three. My standing shoot was almost as bad with two loops to run. I hung my head despondently when I crossed the finishing line. I had never shot so badly in my life and while I simply was not going to make excuses, I secretly put the blame on that tumble and the jarring my rifle must have received—though any amount of rationalising did nothing for the depression that overcame me that evening. It was a poor note on which to end the competition season and all I could do was look ahead to Sapporo the following year.

We flew to Olso to wrap up the season and go home. I went up to Rjukan to see Rod Tuck and enjoyed spring snow, warm sunshine and fun for a few days before my ferry left for Newcastle. The day I left I skied 30 kilometres which rounded the total distance during the season nicely to 2,550 kilometres. If satisfied with nothing else, I was satisfied with that and also with news of my results in the staff exam I had taken—a pass with no overkill!

During the 70/71 season I had become very disillusioned with the way the team had trained together. I believed I was on good ground because I could compare it with the previous winter when I was doing my own thing with that individual desire and dedication to get there. Occasionally I had brief discussions with Martin, our manager, when I aired my views and some of them filtered through to the Brigadier in the Ski Federation. Martin supported them but they were largely considered to be in the 'too

46

difficult to implement' category. There were two salient ideas which I believed warranted further exploration within the Federation. The foremost one was for the team members to be allowed to do their own individual training, and to be called together only every three or four weeks for collective sessions, these to be controlled entirely by the trainer. This was how every other nation conducted its team and it would avoid the dreadful hut environment where the cramped conditions and the competitiveness unavoidably created clashes of personality and a tense atmosphere. Not the most conducive or effective manner to house nine or ten international level sportsmen, I argued. The second point was the necessity for selection races. Hitherto, and certainly in my short experience, it was the Brigadier, trainer, manager and team captain who sat down behind closed doors and deliberated who was to go to this or that particular championship. Undoubtedly, results of any earlier competitions were considered, but there were no 'open' criteria known to the competitors themselves, upon which decisions were to be based. This, I contended, was wrong. The Norwegians, Swedes and Finns, and undoubtedly the other European nations, all had their selection races where results were the criteria for nomination.

Martin explained the difficulties that were perceived with the first point but I was encouraged by the flexible line that the Federation was taking. Towards the end of the summer, when it was time for the team to gather again, that flexibility was demonstrated when the Brigadier announced a scheme that would enable individuals to draw upon some of the team finances to help them get away for ten days at a time to do their own training. At the same time Anders Besseberg produced a list of three competitions in late December 1971 and early January 1972 which would be adjudged as selection races. Good consistency over those three, he said (barring illness and resultant poor form), would be the criteria of selection for Sapporo. With these two concessions I felt justice had been done, although on the last point I had originally suggested that five races ought to be the minimum.

The opportunity for an individual to do his own thing was only taken up by one other besides myself in that 71/72 season. It seemed that the team, without exception all soldiers, preferred to be organised.

Anders sent us our summer training programme and while it remained similar to the previous year's, the emphasis was now on increased weights for the strengthening exercises and extra effort during interval training. It was six days a week from 1st May and demanding. Fortunately, my job at RAF Brize Norton which filled the summer months, gave me the time to follow it almost to the letter. Most of the distance training was done on the Ridgeway in the heart of the Lamborne Downs in Wiltshire, and it was delightful running country. Three weeks of August in the Alps with Douglas Keelan and Mike McMullen were a welcome change to the rigid routines of training, although they were in themselves a demanding physical trial as well. Among other things we traversed the Breithorn, Castor, Pollux and the Lyskamm with Mick Tighe and Tim Walker. John Barry was down and we did the North Face of the Tour Ronde; not a difficult route but a wonderful one. Mike and I went up the trade route on the Matterhorn deliberately starting after breakfast so as to be the only climbers on the mountain. We were, although on the descent we met a Swiss couple on honeymoon who told us they were going to spend the night on the summit! It was a lovely holiday. Refreshed and tanned we returned home and entered the final two months of the purgatorial discipline that Anders had set us.

Anders came over to England at the end of September and he arranged for all of us to do oxygen uptake tests on a treadmill. This provided him with data from which he produced an individual interval programme; all in all this provided a more scientific approach towards our training than before.

We knew the hills around Towyn in Wales like the back of our hands before we descended onto Longmoor in Hampshire where the rifle ranges were soon shuddering under the rigours of combination shooting. Not content with that, he put us through an endurance treadmill test on 4th October. This test was the image of a biathlon race and was run on the treadmill at 9 mph at $12^{1}/_{2}$ per cent gradient. He specifically wanted a non-negotiable 12 minutes, $1^{1}/_{2}$ minutes' rest, repeated 4 times with a final 12 minutes. This, he declared, represented a biathlon race pretty accurately, but he also wanted us to go on after that as long as possible to see how high our pulse could go before exhaustion. It was an uncompromising order and each of us dreaded our turn.

I have little recollection of that test save the apparatus that was wired to chest and back and the ugly mouthpiece and tube that hung down at face level. I fell off the mill at 1 hour 28 minutes, gasping for breath and lucky not to get damaged on being spat off the machine. My pulse reached 202; no consolation for what I felt like at that moment, but just what Anders needed as the factor upon which to base his programme for me.

Biathlon Team Training Programme for Guy Sheridan
5th October–6th November, 1971

1st Day— Morning *Combination training. 3 mins' running before shooting. Pulse 195.*
Afternoon *Distance training. $1^{1}/_{2}$ hours' skigang and running in hill-country. Pulse 175.*

48

2nd Day—**Morning** *Combination training. 7 to 9 mins' running before shooting, and also 7 to 9 mins' running after the last shooting. Pulse 190.*
Afternoon *(a) Grass-ski training. 1 min x 15, 1^1/2 mins' rest between each repetition. (b) Strength training as for August.*

3rd Day—**Morning** *Shooting to directions given by Sid Sidall*
Afternoon *Distance training. 2^1/2 hours' skigang and running in hill-country. Pulse 170.*

4th Day— **Rest** *(Jogging for ^{1}/2 hour, grass-skiing 1 min x 10, 1^1/2 mins' rest between each repetition)*

5th Day— **Morning** *Combination training. 5–6 mins' running before shooting, and also 5–6 mins' running after the last shooting. Pulse 195.*
Afternoon *Skisprint training with 35-lb rucksack uphill for 30 secs, 8–10 repetitions, 3-min rest between each.*

6th Day— **Morning or Afternoon** *3–3^1/2 hours' distance training in hill-country, skigang and running. Pulse 165–170. Remember to take with you something to drink.*

7th Day— **Morning** *Combination training. 5 mins' running before shooting, and also 5 mins' running after the last shooting. Pulse 195.*
Afternoon *(a) Grass-ski training. 1 min x 15, 1^1/2 mins' rest between each repetition. (b) Skisprint training with rucksack 35-lb uphill for 30 secs, 10 repetitions, 3 mins' rest between each.*
Note: *Do the combination training as interval training. On morning of third day do ski sprint training session in addition.*

Training Programme
7th November–18th November

You should follow the programme for the period 5th October–6th November, but instead of doing combination training you should do interval training. That means you are resting for approx 2 to 3 mins instead of shooting.

So preparation for the Olympic season reached its climax and after an anti-flu injection the team once again trod the same path over to Nordsaeter. There was a stronger sense of purpose surrounding everyone as skis were donned and the transformation from the most rigorous training schedules any of us had experienced began. The ambitions of ten people were just around the corner; the Olympic Games on the northern Japanese island of Hokkaido were a mere eight weeks away and the knowledge that only six of us would make the journey preyed heavily on our minds.

The relentless Anders kept the pressure up right through to Christmas to the point when most of us wondered whether he was becoming masochistic. He would stand at the bottom of a hill and drive us up it with healthy encouragement. Harder, harder. Again and again, 30 seconds' explosive uphill skiing with a 15-kilo rucksack, 8 repetitions, 3 minutes' rest between each.

I took one of the options provided by the Brigadier for individuals to get away from each other and the intensive collective sessions under Anders and went to stay in Lillehammer. Diligence and devotion to the programme were possible through the flexibility of having a car, then in its third winter and still free of damage from icy roads and associated driving hazards. These short breaks were no panacea, one still made the most of one's time but they were certainly refreshing and invigorating.

It was during these breaks that I used to go up to Pellestova, where I could do my combination training on a 150-metre range. My own rifle was in the hands of Sid Siddall, the team armourer and one of those quiet individuals with a wealth of knowledge and weapon experience which was difficult to top. While he was working on it, I borrowed one of the team's 6.5-mm Carl Gustav Swedish rifles. On one particular day up at Pellestova I had begun a combination session, had been round the 10-minute loop once, fired 5 rounds in the lying position and had come onto the range for the first standing shoot. The bolt action of the Carl Gustav was noticeably more stiff than my own Mauser and it required a forceful wrist action to unlock the system and reload. I fired the first standing round without incident and the shot went where I wanted it. A sharp, hard wrist action to reload was the last I remembered. A huge explosion, amplified because it was so close to my ears, knocked me unconscious and I woke up some seconds later sprawled over the firing point. Shaking myself free of snow and recovering my senses, I picked up the rifle and gave it a quick visual inspection. The bolt was missing and must have been buried deep in the snow somewhere nearby. I needed a shovel to dig for it so I skied up to Pellestova to borrow one and then returned to the range to reconstruct those last seconds and try and analyse where the bolt must have gone. I found it about 7 metres behind and under a metre of snow. The firing pin was broken and I knew then what had happened. The fast, hard wrist action had caused a premature explosion of the bullet before the bolt's locking devices were in place. This caused the bolt to blow back, breaking out of its retaining catches and, missing my ear by fractions, to bury itself in the snow behind. I had been fortunate since, if I had been in a lying position, the bolt would have struck my head.

Martin and I went to the midnight service on Christmas Eve in the attractive triangular church in Nordsaeter. It was a lovely service, though we didn't understand much of what was said or sung, and I unashamedly recollect calling for divine assistance to get through the pressures of the four weeks ahead. Three days later the first selection race was held in Nordsaeter. This was amongst ourselves which in a curious way bore neither the atmosphere of a serious competition nor the reality of what it auguered. It was a Sunday and half the population of Lillehammer seemed to be out on the tracks enjoying a family day out. Nonetheless, even if it was necessary to shout 'track' or 'løype' continually to ask people to move to one side of the track, this had been declared a selection race. To say that the race was badly organised is not to belittle Anders' efforts in meeting the Federation mandate to have nominated selection races. It was the timing of it, on a Sunday and without the aura of a serious event, that did little to justify the phenomenal work-up that Anders had put us through.

A midfield result with a two-minute penalty secured a place for me in the first six. Disappointing maybe, but with one down and two to go, the next race was going to be important, and the one after that vital. The results of the second were jumbled and hardly made the management's job of determining consistency any easier. Everything now depended on the final race held in mid-January at Pellestova. This naturally did nothing to ease the silence and tension within the confines of the hut. On the morning of the race I awoke with a sore throat, feeling very 'flu bound. It was not the day to feel sorry for myself, yet the dilemma was upon me. I had to start. It was the only opportunity to produce that consistent form for which Anders was looking. For me that morning, it hinged upon good shooting entirely, because joints and muscles were stiff and sore with a virus.

I started, finished, and achieved a five-minute penalty which would have been just the ticket. This time, though, one or two others had a good shoot as well and positions hung on running times. My remembrance is of utter weakness and an overwhelming desire to get to bed with a hot toddy. I had a temperature and, with a week to go before the day of departure for Japan, I was hurriedly moved out of the hut into a room in the Nevrefjell Hotel and into splendid confinement.

The Brigadier came up to see me and told me that I had not been selected; the last race had clinched the decision. A mixture of frustration and anger overwhelmed me and, had I not been so lousy, I feel certain I would have reacted more vehemently than I did. I cursed the inventor of the 'flu-jab and realised that I had been 'hoist by my own pétard'.

The team did remarkably well in Sapporo with Keith Oliver achieving the best ever British placing in the 20-kilometre biathlon. He was 11th and a fraction from scoring the first Olympic point in skiing for the country. While they were enjoying the experience of a northern Japanese winter, the British Championships were run in Oberjoch. Of course without six of the best members there it was a misnomer to call them the Nationals. A three-minute penalty and a good run won me the race by a margin of 14 minutes. However, that short-lived achievement could never have outweighed and compensated for my disappointment at the height of the winter of 1972. *'C'est la vie.'*

Fifteen years on as I write this, there exists a handful of characters, working considerable overtime, hoping for the consistency of form and good shooting that evaded me all those years ago. The rules have changed since then; there are roller skis for summer training, the shooting has gone from full to small bore, the range from 150 metres to 50, and diagonal gait has almost become a thing of the past. Skating is in, and with it almost a new discipline. Although those changes have been a mini revolution in themselves, the demands of biathlon as a sport on the individual remain the same. Perhaps they are even greater. Whatever the sentiment of a 'has been', the four winters of my racing experience became the foundation for the pursuit of cross-country skiing in its other forms; with map and compass, with friends in the forest, in the mountains, east or west, north or south. I am still in love with Norway, the affair having stood the test of time.

Ski, Map and Compass

'I know not whence I came,
I know not whither I go,
But the fact stands clear that I am here
In this world of pleasure and woe.
And out of the mist and murk,
Another truth shines plain,
It is in my power each day and hour
to add to it joy or pain.
(Ella Wheeler Wilcox, *Poems of Power*)

The bramble-bashing, sheeny-suited tribe that take to the forests every weekend call it 'cunning-running' and stickers abound in the rear windows of their cars—'Give me a map and I am magic', 'Orienteers do it in the forest' and many other messages of an equal or even more suggestive nature! The 'sport for all' wasn't alive when Ella Wheeler Wilcox put those poetic words together but if it had been, she could well have been writing about orienteering. It epitomises, for me at least, the strength of the game; it reminds me of that, momentary loss of concentration which catapults you into a feeling of desperation, cursing the situation which it was in your power to prevent: the pleasure of hitting the control bang on, the personal despair when you don't and the physical discomfort of running unrhythmically, perhaps floundering, through bracken, brambles and heather and vaulting fallen trees. Yes, all of it within your power to experience: joy and immense satisfaction when it all goes right, pain and anger when it does not.

Jonathan Thomson taught me how to orienteer in the summer of 1973 in Montreathmont Forest in Angus. I had taught Jonathan how to ski in Drevjamoen that winter and there was no doubt that he took more quickly to skiing than I to orienteering. I could not have had a better teacher though, because in 1972 Jonathan had won a place in the national orienteering team in the World Championships held in Czechoslovakia and was ranked well up amongst the British boys.

Although my own Olympic disappointments were still reasonably fresh in my mind, the desire to get back into something competitive was strong. Training was still a five-days-a-week routine, instilled forever by the rigorous programmes of the previous four years. It took little persuasion from Jonathan for me to take orienteering a little more seriously because I certainly enjoyed that first lesson in Montreathmont. Fitness was no problem; it was the new dimension of reading a map and using a compass on the run that was going to need some practice. So when Jonathan took me down to Kielder Forest that autumn for my first event, I went sure in the knowledge that I couldn't have got a better grounding from anyone else. The results of that event on a cold grey autumn day when pockets of snow littered the forest rides do not merit recollection but the experience had fired a masochistic enthusiasm to join the tribe, buy myself a sheeny suit and get seriously into bramble-bashing.

Pilgrimages to events around the country filled practically every weekend thereafter and the game dominated all leisure activities throughout 1974 while I was studying at the Army and RAF Staff Colleges to try and further my Service career! In the summer of that year an article appeared in *Compass Sport,* the official magazine of the British Orienteering Federation. Written by Roy Whitehead, it described a ski-orienteering event held in Scandinavia the previous winter. I read with increasing interest that the World Championships, the first ever, were scheduled to run in Finland the following winter in Hyvinkää, not far from Hämeenlinna, a place which for me, still had a magnetic attraction. I could ski, and map and compass skills seemed to be improving every weekend so Molly, shortly to become my wife, urged me to go for it. Next, I needed a team. I rustled up that old man of the mountains, Rod Tuck, who answered eagerly with an enormous epistle despatched from Kvitåvatn in south Norway. Then I banged off a letter to Corporal Neil Bowman and Bombardier Brian Desmond, friends from Arbroath days and both very good skiers. They replied positively and agreed to start some orienteering practice in the forest over a few weekends to knock the rust off their dormant navigational ability.

Rod and I had joined the ranks of the 'has beens' as far as ski-racing was concerned, but competition was still very much in our blood. As the Inspector of Physical Training in the Royal Marines in 1967, it had been largely his influence that had encouraged Jonathan to get into orienteering. Rod had managed the men's team for the 1968 World Championships and had been a regular attender at Badge events around the country since then. His own ski-racing experience was legendary (see Chapter 4), and combining the two skills for him would not be so difficult as I envisaged it would be for myself. Rod had characteristically suggested a ladies' team be gathered together as well, with Patricia Murphy as the lead personality and strongest contender for good results. She had been prominent in British ladies' cross-country skiing efforts over the years and was a competent orienteer as well. Later on, Frances Murray and Isobel Inglis agreed to join her in the ladies' team.

My efforts to recruit Jonathan into the team failed when he wrote with regret that the Royal Naval College at Dartmouth was not prepared to release him from his work. But the remaining two were positive: Roy Whitehead and Alan Mason, who had already been involved in the ski orienteering training events, agreed to come. As the autumn of 1974 turned into winter, so a plan evolved that eventually gathered up six men and three girls to travel to Helsinki in mid-February 1975. The British Orienteering Federation (BOF) somehow had found some money hiding away in the crypts of the Sports Council to pay for the return flights for five of us from London and the remaining four from Oslo. I was lucky to find a gap in between courses preparing me for a $2^1/2$ year tour of duty in Iran, but there really wasn't the time for those of us travelling from London to do anything like enough ski training before the main competitions.

My own experience of ski training rang a warning bell, and I sounded it in correspondence with BOF. It was essential that the UK-based team members got onto snow for a minimum of ten days before the races. This was not going to be easy for some. BOF pushed the point with Roy and Alan and we soon had reservations in a small sports centre at Solvalla, a little village north of Helsinki. Meanwhile, Rod wrote to BOF and tried to crank all of us up to getting some sort of team uniform. Blazers and slacks with matching girls' uniforms were out as funds simply could not run to that, but BOF was able to get hold of some track suits with GB embroidered on the back. They were admirably suitable and when we left London on 14th February, even though our standards of skiing were poles apart (not to mention our orienteering competence), at least we knew we could look the same at the opening ceremony!

When the first bulletin for the Championships was sent over by the Finns, with it came some model maps for us to scrutinise. At 1:40,000 scale, they were a new experience for nearly all of us. The detail was very good and really no different from that of normal orienteering maps, but it was the scale and the distances to be run that were viewed with a certain amount of trepidation. For the men's race we could expect 22–25 kilometres and for the ladies' about 12–15 kilometres. Just to race over these distances indicated to us that really we should have a minimum of 500 kilometres of ski training under our belts, which simply was not possible for most of us. We also had to grapple with the marking system for the ski tracks which were overlaid on the maps. A good ski track was marked as a continuous green line; a less good one as a green broken line. Roads and paths covered with snow had a green mark at right angles across them and those which were snow-free or had been sanded had a green 'V' across them. The maps, we were informed, would be large, a minimum of 30 centimetres square for the individual and a minimum of 40 by 22 centimetres for the relay race.

Rod had given the prickly problem of how to carry the map some of his imaginative time. Arms and hands of course were fully occupied holding ski sticks, so something had to be found to hang from the neck. It was a bit late in the day to start worrying about this fundamental problem but it preoccupied us all. The compass was best kept in a top pocket, if you had one, or in a hip pocket. 'Just tuck in behind a Swede, put the map away, put your head down and don't let him out of your sight!' was Rod's solution but one probably beyond the skiing ability of most. His humour did little to brighten the serious pensive faces sitting in a circle around the imaginative man. 'You've got to enjoy this game, life's too short', he reminded us. Something told me to go it alone and there was a chance to try out a couple of ideas in a practice event around the thick forests surrounding Solvalla and also at a local Finnish competition to be held near Lahti which Alan, Neil and I had entered. In the first I held the maps in my left hand, but in order for it to be held firmly while still allowing a good grip of the stick while, it meant getting the map into a small enough package within its polythene container. For the longer stretches between controls, frustrating stops were necessary to refold the map and all in all it was a waste of time and no good for competition work.

It was at Lahti that we were able to see the devices that the Finns used and it was a cruel reminder that we were light years behind in this particular game. Some of the top Finns were there wearing aluminium contraptions attached to a chest harness. Through a simple system of hinges, a flat square tray with a clear perspex cover could be pushed out at right angles to the chest and far enough out to glance down to look at the map under a clear celluloid sheet. The folding action, either down or up to flatten the tray against the chest or stomach, was a useful function for downhill work where the body would be crouched and leaning forward for extra speed; useful too for us Brits who needed something that folded up on falling! Another interesting feature was that the tray could revolve so the map could be orientated to the way you were skiing. The tray too was large enough to take the map with only one fold. Because it was too complicated a contraption to contrive in a few days, we settled for a functional map case that suspended from the neck and had a retaining elastic garter around the body to prevent it banging to and fro with every stride of the ski. We bought one each at the small traders' stalls in the start area of the Lahti competition—just like home, I remember thinking—where van loads of orienteering paraphernalia were hawked at discount rates. We were happy nevertheless, and they worked.

Roy, our team manager, gathered us up on Monday 24th February and we drove over to Hyvinkää in a bus and booked into the rather luxurious Rantasipi Hotel. Rod, Frances Murray and Isobel Inglis arrived from Oslo that afternoon to join Patricia and the rest of the men just before a reception provided by the Hyvinkää town authorities for all nations entering the competitions. The Swedes were there in their blue and yellow national colours, together with the Bulgarians, Austrians, Swiss, an East German, one American, two Canadians and the Finns—who were openly being cast as the favourites in both disciplines. There were nine nations in the men's, six nations in the ladies' including Sarolta Monspart from Hungary who had been very prominent in the World Orienteering Championships a year or two before.

The opening ceremony was in the evening of the same day and on a moonless cold night, in temperatures of $-8\,°C$, we took up our position among the other nations in front of the Welder Statue in the town square. The short welcoming speeches in German, Finnish and English reminded me of those Championships in 1971 where I had shot so disastrously in the relay and those thoughts were difficult to cast out of my mind.

The start draw took place in the hotel the next afternoon. We had spent the morning out on a training run near the competition area to familiarise ourselves with the map, its scale and the track-marking system. We played with the map cases and practised relating map to ground in the unfamiliar white surroundings where all ground features like tracks and streams were under deep snow. Going downhill we realised was going to be the thing to watch and would need tremendous concentration; the speed over the ground, related to distance on the map and the quickness of decision to turn to left or right were going to be critical. A moment too late and it would be easy to find oneself 100 metres too far down the track and faced with a weary sprint back up the hill to get on line again. Rod agreed and we returned to the hotel to wax up our skis, relax and get a good night's sleep. I was thankful that Rod was not drawn to start just behind me!

Breakfast on 25th February was early and quickly finished in a nervous silence, except for the indefatigable Rod whose laughing made heads turn and stare from the other tables. His mind was probably on activities planned for that evening, far from thoughts of the 3-hour race ahead. The competition area was a long drive from the Rantasipi and we were urged to see to morning and pre-race nervous constitutionals before departure. That announcement alone caused another of those Tuck giggles.

We had managed to get a glimpse of the profile of the course the previous evening and without exception, I recall we were all surprised by the distance of the optimum route. It was 29 kilometres with a total climb of 226 metres, and it was 6.1 kilometres longer than we were expecting. The terrain, we were told, was typical Finnish forest, and dense enough that, even in the most favourable skiing conditions, the area might be difficult to cross. We were assured, thankfully, that there were a number of fields and a few roads, so if nothing else, verification of where one was would be a little easier than it would have been if it was dense forest throughout. Small beer really, but a little consolation nonetheless— although it hardly calmed pre-start nerves.

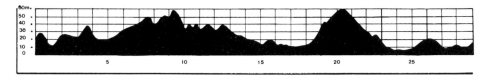

Profile of the men's individual ski orienteering race in the World Championships, Hyvinkka, Finland 1975. Length of course 23.4km, optimum route 29km, 226m of climbing.

The first man was away at ten o'clock by which time I was well into my warm-up and satisfied with the wax. Drawn 5th to start, I went into the box 9 minutes later where it was possible to conduct a nervous study of the competition map for three minutes before the whistle blew. Three minutes ahead of me was the American and three minutes behind, a Bulgarian with a KGB-sounding name. I lurched forward bent on catching the Yank.

Neil, Brian, Alan and Rod were spread right through the field of 34 with Rod starting at 30th. I was thankful that he, at least, was well clear of me as we were vying between ourselves for the British laurels.

It was almost 4 kilometres as the crow flies to the first control, a house courtyard, and however much I had convinced myself beforehand to take it easy at the early stage to make sure I got used to the scale of the map and ground, it didn't seem to temper my eagerness to catch the Yank, and I drove arms and legs almost into oxygen debt in every stride of diagonal gait. Loss of concentration in the chase caused me to whizz past a turning which I should have taken. The overshoot cost me four or five minutes as I returned and got back on route, bending and leaning forward, shortening the ski stride as I entered the hill. I cursed myself for being so careless. The leading Finn made the first control in a fraction under 21 minutes, a whole 9 minutes faster than my clumsy efforts. Thereafter though, it all seemed to flow nicely and route choice, the rhythm of diagonal gait and excellent wax, all seemed to gel. The second leg of 8.2 kilometres was cleared in 45 minutes 35 seconds, the third in 13.62, the fourth in 37.4, fifth in 18.07 while the final exhausting 1.5 kilometres seemed to go on forever. A total running time of 2 hours 42.57 minutes pressed me into 17th place. Olavi Svanberg came in first for Finland in an astonishing 1 hour 49.56 minutes, well ahead of his nearest team mate. The gap was enormous but as the hours and minutes went by and the individual placings were being slipped up and down on the results board, it became clear that Svandberg had had one of those incredible performances of a lifetime—like Bob Beaman's in his long jump world record.

I watched the clock, anxious that Rod was going to pip me, but the minutes ticked by and passed the point when it would be possible. He came in 25th in 3 hours 8.40 minutes, still grinning from ear to ear, and with a chuckle announced that he had been caught short in the forest! Neil was 29th and Alan 30th and the American failed to materialise.

It was fun 'post morteming' that evening in the warmth of the Rantasipi; retracing routes was almost as exhausting as the competition itself, but like orienteers everywhere, we patiently listened to each other's descriptions of where and what went wrong. 'If only, if only I hadn't done that!' seemed to be the chant as we dispersed for a good night's sleep. Curiously, there was no talk about the skiing, but all the tracks had been well prepared and I found it satisfying to stride out, arms at full stretch, triceps tense with exertion, to generate the last centimetre of push from the ski sticks.

The girls had a hard race as well. Their optimum route was 17.8 kilometres, a daunting distance for them.

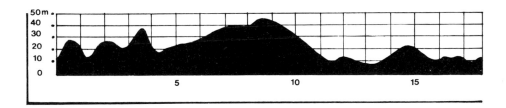

Profile of the ladies' individual ski orienteering race in the World Championships, Hyvinkka, Finland 1975. Length of course 13.8km, optimum route 17.8km, 110m of climbing.

Out of 16 starters, Patricia came 10th ahead of Sarolta Monspart and all the Bulgarians. It was a 'whoopee' result and she was only a minute or two behind a Finn. Isobel was 13th and Frances was 16th; no doubt disappointing for them but if anything it was their skiing that had let them down. Patricia's own cross-country racing experience had blasted through in her favour. The other two, whose orienteering competence was without doubt, clearly needed more time on skis to master the techniques of diagonal gait.

The relay was run on 28th February and we drew lots for our start order. Rod would go in the mass start, then Brian to hand over to Neil and the anchor leg would be mine. Optimum routes for each were 22.0, 20.5, 20.0 and 23.1 kilometres. The first two each had four controls, the remainder five. Maximum climbs were 150 metres except for the second leg, which with 50 metres was virtually level. The girls had optimum routes of 14, 11.6 and 12.3 kilometres. They opted for Patricia to go off first with the mass start, and Frances running the anchor leg.

Rod went off like a train, still chuckling to himself, and got out of the bottleneck in third position. At the end of his leg he was lying fourth and over 11 minutes ahead of the Austrians and 48 minutes up on the Bulgarians. Those two caught up with Brian on his leg and the Austrian was a minute up on him. Neil had a disaster between his first and second controls which he was never able to make good and he handed over to me 21 minutes after the Austrian went out. I was unable to catch him, the gap alas was too large but I gained some satisfaction in having almost the same running time. Great Britain came in 5th leaving the Bulgarians still in the forest with all the blame, no doubt, being poured onto the fellow with the KGB-sounding name who never emerged from Leg 3. The girls fared a little better. They beat the Bulgarians, who retired from the competition, and they won the bronze medal! We all celebrated their rather spurious victory that evening and agreed to gather together in Bulgaria for the world meeting in March 1976.

It certainly had been fun, we had discovered another dimension to cross-country skiing and one which demanded an inordinate amount of concentration. Cunning-running, yes; cunning-skiing, yes and as we waited for the plane at Helsinki airport we could justifiably say that cross-country skiers really can do it in the forest! We went our separate ways and Rod agreed to take the lead in the design and production of a map case contraption which we were all convinced was worth five minutes off our running times.

Life assumed a different proportion in April when Molly and I drove out to Iran. Skiing in one form or another was dominating our activities and plans for the future. There were limitless skiing possibilities in Iran (one particular ski tour there has been described in Chapter 4) but behind the incessant adventurous contrasts, lay the fixture of the World meeting in Velingrad, Bulgaria in February 1976. Being a serving officer in the

Royal Marines, I was under remit to obtain special clearance if I wanted to visit a country in the Eastern Bloc. It is, by necessity, one of the bureaucratic mazes through which service people have to trudge, and it depended on early submission for a request to receive its formal processing. To submit the application from a smelly, hot and humid seaside town on the Persian Gulf made it even more of a protracted exercise and for those in our Embassy in Tehran, something of an incongruous subject.

'Ski orienteering, what do you mean?'

'What, here in Iran; you must be joking!'

'What did you say your name is?'

'Sheridan, did you say. Oh you're a Marine are you?'

'God whatever next—where *is* this place?'

'Bulgaria did you say? They don't have snow there do they?'

I didn't dare tell him I was planning to traverse the Zagros on skis with a Norwegian for fear of immediate dismissal as a crackpot. I plugged away and I guess that because I was not prepared to let go, back came the green light.

The summer in Bushehr, up at the top end of the Persian Gulf coast, was torrid. Training on the salt flats on the peninsula was purgatorial and much worse than I could recall from a few years before over similar countryside in Muscat. The weekends in Shiraz were a welcome break from the humidity and an opportunity to do some beneficial hill work and take on some longer distances without succumbing to the heat.

By a stroke of good luck the first winter snows arrived a couple of days before our Christmas break and had settled nicely above 2,200 metres. Skiing was high on the agenda over the Christmas weekend and we were able to drive up to Dasht-e-Arzan and get up a stony track onto the edge of the snow. The Range Rover coped with any mud and slush in low ratio gear and the back-up of using the differential lock was practical insurance up our sleeves if we got into deep mire. Dasht-e-Arzan is a green fertile bowl, bordered on its west side by a steep cliff, at the bottom of which gurgled a river of cool, clear and purest water. A village straddled the river under the cliff and it was the village folk who told us how to get to the track which would take us high up to the snow. It was they too, who told us about the wolves that lived in the rocks up there. 'Beware of the shir,' they warned us.

The 'shir' is the Persian lion, thought for a long time to be extinct. I had got a glimpse of an animal with what seemed to be a mane one night two or three months before. I was driving through torrential rain at about two o'clock in the morning and some 20 kilometres from Dasht-e-Arzan, and saw this creature walk slowly across the road and disappear down an embankment. It was a large beast whose head disappeared into a massive neck which almost merged with its shoulders. It had a long tail and showed no fear of the lights of the jeep. I thought to myself, rather unconvincingly, that our dog, Shammy, would see wolves or the shir off if they ambushed us.

The skiing was marvellous and almost always on good hard snow. The ridge was sharp with a precipice on its southern side but to the north there were undulating slopes that stretched for at least 20 kilometres and as they were in the shadow of the ridge, they held the snow normally until the end of March. It was all quite high and I was unable to get used to the thinner air of 2,400 metres since I was working at sea level all week, and never had enough time to acclimatise properly. With the Championships in Bulgaria set for the end of February, training up there was vital every weekend as I was trying to build up to a distance of 500 kilometres before departure for Europe.

It was far from easy. Interval training was more painful than that awful experience on the treadmill a few years back. At the top, and sometimes halfway up each hill, body and mind would contort, gasping for cold thin air, the weight slumped and supported by the ski sticks. Shammy, the dog, seemed to show no sign of weakening at the altitude. 'Lucky bitch! I wish I could run around like her', I remember thinking.

At Christmas Rod sent his design for a map case in his card to us, but I had already started my prototype. Using a piece of aluminium from a portable shooting target mechanism, a small contraption was soon taking shape in the confines of a small office in Bushehr, but to slightly different measurements to Rod's plan. The problem of the swivelling flat plate for the map was solved by using an old scratched 33-rpm record and carving it into a square. A botch job with araldite and some velcro soon had a polythene flap covering it under which the map would go; Heath Robinson would have been proud of the invention and, to spite my sceptical friends, it actually worked and folded up and down as well.

The flight from Abadan to Athens, where an Aeroflot connection took me further on to Sofia, coincided with Molly's departure for Tehran and hospital to have a baby. She had urged me to go off to Bulgaria during this time, reassuring me that, given good timing, there would be a little one awaiting my return twelve days later. She was to stay with Sam and Tulip Bemrose until she was forced to go into hospital. When I arrived in Sofia I was met by the Military Attache from our Embassy.

I collected my skis and baggage and checked through Passport Control. I remember thinking that all this was strangely the wrong way around. My visa, obtained through the Bulgarian Embassy in Tehran, caused some interest to the controller who made a short telephone call. Colonel

Chappel led me through the arrivals lounge and as we got outside he pointed out two sinister-looking and rather stout men in dark coats and fur hats.

'You'll get to recognise these two pretty well over the next ten days', he said, turning to look at me with a slight smile. 'Because I've met you they will follow you wherever you go'.

'To Velingrad?' I queried rather disbelievingly.

'Yes, they'll have breakfast at the same time, they'll watch every move you make, but I think they'll draw the line at following you on skis.'

So this was Eastern Europe!

Colonel Chappel had booked me into the Hotel Zdravetz in Velingrad for a week and had arranged for his staff car to take me there the next morning. He said he would meet Rod Tuck and the remainder of the team when they came in and send them on their way. As a parting shot, he invited us all to stay the night with him and his wife on our way home. He had been very kind and his assistance had certainly smoothed my arrival and first visit to a totalitarian state.

The staff car was shadowed by a black Moskvitch and its two sombre occupants for the four-hour drive to Velingrad, where I was deposited at the state-run hotel in the centre of the small mountain town. It was a pretty little place, but, even at an altitude of 1,000 metres, there was not much snow to be seen. However, during a lengthy discussion with the receptionist under the ever watchful eye of one of the secret servicemen, I discovered that the main ski area was half an hour's drive away by bus and a few hundred metres higher up. That evening the Moskvitch departed leaving the more gruesome looking of the two men behind. He had booked himself into the room next to mine and he watched curiously as I waxed my skis out in the corridor.

I reached the breakfast table before the grumpy agent and I thought for a moment that I had managed to give him the slip by getting up early. No such luck, however, there he was at the hotel entrance when I clattered down the stairs carrying skis and sticks. We both caught the bus and sat at different ends, each by an exit. He was clearly going to get out when I did but from then on I would be alone because he had no skis and was still wearing his suit and dark coat.

As the bus roared up the winding road, so the snow on either side became deeper and after 25 minutes we edged into a picturesque valley with open fields nestling between high forested hillsides. I jumped off the bus at a small lay-by where there was a small wooden lean-to shack with a rusty pipe sticking through the roof. Smoke curled upwards in the still cold air and the two small windows were misty with rivulets of condensation. A ski track led off into the fields to one side of the hut. As I clipped on my skis, my KGB-style companion, who had got out of the rear exit of the bus, clomped up two creaky steps and disappeared into the hut, releasing, through the open door, a shimmering cloud of warm smoky air into the cold atmosphere. I was on my own again and could enjoy the strange sensation of skiing in a remote Bulgarian mountain valley entirely alone. As I took off along the track, I thought no more of my follower. I made up my mind that I would do four hours' distance training and as arms and legs got into their rhythmical stride, I wondered and worried about how Molly was getting on in Tehran.

The track wasn't bad and although the valley was 2,100 metres up, the thinner air was no deterrent to completing what I set out to do that day. It was a circular route, about 8 kilometres long and to break up the monotony of the circuit, I went anticlockwise for the last two hours and curiously enjoyed turning the thrill of earlier downhill stretches into oxygen-starving effort and vice versa. The small rickety hut in the lay-by became a warm haven in which to wait for the bus and when I pushed the door open, silence fell on the half dozen occupants. The air was thick with smoke and the smell of beer and Slivovitch was ample evidence that my friend had been relaxing with some of the locals. When the bus arrived a little later, he walked to the door and onto the bus with a slight stumble and I saw him smile for the first time. 'They are human after all', I thought as the bus returned down the hill to Velingrad. He must have gone to bed to sleep away his over-indulgence because I didn't see him until breakfast the next morning!

Bad news arrived on the third day. The Embassy telephoned the hotel in the evening and Colonel Chappel told me that Molly had been delivered of a still-born baby that morning. It was devastating news. The telegram from Tehran had said Molly was fine; the Bemroses were extending their enormous kindness and it stressed that Molly did not want me to quit and board the first plane back as she wanted me to see the Championships through to the end. I took up Colonel Chappel's offer of sending a message of sympathy and loving thoughts through his Embassy to Tehran. The next three days were lonely with only the ski training to take my mind off the agonising news and it was a relief when Rod Tuck and the rest of the team pitched into the hotel. With them came a replacement for my secret serviceman who checked out of the hotel and without acknowledging my 'goodbyes' left in the same black Moskvitch car.

During the week's ski training based on the Hotel Zdravetz, I came to know that 8 kilometres ski track extremely well, and I made contact with some of the Bulgarian instructors at the Central School of Orienteering, Kislovodsk Sport Centre in Velingrad. They took me to their own National Ski Orienteering Championships at Borowitz where they arranged for me to enter the competition. Because I was not physically ready for a serious race, I chose to do the men's 19-years-age group course and use the event as a training session to get used to the map case. The terrain was fierce both up and down with one hill having over 175 metres' height gain but the detail on the map didn't have the clarity of those we had used in Finland the previous year. The event was useful and it enabled me to pass on some information to Rod, Neil, Brian and the girls and voice a warning that it was going to be technically harder than Finland, and very demanding both physically and in downhill skiing complexity.

The profile for the men's and ladies' individual races was distributed that evening to the five nations taking part and it certainly endorsed that experience at Borowitz. Without exception we were astonished at the optimum routes—a grizzly 31.7 kilometres for the men and not such a stupefying 15.8 kilometres for the ladies. The height gain was horrifying!

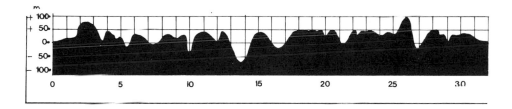

Profile of the men's individual ski orienteering race in the World Championships, Velingrad, Bulgaria 1976. Length of course 24.4km, optimum route 31.7km, 780m of climbing.

The Kislovodsk Sports Centre was a comfortable residential hall and unlike the Hotel Zdravetz the plumbing worked although with resounding gurgles and coughs day and night. We were all billeted in twin-bedded rooms and I found myself sharing with Rod. We had a pleasant English-speaking Bulgarian from Plovdiv University as our guide and general factotum and he joined us for every meal and race briefing. All the time in the background, though, was a secret serviceman who at least possessed a more human approach to his task than his predecessor.

The chance of a training event was available the next day in the neighbourhood and most people took the opportunity to shake off the effects of their long journeys. The opening ceremony was conducted outside the Hotel Zdravetz but unlike Finland the year before, there was no snow in Velingrad. It felt strange to stand there in those circumstances and because there was not the local support for the ceremony, it seemed to lack that welcoming atmosphere so openly portrayed in Hyvinkää.

'Oh well, it's totalitarian, isn't it?' Rod was directing his words towards our 'man' who was standing close to the Chairman of the Championships, but they went unheard. His chuckles however, caused the Finns on our right to turn their heads.

It was a two-hour drive to the competition area which lay at altitudes between 2,000 and 2,300 metres, and by the time we got there, it was a few minutes before ten o'clock when the first man was off. Drawn number two to start, it was difficult not to panic with so many preparatory things to do, the most important being to select the right wax and apply it, something which simply hadn't been possible the night before. Although it was cold, $-8\,^{\circ}$C, it was a gloriously sunny day and at the latitude of the Bulgarian mountains, the sun's warmth was sure to play havoc with the snow around noon. The distance and an anticipated running time of $2^{1}/_{2}$ to 3 hours was going to make this the most critical decision.

Rod, who was drawn 10th, lent a hand and tried out a couple of wax combinations on a spare set of skis that we had taken with us. Neil and Brian also joined in the elimination process. They both had time on their hands as they were 15th and 19th away, and it was of equal interest to the three of them to help get it right. With time almost up, decisions had to be made and that moment of commitment arrived. I put blue Swix underfoot, green Swix on tip and tail and a stick of red Exelit in a pocket which would hopefully deal with the soft snow expected later on. If it went to slush and ice then it would be a matter of hoping that someone had the wax for that at a feeding control during the race.

With a 'Here goes!' I went into the start box, checked that my compass was in my hip pocket, stole a half-minute glance at the map, folded it and slid it under the polythene of the map case and waited for the slap on the back, 'Go'.

The number one away was a Swede and I remembered Rod's commandment in Finland. My inclination was to try and catch him and then sit on his tail all the way to the finish. Judgement and inclination fought a momentary battle in my mind; judgement won and I reckoned it was the right way to go. He would be a little faster on his skis than I and thus the chance of losing him would propel me into becoming Ella Wheeler Wilcox's subject for her first two poetic lines.

The first couple of kilometres were over open areas and I had to make a conscious effort to suppress the desire to go flat out. Now was the time to go at that optimum speed where the mind could relate ground to map and apply it without making an error. The wax was doing its stuff but I wondered for how long and apart from one fall on a steep section, which proved fortunately that the folding system on the map case actually functioned, the early cautious speed enabled a faultless entry to the first control positioned on the corner of a wood. To my utter astonishment there was the Swede having just skied in from another direction. He stamped his control card a few seconds ahead of me and sped out. In an instant I was after him. Throwing caution to the wind, and following Rod's eleventh commandment, I sat on his tail for about 5 kilometres until he disappeared over a steep embankment above a road, ending up in the middle of it in a bundle of arms, legs, skis and sticks. It was only a deliberate sit-down fall on the brink of the drop that prevented me from joining him in similar fashion.

Svensson was the Swede's name and his fall had dislocated his shoulder and broken one ski. He was in some pain so I got him into a comfortable position and told him that I would alert the race authorities at the food station which was a further 2 kilometres down the road. Reassuring him that someone would be with him in ten minutes or so, I skied off down the road using long skating strides, pushing hard on the arms and going at a good pace. The incident had delayed me by two or three minutes. It was only with difficulty that I got the people standing at the food station to understand that there was an injured skier up the road. Gesticulating and pointing and with my own impatience to get on, I eventually got the message through and after quickly swallowing a rather sickly sweet orange drink, I skied on and out of the valley to the start of a long climb. I turned to look back before entering the forest just in time to see a car swinging round to drive up towards the Swede. Now I could forget about him.

It was at least 8 kilometres uphill to Control 2 with a height gain of a little over 500 metres before a steep traversing descent gave an opportunity for a breather. I was overtaken by two Swedes towards the top but was too extended to sit on their tails and only caught sight of their backs disappearing out of the control as I descended towards it. That leg must have been nearing 17 kilometres and I was reasonably happy in covering the distance in 1 hour 31 minutes. I have a dim memory of fatigue, rasping thirst and the onslaught of dehydration which caused mental distractions. I missed a vital turn and sped off down an increasingly narrowing valley for about a kilometre before I realised it. The return was one of the weariest I can ever recollect and I was infuriated for allowing myself to waste such a lot of time.

'It's all part of the game', Rod would say, and of course it was. It was my own careless error. That wasn't the end of it though and when I skied up to the next control, stamped my card and raced up a hill thinking I was heading for Control 4, I came across a track which shouldn't have been there. Comparing the map and ground about me I realised I had failed to check the code on the control and had visited the penultimate control of the ladies' course. Another wild curse rent the air as I poled off, skating down to the proper Control 3, schussed to a stop and stamped. It was only 300 metres from the ladies' controls yet I had to ski an extra kilometre because of the error. From 3 to 4 and 5 was straightforward but I was exceedingly glad to get to the finish in 2 hours 55 minutes 44 seconds. The wax had worked a treat with the sun hardly affecting the snow within the shadows of the forest.

It was possible to analyse the times between the controls later on because, at each, the arrival was recorded by an official in wireless contact with the finish. In the final result list and lying 11th out of 24 at Control 2, I was on for a good result but the loss of 8–10 minutes between 2 and 3 dropped it to 13th and the hiccup of stamping the wrong control took it down to 14th; a striking example of what carelessness can do. 'It's all part of the game, it's all part of the game' was repeating itself over and over again in my mind while I changed out of my soggy sweaty clothes to wait for my team-mates to pole around the corner to the finish.

Neil and Brian both finished but were disqualified for not visiting and stamping a control. They were far from happy with their performance but they were not alone, being joined by a Bulgarian, an Austrian and the unfortunate Swede in the ranks of the non-finishers. There was no sign of Rod and the small crowd of spectators and waiting racers had dwindled to the GB team and a few officials when an announcement, in broken English, was made over the public address system.

'Competitor No. 10 has just arrived at Control 1.'

There was a crackling pause on the speakers while we waited for something else to be said, expecting Rod to retire.

'No. 10 has asked the controller for a cigarette and drink!' Pause. Laughter and disbelief!

'No. 10 is smoking his cigarette and having a rest at the control but there is no drink.'

A few minutes passed.

'No. 10 has finished and has left for Control No. 2.'

We all looked at each other and tried to reason amongst ourselves why Rod should suddenly display such irrational behaviour. His progress through the other controls was monitored and reported back and 5 hours and 46 minutes after starting, Rod skied round the corner and into the finish. As he crossed the line, the race secretary came out of the time-keepers' tent carrying a tray. On it were two glasses, two cigars, a box of matches and a bottle of Slivovitch, the local spirit distilled from plums.

The secretary poured a healthy dollop of spirit in the glasses, offered one to Rod, took one himself and said 'Now, you have a drink and cigar; now you rest.'

Even our secret serviceman was almost in tears with laughter. The salt of dried sweat on Rod's face cracked as his frown spread into one of those huge grins and he joined the laughter.

'What happened then, Rod?' Another chuckle.

'Oh nothing much, I just skied off the map. Bloody awful, eh! How about living that one down! Nearly 6 hours! Quite quick for an old man don't you think?'

The relay was run two days later in the same area in weather that was equally as gorgeous. The courses were much shorter than in Finland and there were only three legs. Neil ran the first and I handed over to Rod but we were not quick enough to pip either the Bulgarian or Austrian teams. The expected winners were the Finns.

A party in the evening at the Hotel Zdravetz virtually became the final competition of the Championships as the bachelors tried to win the favours of all the pretty girls in the ladies' teams. Towards the end of the evening our secret serviceman, who was almost ten parts to the wind, grabbed me by the arm and pulled me over to the bar where there were two large glasses of Slivovitch.

'Sheers,' he said with a big boozy smile.

'Cheers, I am glad your chum left and you took his place.' My words passed with not a word being understood.

'Sheers.' He was now almost eleven parts gone. I shook his rather tubby hand and bade him good luck, good promotion and a nice retirement. It was time to go to bed and to turn thoughts toward Molly in Tehran.

Colonel Chappel put up with the crowd of us for a night in Sofia where we met the Ambassador and were given a right royal send off. An empty Aeroflot plane sped me to Athens for a connecting flight to Tehran and a longing reunion with Molly. Sam and Tulip had been quite marvellous looking after her. The next day the two of us drove 1,000 kilometres to Shiraz and a warm welcome from our Persian mongrel, Shammy.

Ski orienteering as a competitor was certainly over for me and I had told Rod that I thought we both ought to bale out and make way for younger blood. The two championships had been very different experiences and although undoubtedly our own biathlon racing years had paid us a handsome dividend, the fiendish difficulty of dovetailing both cross-country skiing and complicated navigation had earned our deep respect.

It was to the direction of ski orienteering in Great Britain that Rod and I now turned our attention. It had to wait, though, until my return to England from Iran in the late summer of 1977 when I agreed I would take on the chairmanship of the Ski Orienteering Committee in the Federation.

It sounded a very grand title indeed but it was far from that. What was wanted was presence within the general meetings and that was important if we were to spread our knowledge, gather in recruits to the sport, get the right advertising support and most vital of all, obtain financial sponsorship for the International Championships in the future.

There was undoubtedly a lot of talent available in the Army and my own Corps and it was to these people that we directed some extensive advertising. It was important not to forget that, politically and to keep on the right side of the Federation, we would need to blend those efforts with wide recruiting among orienteers and the cross-country ski clubs which were beginning to sprout in the north of England and in Scotland. To launch this side of the campaign, Rod offered two cross-country skiing scholarships at his lodge near Rjukan in Norway. Together we evolved some selection criteria and then called for applicants through the columns of the Federation's own magazine *Compass Sport*.

Rod and I had been convinced for some time that it would be easier to teach a good, fast, competent orienteer how to ski rather than the other way round. Neil Bowman and Brian Desmond both had excellent skiing ability but they had experienced difficulty in combining the skill of using map and compass at the *moment critique* and were inconsistent. There were similar arguments in the sport of biathlon although by and large those in that sport hadn't been given a test. We based our criteria on this opinion and if an applicant had managed to accrue some cross-country skiing experience it would clearly be in his or her favour.

The response to our advertisement in *Compass Sport* was most encouraging and Peter Haines and Pauline Hutchinson were selected. There were many others who showed interest in travelling to Norway over Christmas and the New Year in 1978, among whom were Mike Winpenny, John Rye and David Marshall, and Wendy Dodds, Ros Coats and Izzie Inglis. Mike, John and David were all in the Forces and were, without exception, very competent consistent orienteers. They could all ski pretty fast as well. The reputation of Wendy and Ros as phenomenally strong and fast mountain marathon runners preceded them and clearly if they could pick up the techniques of skiing they would be a real prospect for results at the next World Championships in Avesta, Sweden in February 1980.

It was for those World Championships that we geared our meetings and skiing work-up for that and the following winter. The field of interest was quite small and the problem of selection events, should there be an oversubscription of talent, had been a backstage thought up to now. But with only four places in each event available to both men and ladies, we had to have some form of elimination process, agreed by everyone at a general meeting. To assemble everyone from all points of the country became an almost insurmountable problem and the venue for that meeting wasn't decided until the start lists for the 1979 Karrimor Mountain

Marathon had been produced. On glancing through the lists, it wasn't difficult to see that almost all of our ski orienteers were starting in the Elite or 'A' classes. The line to take was decided for me. I sent a hasty letter off to each, backed up by a telephone call and convened the meeting at the overnight campsite for the Elite and 'A' classes.

The Mountain Marathon was held in the Rhinog Mountains of North Wales and just as I had confidently predicted, everyone made it to the campsite except Izzie whose companion had twisted an ankle. They bivouacked on the hill somewhere and retired from the marathon the next day. If the truth be known, if anyone was going to have any difficulty getting there on time it would be me, the Chairman. I and my partner, Douglas Keelan were on the verge of saying that we were too long in the tooth to continue doing the 'A' courses and 1979 would be the last one. And so it was.

We all agreed at the meeting that I should be the person to make the selections using known form and results from two local events in Norway and Sweden for those who were able to make them. The Swedes had asked me to be a technical delegate at the Championships and therefore I would best be able to provide the most impartial decisions. I offered my job as Chairman to the floor and Mike agreed to take it on. The final call was for a team manager to take on the task of co-ordinating the arrangements to get everyone over to Sweden for the Championships themselves. Thus the strangest of meetings ended and everyone wearily dispersed to their tents.

The Championships in Sweden came and went and Mike took the reins firmly in his hands after them. An ambitious plan hatched in Oslo that winter with a couple of Norwegian friends was taking shape and was beginning to occupy most of my spare time. It was a plan in which complicated navigation and route-finding would play a dominant role. It had nothing to do with ski orienteering although I was convinced my own particular experiences of skiing with a map and compass would help to provide a greater understanding of what we were just about to embark upon. We were planning to make a winter ski journey across the Western Indian Himalayas. It was a different kind of ski marathon, far removed from the three hours of 31-kilometre optimum route in the mountains and forests of Bulgaria.

It is easy enough in this world to make haste
If one lives for that purpose—but think of the waste
For life is a poem to leisurely read,
And the joy of the journey lies not in its speed.

(Ella Wheeler Wilcox)

Iran: A Winter Arrest

It had been a long haul to the top of Gaustatoppen (1,883 metres); more strenuous, I thought, than the longest ski race I had ever done—but I had got there a couple of minutes ahead of Rod Tuck, and it had been a race, one which Rod had run for the first time two years before. My satisfaction in beating this legendary character to the top was smartly removed by the shout, 'Buy me a drink, will you?' Obligingly, I disappeared into the small hut at the top of the highest mountain in south Norway and bought two bottles of Vørterøl, a thirst-quenching energy-giving malt beverage. When I emerged Rod had arrived; he grabbed a bottle and cast off down the steepening slopes clutching ski sticks in the other hand. 'First one back to Kvitåvatn!' he shouted as he disappeared from view. The man had fooled me and I never caught up with him on the 8-kilometre ski chase back to the lodge. He was smug when I got in two or three minutes after him but he gave me a drink and I consoled myself that at least I had pipped him on the hardest part. Not bad for an old hand such as he, I thought, as we sat relaxing in the hall. He must have been forty years old then, and he still displayed that competitive urge that had enabled him to be the first and probably the only Englishman to have raced in a Summer and Winter Olympics (Innsbruck in the Biathlon and Tokyo in the Pentathlon, 1964).

Whilst we were talking, in came a tall, blond Norwegian dressed in blue dungarees, carpenter's ruler and hammer protruding from the slim pocket on his trouser leg.

'Hei Odd' said Rod. 'Guy, have you met Odd Eliassen?'

'No' I said, getting wearily to my feet.

'Odd is up here building my staff quarters' Rod explained. 'We met through an old school chum, Peter Steele; Peter was the doctor on the International Everest Expedition in 1971, and Odd was one of the two Norwegians that went along. You know—that was the expedition that ended up in a drama and half the team deserting!'

'Oh yes.' I could recall something about it.

72

That evening we sat together for supper, and were joined by Erik Dalhl, Odd's assistant for the staff quarters project. We agreed to go out for a short ski tour the next day after lunch. 'Just something in the immediate vicinity of the lodge', Odd declared. That short tour was well over 40 kilometres and found me exhausted bringing up the rear, but the three hours that we were out were the first of many more 'short' tours to come and saw the foundation of a team that would take us into the next decade and to many different parts of the world to ski.

The next day I went by train to Asker, a suburb of Oslo, where I discovered that I had left my wallet behind in Rod's lodge and therefore had no money. I rang Odd who collected me from the station and invited me to stay the night at his home, offering to lend me 500 kroner and to drive me to Oslo the following morning to catch the boat to England.

Odd had not long returned from a successful expedition with chums from the Norwegian Alpine Club (Tind Klubb), that scaled Noshaq, in the Hindu Kush. They had driven out and back through Turkey and Iran, and now Rotraut, his Austrian born wife, was preparing an Iranian dish for supper. After a few very tasty helpings, Odd explained that what we were eating were sheep testicles and he had first experienced the treat in Tehran. I do not remember my reaction to this announcement—but the food was, on reflection, quite delicious. I told Odd that I was just about to go out to Iran to work and how sad I was to be hanging up my skis and boots for two years.

'Why?' remarked Odd.

He had flown over Iran in February 1971 on his way out to Nepal for the Everest Expedition, and from the plane had seen mountains and lots of snow. He convinced me I should take skis with me. Molly, however, wasn't so easily persuaded and I had to enter into protracted negotiations with her as I haggled for space in the car for skis and waxes. The drive out to Iran in April 1975 was an eighteen-day honeymoon. Stops in Geneva and a brisk ski down the Mer de Glace from the Aiguille du Midi to Chamonix on cross-country skis provided the thrill of a lifetime before we drove on to Brindisi for the ferry to Corfu and the winding drive over the Pindos Range. Spring eased into summer the further east we drove, snow receding to greater altitudes until, upon our arrival in Tehran in early May, there were only patches on the northern slopes of the Elburz mountains.

Our Ford Cortina Estate creaked under the weight of luggage when we drove out of the smelly southern quarter of Tehran on the last leg of our journey to Shiraz which was still 1,000 kilometres away. It was very hot and the frequency of *Chai Khanas* on the side of the road provided welcome stops for an iced Coke and a chance for me to practise my Farsi.

In March I had been sent on a language course in London, just off Oxford Street, and spent six weeks struggling over a new alphabet and trying to remember always to put verbs at the end of a sentence! Distracted by the pace of London and our teacher, a 22-year-old Persian lady, who never wore a bra and insisted on wearing a see-through blouse, my progress wasn't so fast as it could have been and it took me a good fifteen minutesto order yoghurt and a boiled egg in the roadside tea house.

After Tehran we stayed in the Shah Abbas Hotel in Esfahan and it was an example of the opulence and extravagance of the golden years of the Pahlavi dynasty. Carpets of every size and intricate design festooned the walls, covered the floor and even lay beside the swimming pool. There were the tribal designs of the Qashgai and Fars, the detailed floral emblems of Kashan, the ochres and deep blues of Baluchi, the animals and wild flowers of Tabriz, each one with its own density of knots and rich in the vivid colours of natural vegetable dyes.

At Abadeh, half way to Shiraz and considered to be the home of backgammon, we caught a glimpse of a 4,000-metre peak, Kuh-e-Sefid (The White Mountain), one of the most southerly sentinels of the Zagros range. Through the late forenoon haze, a few white streaks of snow were visible near the summit. At this latitude and for this time of year, this was remarkable and confirmed that there would be a great deal of snow here in the winter.

We clattered our way on the potholed road down past Takt-e-Jamshid (Persepolis to the Westerner), and the ruins of King Cyrus the Great's Centre of Empire, to Shiraz, a city of roses and gardens, which was to be our home for two years.

The months passed and summer cooled into autumn. The winter of 1976 disappeared almost as quickly as it had arrived but not before our Range Rover had provided the opportunity we had sought to explore the Zagros mountains. I was training hard for the World Ski Orienteering Championships in Bulgaria and every weekend found us in the mountains above Dasht-e-Arzan at 2,500 metres above sea level. The hard névé snow was magnificent for skiing though greedy for Klister wax which was so necessary for good kick off and grip on this sort of surface. To experience the hard snow before the sun turned it into a sugary soup, we used to leave before dawn, and plan to be on skis within two hours' drive. A three-hour training session, which often covered 50 kilometres in good conditions, was followed by a picnic and some relaxed skiing on a nearby slope before the weary return to Shiraz. But it was during that first winter in Shiraz that I conceived my idea for an exciting cross-country ski trip. It had come to me as I had watched a tribe of people pass through Qasrodasht, a rural suburb of Shiraz, on their biannual migration.

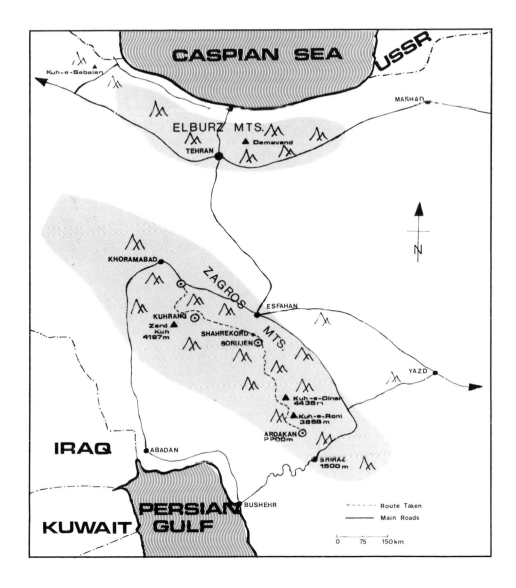

The Qashgai, a large tribe of Turkish origin, migrate to and from the warm coastal regions of the Persian Gulf into the mountains every spring and autumn. Their six-week journey, with thousands of animals and all their wordly possessions, takes them from the searing heat and humidity of the Gulf coast to the green pastures fed by melting snows high upon the slopes of the Zagros. Here they graze their animals and weave their rugs, moving from pasture to pasture and at heights that vary from 2,400 to 3,400 metres where it is delightfully cool. Their routes have been the same for centuries and their tracks have carved wide paths over high passes under great mountain cliffs and into high valleys and alps often dissected by cold clear rivers of the purest water. In early October these hardiest of people pack everything, load their camels, donkeys and horses and retrace their steps down to their lower warmer winter quarters. My idea was to follow their route, in winter, on skis; it promised some exciting skiing.

At the end of that first winter's experience in Iran, I was able to write to Odd (now working for a Norwegian Aid Development project building huts on Mount Kilimanjaro in Tanzania), to tell him that I had worked out a line about 600 kilometres long which would take us through the heart of the Zagros. All that needed verifying was a tricky part near Zard Kuh (at 4,197 metres, the second highest massif in the range), which was in the centre of Bakhtiari country. I reassured him that I would be able to go up there sometime in the summer to check it out and suggested mid-February the following year for the trip.

His reply, in delightful broken English, arrived on 27th August:

Dear Guy   *Marangu 27.7.76*
Thanks a lot for your letter which I just received from Norway. These mountains look fantastic. I thought the hills would have been much more rough. The bloody thing is that I cannot leave this park before June '77 when my contract expires. I have been thinking about this trip since you left Oslo, and I was very glad to hear from you. What you tells sounds fantastic. I did a similar trip on skis in the atlas mountains in Maroc two years ago where we went 400km on skiis in 4 weeks. We also lived in the mountain villages or tents and cooked all our food on open fire, to save weight. With food for about three weeks and all other equipment in the rucksack it was not heavier than 40kg to start with. (but that was in fact too bloody heavy the first week). Guy, I cannot join you on this trip this winter cause of my contract here on Kilimanjaro, but what about the next winter? I know this is far in the future, but I have been thinking so much about this trip so I won't ever give it up. Not after I have seen your pictures. We were three in Maroc, but found out that we did not save any weight in that way. If this have any interest let me know, but if you can wait one more year I'll join you. I have done some skiing here on Kilimanjaro also but it is not enough snow to do longer trips. I can just run around on the summit glacier till I get exhausted cause of the altitude, but it is great fun still. I hope to go to Ruwenzori in Christmas and I'll take my skiis with me there. I have a fine job here. My work is to supervise the construction of the new tourist huts on the mountain. I have to walk up and down on the mountain up to two times a week, and I am now in a very good fysical condition. The salary is good and we are living in a nice house high up on the slopes here. There is mountain trout in the rivers around and snow higher up. So it has been a very interesting job down here. I have

not had time to do so much climbing but when the houses are finished in September I am going to make a guide book for climbing and walking and then I have to do all the routes here. That work will be like a holiday. Do you know anything about the snow conditions in the central Hindukush in Afgahnistan? I mean then the area between Herat and Kabul. I heard there is plenty of snow there in winter and I have been driving parts of it in summer, that looked also very good for skiing. So if you do the Zagros mountains this winter, may be we can do the Hindu Kush next year? At least it is great fun to make plans.

Let's keep in contact in the coming months. If I can escape here for four weeks I'll join you.

I will let you know soon.

Thanks a lot for your letter again.

All the best from 'Odd'

This was followed a month later with confirmation that he could take some leave and join me for the trip:

Dear Guy   *Marangu 29.8.76*
I have now made up my mind, I will be coming definitely. I have arranged with my leave, so it should be no problems in that way.

I really look forward to this trip, but there will of course be some correspondence back and from in the coming months.

This is not my strongest side, but what to do? What kind of skis are you going to use. I will prefer a little more heavy skis. 'Turlangrenn' with Kandahar or Tempo bindings. I have used this always in the mountains and they are okay.

Is there any possibilities to buy food locally while we are going? This will save the weight quite a bit. How cold can the night be up in the mountains. In the Atlas we did well with very little clothes, and I think the temperature will roughly be the same there. As long as the sleeping bag are warm enough there will be no problems.

If we cannot rely on buying food locally, are there any possibilities of getting air drops one or two times? How are the locals when they meet forengiers. I have heard so much about the Kurds but I believe they are like mountain people all over, nice and friendly. Can you send me your plans as soon as you can. Do you have some maps of the area which you could send me?

Looking forward to hear from you soon.

Is it possible to reach you by phone?

Hilsen

'Odd'

While correspondence flowed erratically from Shiraz to Marangu in Tanzania, Molly and I used every weekend to explore and find out a little more about the routes used by the Qashgai.

We went up to Shahreza, a small town not far from Zard Kuh and quizzed the local Bakhtiari tribes on snow depths, temperatures, and a host of other pertinent points. Slowly the jigsaw puzzle of a route was pieced together and it was time for me to get leave and gather up food and kit for the adventure that lay ahead.

Maps were difficult to obtain and in traditional Middle Eastern fashion, they were given a confidential classification and were only available through the Military. We badly needed 1:50,000 cover of the trickier parts of the route but the only way I could get hold of them was by subterfuge—a risk worth taking! In the end I could only find two so I resorted to using 1:500,000 tactical pilotage charts. This was far from ideal but I had no option. Our Embassy in Tehran now became concerned and because I had diplomatic status, they were worried about clearance with the Iranian authorities and, more particularly, the inherent suspicions towards foreigners in the remoter areas of this country especially at an unusual time of the year. I cursed the bureaucracy into which I was now drawn and the extra effort it all generated to convince the office wallahs in their air conditioning that Odd and I were quite capable of looking after ourselves and completing the route. It was all rather tiresome and the inevitable compromise was reached. The green light was on.

Odd flew into Shiraz on Monday 6th February 1977 and Molly took him out to Dasht-e-Arzan for a couple of mornings' skiing before we started. I flew in at the beginning of the Islamic weekend and the flight over the mountains confirmed that there was ample snow down to about 2,200 metres. This was a great relief and removed my main concern of there being inadequate cover; my rehearsed answers to justify the expense of Odd's long flight from Tanzania were cast to the wind! Over dinner on 9th February, we discussed and agreed what to take, packed six days' food and a petrol primus stove and decided not to take a tent. In a separate box were provisions for the second leg which Molly was to deliver to Borujen, a small town some 300 kilometres away to meet us on 16th February. I had prepared some emergency instructions for her to follow. The Naval Attaché in the Embassy had insisted on this, although knowing the remoteness of the route ahead, my confidence in transmitting messages should we have an accident was hardly very great.

Two empty wine bottles confirmed the reason for a slight hangover, and after a hastily prepared breakfast, the three of us left for Ardakan, a small village on the bumpy road to Yasuj. It was about one hour's drive and the village was silent and deserted when we arrived at dawn. It was − 5 °C with a patchy sky, and there had been one centimetre of snow during the night. This was indeed good news because the first few hours would see us climbing from 2,300 metres up to a pass a fraction below 3,000 metres. With new cold snow and blue ski wax this climb would not be difficult but we would need to get up and over before the sun climbed too high and melted it. A farewell to Molly and after encouraging her to take extra care, because she was now five months pregnant, we swung rucksacks on, clipped on the skis and departed.

The wax worked extremely well and it needed to; any extra effort with 23-kilo rucksacks created by slippery skis would be compounded by the altitude which, as we climbed, I began to feel. Odd was fresh from the thin air of Kilimanjaro but for me the effects of having to work at sea level on the Persian Gulf coast quickly began to manifest itself. The sun was soon warming the South Face of Kuh-e-Roni (3,840 metres), which I had climbed by an easy route the previous summer. The sheer face of this impressive peak dominated the pass up ahead and as we toiled up the steep slopes so the sun descended to greet us. It was going to be a hot day so it was vital to push on without a rest to gain the pass as early as we could. We were there shortly after 9.30 and it had taken us a little under four hours—we were well satisfied with the wax. Ahead lay an undulating valley which after several kilometres dropped down to Komehr, a small, mud-walled hamlet surrounded by tall tabrizee trees, which are a type of poplar. Both Odd and I were impressed by the fact that here we were, a crow's flight distance of 150 kilometres from the heat and smell of the Gulf littoral in a mountain wilderness and skiing on impeccable snow. And not a soul in sight!

Komehr was deserted but there was an open stream trickling down one side of a copse of tabrizees and we were able to replenish water bottles and quench raging thirsts. The stream was the life essence of the tall slim trees whose trunks are used as supporting rafters in these characteristic mud houses, for in this dry desert scene, there are no other resources. In the summer they form little oases of green in the harsh brown landscape and provide welcome shade. Now in mid-winter their silhouette was skeletal against the bright reflection of the sun on snow. We had come 25 kilometres since leaving the Range Rover and the heat of the mid-day sun was astonishing. Our efforts up to that first pass and beyond to Komehr had dehydrated me so that I had that heavy-legged feeling of weakness. Odd was feeling as strong as a horse however and had forged ahead to spy out our route. A lunch break with hot, sweet tea provided a resurgence of energy for the second part of the day.

Centuries ago Alexander the Great marched down into this valley with his armies on his way to raze Persepolis and as we reached a small pass some 10 kilometres ahead, by glancing back the way we had come, it was easy to see how the bulk of Kuh-e-Roni had forced him to track to the east to the Rud-e-Kar (River Kar) valley. To his good fortune this valley funnelled him in a south-easterly direction for 100 kilometres directly into Persepolis. Today the valley is blocked by a dam with a long azure lake of sweet water snaking away behind it. It is called Darius and in the Shah's day boasted a sailing club. Alexander, however, did not have to contend with snow when he was here, nor the obstacle of a man-made lake!

The lengthening shadows jolted us to our senses and told us we must hasten. Darkness suddenly descended as it always does at these latitudes and we were still several kilometres from a Gendarmerie post where we were hoping to spend the night. We descended for 2–3 kilometres at a speed exaggerated by the failing light. Odd had disappeared from hearing below while I gingerly snow ploughed my way down tensing myself to maintain balance and remain on my feet. I was exhausted and the combination of heavy rucksack, dehydration and such a long first day was taking its toll. Odd waited patiently at the bottom and together we skied towards a twinkling light. In the darkness we had no idea how far away it was. It seemed an age but the sound of dogs barking, alerted no doubt by the noise of skis and sticks creaking on the crusty snow, indicated that we were getting close. A small hill led up to the light which was hanging outside the front door of the Gendarmerie post. We knocked and went in and I collapsed onto the fine tribal rug covering the mud floor. A drink of sweetened tea and lots of it was what I wanted more than anything at that moment. Odd murmured that he thought we had covered 55 kilometres and when I had recovered some of my composure I asked the Gendarmerie if that was so. *'Bali'* (yes) they replied.

They fed us *Chelo Morg,* a lightly-spiced chicken dish and I remember little else as my eyelids slammed shut and didn't open again until dawn the next day.

The bulk of Kuh-e-Dinar (4,435 metres) barred our way ahead. Alexander had been forced to circumvent its southerly 1,000-metre precipice, which stretched unbroken except in one place for 50 kilometres, until he found a gap which led him straight into the valley in which we now stood. Our route was to the east and, refreshed by an immaculate night's rest, we headed out into the cold and a temperature of $-18\,°C$. But the skiing was superb, and being at a slightly lower altitude than the previous day I felt good. The south-facing slopes at the lower altitude (2,400 metres) were often free of snow but we were able to pick a zig-zag route around most of them. Sometimes we walked up a bare slope, carrying skis, but only when it was necessary to return to the line of our route. Once over these bare slopes, the northern sides provided that exhilarating descent, where the snow was cold and control on hard névé that much easier. Odd exercised his patience at the foot of each of these slopes having so often demonstrated his mastery of downhill skiing on cross-country skis with a heavy rucksack. I would arrive almost every time in the most ungraceful manner, pleased that I had not cartwheeled several times. It would have been nice to have some style and to do it at speed; I still had much to learn from him.

Village folk came out to see us pass by and we were often followed by hordes of giggling, excited children who would run after us, up to their ankles in snow, some in bare feet! They had never seen such a spectacle before. We lunched by a small stream and enjoyed the warm sunshine before heading northwards with Kuh-e-Dinar to our west. As the sun descended and the highest summits of Kuh-e-Dinar cast shadows about our feet, we searched for a suitable night site. With no tent we focused our search on deep snow drifts. We had no intention of digging a snow hole because it takes some time and more often than not, you became very wet in the process. Instead, Odd's plan, which he had explained briefly before we left Shiraz, was to make a small shelter using snow bricks for the walls. We used our skis and sticks to form a lattice work for the roof and over that we stretched a space blanket. This in turn was anchored down with a layer of snow bricks, and once erected, the whole structure froze together. For a door we had a single 60-centimetre wide strip of clear polythene which was suspended from a ski stick up in the roof. Once inside with the primus going and a candle alight, it made a warm and cosy home. Snow from the floor or walls was close to hand to melt on the stove into water for our dehydrated food.

Our first night in such a shelter was extremely cold and it was −26 °C when I was woken in the early hours of the morning by uncomfortable pains in my stomach. Within seconds I was retching with no time to get to the door. The patch of snow at the foot of the wall on my side became an aiming mark. The *Chelo Morg* from the previous evening had failed to be digested and had clearly disagreed with me. The effort of it all weakened me considerably and when we set off before dawn I did not relish the thought of the 50 kilometres of hard skiing ahead of us that day. Whatever had affected me had avoided Odd and we resolved that wherever possible we would fight shy of eating village food and rely completely on our own supplies.

That day was a struggle and I was very worried that I was impeding our progress and that perhaps we would not make Borujen on time. The worst section was a plateau, some 15 kilometres wide, over which we skated with a kind of kick and balancing act on one ski and a push with both ski sticks behind; I tried to imitate Odd but could not find the rhythm that seemed to

81

propel him effortlessly. We arrived at Khosrow Shirin with Odd insatiable for more skiing like that, while all I wanted was gallons of something sweet. A longish stop produced the remedy and I reasoned that all the vomiting during the night coupled with the effort of the last 25 kilometres had weakened me.

To our west the summit ridge of Kuh-e-Dinar was silhouetted against the bright sky. This mighty ridge averages 4,000 metres for its entire length of 50 kilometres and its numerous summits rise to their highest at 4,435 metres. I had not seen this side of the mountain before and although it was less precipitous than on the west it was nonetheless still most impressive. The gap in the centre of the ridge was more noticeable from where we now stood and we had to resist the temptation to divert from our route to get up there. Alas it was a good 20 kilometres away and we had not the time. It was a sensational sight from the spot where we built our snow shelter that evening. There was a trickle of a stream close by and we were able to cook our supper in the warmth of the evening sun before the sudden drop in temperature heralded sunset and drove us into our sleeping bags. Later that winter, not long after Odd's departure for Tanzania, I was able to ski up onto that ridge and gain a grandstand view of practically the complete length of this section of our route.

Our fourth day out began no differently than the others. The weather was perfect; it was cold when we set off, the snow was still in good condition and we both felt good, the gyppy tummy of the previous days quickly forgotten. It was not long before we had to descend to cross a wide valley which would take us off the snow for about 5 kilometres. A small village straddled a river not far away and, parked beside a house near the centre was a tractor. The sight of this prompted us to descend to try and find some petrol to top up our fuel bottle. As we schussed to a stop, we were soon surrounded by villagers. The headman emerged and we exchanged the customary salaams. 'Will you have lunch with me?' he asked. Odd and I looked at each other and the temptation was too great—we agreed.

We were ushered towards a small house where we shed our rucksacks and leaned our skis against the wall. We removed our boots and entered a room where there was a kerosene stove in one corner providing a little warmth. We sat on the floor on a gaily-coloured tribal rug and propped some woven cushions behind us to lean against. Tea was soon produced and I chatted in Farsi with our hosts, translating into English and passing it all on to Odd as we went along. About an hour passed and I asked when lunch would be ready. I explained that we must get on, we had a long way to go. Our host gesticulated that they had just caught the chicken and were dealing with it now; 'It won't be long' he declared.

Thirty minutes passed and Odd and I now talking in Norwegian, decided that we could not wait any longer. We had to leave if we were to do our distance that day. We made moves to depart, explaining in Farsi and thanking him for the *chai*. As we were doing this, there seemed to be a commotion outside, which was not visible to us through the small window, but I could hear orders being spoken in Farsi. There was a clatter in the passageway outside the room and I heard the all too familiar sound of a rifle being cocked, and then another. I hardly had time to look at Odd and register with him my wide-eyed disbelief of what I thought was about to happen, when the door burst open and two soldiers armed with G3 automatic rifles stormed in and covered each of us. Behind them entered a Sergeant who ordered us to sit down. We did what we were told. Under the muzzles of two automatic rifles, now was not the time to argue! We produced our papers, for me my diplomatic identity card and a letter written in Farsi explaining what we were doing, and for Odd his Norwegian passport.

It was clear to both of us that we were here to stay for some time and we discussed our predicament in Norwegian. We both agreed that I should try and break the ice by asking what had happened to the lunch, as it was for this that they had originally invited us and it was bad Persian manners not to provide it! It seemed to defuse the situation a little, but there was no indication of relaxation on the part of the Sergeant. We soon realised why the waiting game with the lunch was played. The suspicions of the headman must have made him delay the production of lunch while someone was despatched to fetch the Gendarmerie. After a few minutes, lunch was brought in but alas, it seemed not for us. The Sergeant tucked in while we sat, still under the guard of the two soldiers. 'Cheeky sod' I murmured to Odd. We had to do something to retrieve the initiative and a further discussion with Odd suggested that I must use my authority and knowledge of the language to regain the upper hand. It was merely a question of timing it right!

The time came after the Sergeant had downed our lunch and ordered us onto our feet and outside. When he told us to pick up our rucksacks and get into the back of a Russian Gaz Jeep, I stopped, turned, stared at him straight in the eye and said *'Ostavar, man Sargerd hastam. Man moostashahra Takavaran Shahanshahee hastam.'* (Sergeant, I am a Major, an advisor to the Shah's Commandos.) To my relief, he stood to attention and ordered the two soldiers to pick up our rucksacks and put them and our skis into the jeep. It had worked! We now had the initiative and, keen to hold it, I got into the front seat of the jeep next to the Sergeant. Odd was already trying to chat to the soldiers in the back. We were taken to a large village called Hanna where, the Sergeant indicated, there would be a

Lieutenant Colonel from *Savak* to question us. *Savak,* I explained to Odd, was the much-feared State Secret Police, and we agreed that we would pull the same line on him when we saw him.

It did not take long for the Sergeant to find him. Papers were produced and much to our surprise the *Savak* Colonel gave the Sergeant a public dressing down and ordered our immediate release. By this time it was late in the evening and we were driven to a small caravanserai where we were told we could stay the night, at the Shah's expense before being allowed to continue our journey the next morning.

We had about 90 kilometres to go before reaching our rendezvous at Borujen with Molly and the best part of two days to cover the distance. The previous day's drama had been frustrating, especially as we had missed 30 kilometres of good skiing. A five-minute ride in a pick-up got us clear of Semiron and back onto good snow atop the escarpment, where a long plateau disappeared towards Mehr-Gerd, a village some 15 kilometres from us. The plateau continued undulating gently for a further 40 kilometres descending once to cross a river. It was in fact a wide open valley between long mountain ridges, which drained into the centre from the 3,000-metre heights to either side. Another night was spent safely in an 'Eliassen-patent' snow shelter but in the morning we discovered a lot of large animal footprints around the shelter. I knew there were wolves in these mountains because the previous summer I had disturbed seven of the creatures dozing in the lee of a ridge on the western flank of Kuh-e-Dinar. On that occasion I had been on my own and by good fortune found myself above them. They had disappeared when I hurled stones and abuse at them but it was a close skirmish with nature and the memory of fourteen grey eyes following my every move a mere 15–20 metres from me is as vivid today as it was at that moment. We would have to take care from now on.

Now on our sixth day out, we were well satisfied with our kit. Odd was using his Bonna glass fibre skis and I was using a Kneissel plastic pair with metal edges under the middle of the ski. Waxing had not been the problem we had envisaged and from the beginning of the trip we had soon appreciated the need to anticipate the waxing requirement for the next morning. Heat was essential to smooth and spread blue Klister wax, which was the only one able to give us good grip on the icy névé each morning, and we used the warm sun to good effect to do this each evening. For boots, both of us wore rubber, felt-lined ones made in Korea and they fitted the 75-mm Nordic-norm Rottefella binding. The boots were excellent, they were light and their greatest merit was to keep our feet dry for longer than any other boots would have done in the wet soupy snow that we experienced every afternoon.

The extreme limits of the migration of the Qashgai tribe, probably those

84

called Darashiri, were up here and we were shortly to cross their invisible boundary with the Bakhtiari folk, most of whom are still nomadic though there are a few who have become settled in small villages.

A Moslem cemetery marked by small head stones poking through the snow lay on the last pass that we crossed before the beginning of our descent towards Borujen. There was not a village in sight in either direction and we guessed that this was a traditional burial ground used by the Qashgai. It was a lovely spot flanked by two rugged peaks towering 500–600 metres above us, so we joined the dead of many decades, to rest and have some lunch before skimming off towards a re-entrant that dropped steeply to the north.

The re-entrant turned into a gully narrowing into something resembling a cresta run. The bottom was full of snow but the sun had melted it away to only a metre or so up on the left-hand side. A late turn would lead us on to bare mountainside with the pain of sprawling into desert thorns. Odd took it in one, but not me. At the narrowest point I funked it, took off my skis and clambered down for 30 metres.

We could see Borujen clearly below us and about 8 kilometres distant, and there did not seem to be much snow out in the middle of the plain. As the gully opened out into a valley and then merged into the plain, we dropped down to the 2,000-metre contour. We were lucky to find a thin finger of snow which followed a dry watercourse to within 200 metres of the town. There parked outside the Iran Tour Inn 400 metres away was our white Range Rover. Molly had made it safely. Carrying skis, Odd and I walked along the road and as we neared the inn, a crowd of people followed us curiously studying us while chattering wildly among themselves. Feeling like pied-pipers, we swung through the gates of the inn and were greeted by Molly and her friend Shirley she had brought with her to keep her company on the long drive from Shiraz. They had arrived half an hour before us, and Odd and I somewhat smugly concluded that our timing could not have been better. We had skied a little under 300 kilometres in six days.

The memories of that short mid-tour break in the inn at Borujen are blissful. We ate well, Molly had brought some beer and wine, and we relished the rest. It all stimulated our enthusiasm for the morrow and the second leg of the trip.

We drove along a bumpy icy road to Shahrekord the next morning, 17th February. We would start the next leg from there while Molly would drive to Tehran to stay with friends before returning for our rendezvous in six days' time. As we climbed out of the plain, the Range Rover making light of the steep icy road, we saw some boys sliding down a small slope just outside the village. We stopped and were privileged to be given a skiing display by three young Bakhtiari boys who had invented their own skis: strips of wood from discarded fruit boxes on which were nailed small curved tips. Their sticks were anything from broom handles to a bit of a branch from a tabrizee tree. Bindings were leather thongs or pieces of rope and string through which they put any old pair of shoes or gum boots. Odd cast a professional Nordic and carpenter's eye on their handicraft and after we were given a few more demonstrations of Bakhtiari telemark and snow plough turns, he acknowledged that his own country, the inventors of skiing as it is known today, must have been doing similar things on makeshift bits of wood a couple of centuries before.

We were now heading for a village called Kuhrang which a few years earlier had become the centre of an ambitious engineering project. It was the Shah's ultimate plan to build a firm industrial base for his country and a huge steel works, built largely with Soviet aid, had risen out of the desert near Esfahan. For this and other emerging industries water and electricity were needed. A massive dam had been constructed at Chadegan in a deep sun-scorched valley, and to compensate for enormous evaporation during the long summer, a tunnel had been built under the mountain to channel water from the Kuhrang river. This river flows into the Karun, Iran's largest river, which enters the Persian Gulf at Abadan. Its source is high up on Zard Kuh (Yellow Mountain) at 4,197 metres the loftiest peak in this part of the Zagros range. In the summer water cascades out of the tunnel exit but now it was a mere trickle over great mushrooms of blue-green ice.

Since we had left Molly at Shahrekord, Odd had not been feeling a hundred per cent and he had had an uncomfortable night in the snow shelter the previous night. Whatever it was that was gripping him had missed me. As he was running a temperature we chose to spend the next night in a Bakhtiari village, where a little extra warmth and comfort might help towards a better night's rest. The skiing had been good since Sharekord and in spite of Odd's problem we had made good distance through remarkable scenery. That evening, as we approached a hamlet, we were given an aggressive welcome by a group of evil-looking dogs, their ears cut back to better focus their hearing, and in spite of the efforts of their owners to control them, we were only able to keep them at bay by brandishing our ski sticks.

The headman, Habibollah, was very welcoming and asked us to stay the night, and to share his house with his family. He was a tall, tubby man and wore the traditional Bakhtiari cloak of closely woven wool with black vertical patterns. Perched on his head was a black felt pot of a hat. His house was on the edge of the village and was two-storied. The ground floor was a stable of several rooms where all animals were housed in winter time. A set of stone and mud steps rose to a verandah on the first floor with three rooms leading off into the back of the house. The roof was formed by a framework of tabrizee tree trunks and placed above them was a thatch of brush and twigs. He explained that when he was a boy he and his family would set off on their migration to get away from the cold snowy winters. In the 1930s Reza Shah, the Shah's father, instituted a settlement policy for the two main nomadic tribes and the Qashgai and Bakhtiari found themselves being forced to settle and build their own houses. In the early days the rigours of the fierce winters claimed their toll among the people and their animals, and many perished. Today there are more of the Bakhtiari people settled into villages than their southerly neighbours the Qashgai.

We were invited into the main living room where we were introduced to Habibollah's two wives and children from both! In one corner was a stove which was soon put to good use cooking a young fat-tailed sheep, slaughtered for the occasion. In the centre of the room was a charcoal burner over which was draped a heavy thick-padded blanket and we were quickly shown its purpose. The whole family were arranged like a star around the burner, and their feet were thrust under the blanket and up to the smouldering charcoal. It was an ingenious way of warming feet and the male members of the family who were constantly in and out, tinkering with various chores, would thrust their icy feet under the blanket for a brief warming before venturing outside into the snow again. Odd and I were allocated a corner and we were soon touching feet with all the household. The food was good, lightly spiced and served with a little rice. Habibollah was very proud of his new young wife and asked us what we thought of her. 'Khelee gashangi' (very beautiful) we replied. His rather wizened first wife did not agree and she spared no effort in telling us that she did not like being relegated to second place and living in the same house. There were numerous children of all ages, and after supper we negotiated for space to stretch out for the night. Odd took some pills which psychologically made him feel a little better. What we should have taken were sleeping pills but alas we had none, and had to contend with snoring, interspersed with a crying baby being breast fed at frequent intervals, bleating sheep and other noisy animals! Not a minute's silence passed throughout the entire night but it was a rich experience and neither of us would have wished to have missed it.

After a breakfast of yoghurt and boiled eggs, Odd was back on form. Both of us noticed that we had been bitten during the night around our waists and these bites itched incessantly. But bed bugs or fleas, we resigned ourselves to carrying our tiny passengers for the remainder of the trip! Doubtless they were lodged in our sleeping bags as well as our clothes but there was little we could do, save curse the irritation.

We were now into our ninth day of fine weather, and we followed the line of an open river with the bulk of Zard Kuh at our backs. There was at least a metre of snow here—a little more than we had on the first leg and it was still the same hard surface that we had been blessed with throughout the trip. The sun was very strong and extremely warm in the middle of the day, and both of us were getting badly burnt on the nose and ears. Odd manufactured a nose-cover out of a food carton, suspending it from the bridge of his sunglasses by sticky tape.

We left the river and swung north-westwards following a shallow valley flanked by ridges that rose to just under 4,000 metres on one side and 3,200 metres on the other. Here we met an old Bakhtiari man and his grandson. They were walking in the soupy mid afternoon snow and their chatter indicated that they had travelled some distance. Their dark inquisitive eyes were streaming water, the whites more a shade of scarlet than the colour nature had intended. It did not need a doctor to diagnose that they were suffering from severe snow blindness. We tried to explain their problem to them but they would only retort that they had been walking around in the snow all their lives and had put up with the pain and inconvenience. So there was little we could offer them beyond encouraging them to get some sunglasses the next time they went to a bazaar. It was astonishing to us that this sort of elementary precaution was simply not understood, though in summer most Persians wore their sunglasses, indoors and out!

Another 50 kilometres and a snow shelter further on found us nearing the end of our journey. Our flea bites had become more irritating but other than that we were on good form. The rigours of the first few days had long been put behind as we put the kilometres behind and enjoyed the skiing. Every conceivable technique used was a pleasure: skating, double poling, diagonal gait, long uphill zig-zag traverses to reach another pass and the dizzy sensational downhill stretch the other side. Testing turns of every variety: snow-plough, telemark, christie, or just a sideslip were all a delight. And it was those immeasurable feelings of fulfilment and contentment, joint experiences of mountaineer and mountain ski-tourer alike that compelled Odd to speak out: *'Utrolig'* (unbelievable) he said.

Our final and eleventh day dawned glorious with a heavy frost. We tracked eastwards around the flank of a 3,883-metre peak, over a pass and propelled ourselves down a long gradual slope with good speed. Round a corner, across a river, and over a small hill and we were descending to the harsh brown line which marked the extreme edge of the snow. We decided to have lunch there and basked in the hot sun while tea brewed. There was a bumpy jeep track visible a couple of kilometres away, and we walked up this to the main asphalt road between Esfahan and Khoramabad. It was not long before a bus appeared on the horizon and we flagged it down for the 250-kilometre journey to Esfahan.

It was with contentment that we relaxed in the bus. We had had a marvellous 550-kilometre experience and wished we could do it all again. That night, with the euphoria felt by all mountaineers and adventurers after success, and artificially stimulated by nasty local beer, we preyed on the fleas in a manner more akin to a sacrificial ritual. I think we slaughtered most of them, though some perhaps escaped into the grubbiness of the rather dirty inn where we had found two beds for the few rials we possessed. No Shah Abbas Hotel this! A search by telephone tracked Molly down in the cold northern suburbs of Tehran and she said she would be with us at noon the following day.

Odd was never to see the opulence of the Shah Abbas Hotel. Dirty and unshaven, we were barred from entry by a giant of a Persian bouncer, so while we waited for Molly, drinking copious amounts of tea we wondered 'Where next?'

'Afghanistan' said Odd.

The Russians put paid to that plan on a cold wintry day in December 1979.

The Western Himalayas: A 600-Kilometre Winter Journey

'Winter comes to rule the varied year.'
(Thomson, *The Seasons*)

On 31st October 1980 an alarming letter was sent to me from Odd Eliassen. On the reverse face of the envelope, written in bold letters was a cryptic note:

MOLLY. Can you please read this letter for Guy on the 'phone if he is away for a while. It is Urgent.
Odd.

It was midweek. Stationed at Portsmouth, I was a weekend commuter to our home in Devon, so Molly read the letter over the telephone.

Dear Guy,
Bad news, the military authorities here have suddenly discovered that I have not been on 'repetisjøn's øvelse' [3 weeks mandatory military training for all able-bodied Norwegian men] *for fifteen years and they have now called me in on 3 March 1981. I am not willing to give up the trip to India so I need your help, and this is urgent. Can't you write as a Major in the Royal Marines the importance of my being on our expedition and that we have worked and planned this expedition for four years. I think you can head the letter to my Oberst* [Colonel] *who is my regimental chief. I am pessimistic now and very uncertain about the whole thing.*

With a mere ten weeks to go before our departure, and with almost all of the planning behind us, it was a bomb shell! The letter ended with Odd saying he had to send his application within three weeks, so we didn't have much time. I put pen to paper that evening and wrote to Odd's Oberst. The last two sentences of my letter made a simple plea:

For me to obtain leave from the Royal Marines to do this journey with two of your countrymen required me to give notice to my head office two years ago. I am sure you will appreciate how devastating to our plans it would be for Mr Eliassen not to accompany us.

Uncertainty ruled for the next three weeks during which time fingers were earnestly crossed in Devon, Hampshire, Oslo and Asker. If Odd couldn't go the trip would have to be cancelled; we wouldn't be able to find a replacement at such short notice. But luck was on our side and Odd gained his reprieve.

It was in Iran in 1977 that I first mentioned the possibility of skiing through part of the Indian Himalayas. In 1976 Molly and I, joined by Ram Seeger (an old friend in the Royal Marines), had been there to climb Phabrang, a 6,200-metre peak in Himachal Pradesh. While we did not get quite to the summit, and that produced its own disappointments, it had been possible to see far up into the top of the Miyar Nulla with its long gradual sloping glacier and its high wide pass bearing no headwall. Whatever lay on the other side of that pass was almost certainly the key to access to the wide open valley and kingdom of Zanskar. My knowledge of a road connection to Ladakh over a relatively low pass called the Pensi La suggested that from there, access to the Vale of Kashmir would certainly be possible through one of several passes. The more I thought about the possibility of such a ski tour, the greater was my motivation to find out a little bit more.

Ram provided the answer to the key question. In 1978, he returned to India and after several adventures walked over that pass at the head of the Miyar Nulla. It was called the Kang La and, although at an altitude of 5,468 metres, it was a straightforward glacier plod. Ram confirmed that there were no icefall barriers either side but once down towards the main river valley of the Tsarap Lingti Chu, there was a narrow steep defile to negotiate before reaching the open central Zanskar valley. That defile, he explained, boasted a spectacular monastery, perched on a sheer knuckle of rock called Burdem Gompa. He also confirmed that the approach to Zanskar through the Suru Valley was wide, although in one place where it swung in a great zig-zag under the precipices of Nun and Kun, it was narrow and very steep. 'That could be a problem in winter', he suggested.

Ram's wanderings in India and Odd's arrival in England for a holiday early in 1979 provided the impetus for me to suggest that we launch ourselves rapidly into detailed planning. He was keen and he had a good friend who would also want to go along. His name was Erik Boehlke. In concept our plan would vary little from the long winter ski journeys that had been accumulated between us over the previous few years. It would be lightweight, an important factor at altitude. Unlike Iran, we would need the protection of a tent to shield us from any protracted Himalayan winter storms, and because the distance from Srinagar in Kashmir to Manali was almost 800 kilometres we would have to put out food depots about 10 days' skiing apart. The mechanics of doing that were perplexing and although it was early days and we were merely developing and exploring ideas, the cacheing of food became the fundamental and most important issue if the trip were to achieve any form of success.

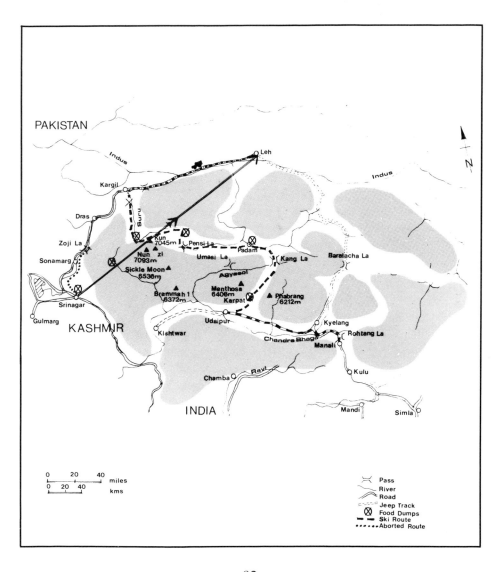

Our concept was to be self-sufficient in food for two important reasons. It would, we believed, be most unfair to rely for food on the local village people as we passed. They were, more often than not, barely able to survive on the meagre crops that they could harvest in the short summer months and even if they were able to help us, the calorific value of the food would almost certainly be too low. But perhaps the most important reason was the likelihood, based on experience, of contracting debilitating stomach disorders.

Meanwhile, equipment and money had to be found: Odd and Erik promised to seduce ski and equipment manufacturers the length and breadth of Norway while the initial task of finding some financial sponsorship would be mine.

At that time I was in a busy staff job in Portsmouth and couldn't get away to join Odd, Erik and two other Norwegian friends on a 400-kilometre ski tour in the Atlas Mountains of Morocco, their second in the area. It turned out to be a very useful evaluation of skis and equipment and proved that the essential element of our plans for India were workable. While they were away enjoying the winter sun of the lower latitudes, I attempted to swing the bureaucracy of the British military system into gear to favour my request for leave during the winter of 1981. The Corps were happy but I encountered a very different reaction from the British High Commission in New Delhi, through whom notice of my participation and the outline plans of the journey had to be passed. The High Commission almost torpedoed the whole plan, and it is pertinent to quote part of their letter because it shows how out of touch some diplomatic people can be with the more simple things in life.

The areas you wish to operate in are probably restricted and possibly prohibited. The fact that you are a bone fide traveller will arouse suspicions rather than lull them. From a purely realistic stand point it would be naïve to suppose that any food dump placed in September in India would be intact when required 5 months later. The Indians are a poor and hungry race in the mountains.

I wondered whether the author had ever been out of Delhi! And that was not all—they went on to point out that my military status required Foreign and Commonwealth Office approval for the journey; that I needed to have the approval of the High Commission in Delhi; approval from the Ministry of External Affairs in India; permission from the Indian Mountaineering Federation (IMF) and to cap it all, we would have to be accompanied by an Indian Service Liaison Officer. I hoped we could find one who could ski! I was wise enough to realise that one knocks bureaucracy at one's peril but to be told all these prerequisites was pretty depressing. I decided not to tell Odd and Erik about these military hurdles because they were my problem and I knew that if I were barred by bureaucracy from going on the trip, they would do it anyway. I was also long enough in the tooth to know that an over-reaction to that letter would almost certainly alienate the people delegated to process my request in faraway India. Secure in that knowledge, another much longer letter went off to the High Commission in Delhi.

In this, I pointed out that ours was a ski trek and thus the word expedition could be misleading; that the trek did not include climbing a peak or using technical mountaineering equipment such as ice axes and crampons which were the usual criteria for IMF clearance and the engagement of a Liaison Officer; that the area through which we would ski throbbed with Indian and foreign trekkers during the summer months and that there was no requirement in the Western Indian Himalayas to have a trekking permit; that our plans to dump food were not naïve because Ram had done it before and had found it safe on his return; that the local folk were Buddhists and Buddhists don't steal—and as my *coup de main,* that if I were barred from going on the trip, my absence would not prevent the Norwegians doing it. With that parting shot, I despatched the letter.

While waiting for their reply I carried on with all the preparations and over the Easter holiday I made a rendezvous with Odd and Erik in Oslo. It was my first meeting with Erik. An established lawyer with a substantial legal firm in Oslo, his speciality was company and business law and he had earned his legal laurels in his handling of a case in north Norway some years before. He was, like Odd, an extremely strong skier and a noted mountaineer in his own country. Shrewd and precise, he also possessed a marvellous sense of humour. Probably the only lawyer who goes to work in the City of Oslo dressed in a sweater and jeans, his outward casualness belies his legal skill, which is formidable.

Ram flew from London with me, and the four of us drove up to Lom on the eastern edge of the Jotunheim mountains. There we turned west towards Sjåk where a small snow-ploughed forest road led us for $1^1/2$ kilometres to the entrance of Lundadalen. The car was loaded with two tents, packages of food and in our rucksacks was a variety of clothes, anoraks, shirts and woollen underwear, all obtained through the diligence of Odd and Erik. We were embarking on a week of mountain skiing, operating from one remote campsite, and by doing 30–40 kilometres a day up onto the surrounding peaks and glaciers, we would get some idea of the amount of food we should need for similar distances and temperatures in India. We all believed it was an important part of the planning stage and although the question of my own participation in the expedition was a nagging and doubtful one, it did not deter me from joining in some of the superlative skiing that is so common in the Norwegian mountains in mid-April. Ram wouldn't be joining us on the main expedition but was there to pass on his knowledge and to enjoy the skiing.

The two tents were of the same design and made by Bergans, a well-known Norwegian mountain equipment manufacturer. One was made of Goretex, a relatively new material that was reputed to allow vapour and condensation to pass from within to the outside yet still provide a waterproof fabric. The other was made of the normal nylon waterproof material. They were actually three-man tents but now Odd and I shared one, Ram and Erik the other.

Strenuous physical effort each day of the week enabled us to table our views on the exact composition of breakfast, lunch and evening meals to satisfy that physical demand. We increased the input where we felt it was needed, removed those items that someone disliked and gradually over the seven days, we were able to piece together a daily ration which we believed would be adequate to meet the physical and climatic trials of a six-week winter journey in the high Himalayas. The last couple of days in Rondana, a beautiful and quite isolated range of peaks rising to 2,000 metres further to the east of the Jotunheim, confirmed our views on the tents; the Goretex one hadn't proved satisfactory and we would use the traditional, well-proven fabric. We decided that about 75 per cent of our clothing would be wool, particularly when worn next to the skin. Synthetic materials were unsuitable even when blended with wool, except for the top insulating layers. There was nothing new in this concept, the Norwegians explained. Wool has been the base upon which people have survived winters for centuries.

That week had been a great tonic but, try as I might, I hadn't been able to forget about the High Commission in Delhi. Notwithstanding the company I shared, the fun of seven days' hard skiing and the prospects of the journey still ahead, it was impossible to shake off the notion that I might not be allowed to go when it actually took place. Perhaps Odd and Erik could sense an agitation, I don't know, but agitation was there for a further two months until 9th June, when clearance for me came in an abrupt postcript from Delhi. Relief would be an understatement.

Now I could concentrate wholeheartedly on our plans. Most imminent was our first trip to the Himalayas when we planned to make all the food dumps. This was to be in August—then we would go out again the following February for the trip proper. For the August trip, though, I had to accumulate all the food needed for the 40-day winter journey, to pack it all up and then divide it equally into five larger packages. They were quite a weight and how to get them out to Delhi now preoccupied my free time.

95

By a stroke of luck a good friend, David Nicholls, was organising a Royal Naval Mountaineering Club expedition to Himachal Pradesh to attempt to climb Tent Peak (6,150 metres) and complete an alpine-style ascent of the North-West Face of Phabrang (6,200 metres). The latter had been at my suggestion following the visit Ram and I had paid to the peak in 1976. David, fresh from his ascent of the North Face of the Eiger with John Barry (a fun-loving team and equal tigers in the mountains), was soon to leave for India and he agreed to take all our food out with his equipment and leave it at the house of one Moti Singh in the small village of Karpat, close to the Phabrang glacier. David drew a map and sent me some notes subsequently which would guide us to the house. It was a very kind gesture and one which saved us a great deal of work.

While all this was going on, efforts to gain some financial support were beginning to make headway. We had applied for the Rolex Awards for Enterprise although we realised our chances of success were remote. An application for a grant also went off to the Mount Everest Foundation (MEF) and in due course I was summoned to appear before a screening committee at the Royal Geographical Society (RGS) in London. It was quite a daunting experience: while I was seated in isolation on one side of a long table, there were no less than twelve interviewers sitting on the other.

'It's an unusual expedition', said one.

'Yes', I agreed, and spreading a map out on the table, I began to explain our plans. They were keenly interested in what unfolded and after the question-and-answer session that followed, I left the RGS with confidence that we would get something—though not so much as the £500 cheque which arrived a few weeks later. The MEF endorsement and support was a great fillip to our endeavour.

With our food safely out in New Delhi, our major logistical problems were over. There remained about 25 kilos of odds and ends that included ski waxes, fuel bottles, spare bindings, 3 snow shovels, a tent and a spare sleeping bag which went out to Delhi over one weekend with friends Ann and David Barraclough, who used their concessionary benefits available to them from their employers, British Airways. The Barracloughs also organised our August flights out to New Delhi and kindly tolerated an invasion of their house in Egham when Odd, Erik and his brother Knut (who agreed to help us) flew in from Oslo prior to our departure.

The Norwegians had with them our skis donated by Åsnes, which had already been fitted with 75-millimetre Nordic norm Rottefella bindings, with metal edges under the middle on both sides. Erik had managed to procure an extra pair which would serve as spares and would be placed in Padam, a larger than usual village, geographically in the centre of Zanskar and coincidentally about the halfway point of the journey. There were five pairs of sticks, cane ones made by Trygve Lilljedahl in Lillehammer. We had decided to go for these for the simple reason that cane was more likely to split than snap and thus would be easier to mend. One stick, as a spare, would be placed with a food depot at Ringdom Gompa, while a pair would go to Padam with the spare skis and we would try and put another in at Sokhniz together with some food.

The day before we left London we received a telegram from Douglas Keelan in Delhi. He had flown out with David Nicholls' expedition stores and he confirmed that our food had been cleared without any difficulties through Indian Customs, that he could take some of his leave and help us put out our food depots, and that we were to be the guests of Tim and Kitty Wilson on arrival in Delhi. Tim, then a Colonel in the Royal Marines was on a course at the Indian Army College of Defence Studies and would provide his car as a run-around for last-minute shopping. The timing of the telegram was just right and the four of us who boarded the BA flight made the most of the free drinks issued on board. We were happy that things seemed to have gone so well and that we were on our way to fulfil the first important administrative element of our ski journey.

Douglas met us at Delhi airport at dawn and had very obviously been enjoying Tim Wilson's whisky. In between hiccups and cheering Queen Victoria (why her in particular the four of us never knew and Douglas cannot remember either), he gave us a vague timetable of things to do before we would have to catch our plane to Srinagar, the capital city of Kashmir. Although the Indian Customs were curious as to why we were taking skis into India in the height of the summer, we had no particular difficulties getting through. We were 240 kilos overweight when we checked in for our flight to Srinagar; it would have been 320 kilos were it not for three sturdy pairs of Norwegian feet wedged under the scales! On arrival we were surrounded by hordes of taxi drivers and houseboat owners touting for business, but looming above them all was a hand-held notice: 'Butts Clermont Houseboats'. These had been recommended by Ram and we were soon barging our way through the hordes to two taxis which sped us recklessly through the crowded streets of the city and out to the edge of the Wular Lake and our houseboat. It was a chocolate-box scene, the mountains enclosing the Kashmir vale reflecting in the dew-pond-calm water of the lake. Chrysanthemums in profusion surrounded two garden tables round which we were soon drinking beer and trying to gather the energy to organise ourselves to unpack, repack, sort out what was needed for the imminent walk in the high Himalaya and make our final plans for placing our food dumps. Part of the reason for doing this ourselves and therefore doing this pre-expedition expedition was that we could use this trip to reconnoitre two high passes we would have to cross to get into Ladakh and Zanskar in winter. Erik, Odd and Knut agreed to check out the Gulol Gali and Rangmarg Passes (both around 4,500 metres), and to dump food at a village between the Gali and Rangmarg Pass. Meanwhile Douglas and I would go by bus and lorry over the Zoji La, a 3,500-metre pass màrking the border of Kashmir and Ladakh, to Kargil and eventually to Padam in the centre of Zanskar. We would dump 8 days' food, fuel, ski waxes and a ski stick in Ringdom Gompa, a monastery perched on a knuckle of rock at the convergence of three high valleys, and another package containing the same items together with the pair of skis at Padam. We would then walk over the Kang La, down the mighty Miyar Nulla to the head of a bumpy road at Udaipur. From there we would catch a lorry, jeep, or perhaps a bus to drive over the Rhotang La (4,050 metres), the final pass into the lowlands and steaming hot plains of northern Punjab. All of us would rendezvous in Delhi at Tim Wilson's house two weeks later and fly home together in time for work.

That was the plan anyway and it worked—with one or two deviations and alterations. It was a lovely walk for all except Erik who had suffered severe concussion when he banged his head on a ceiling beam in a house in the village of Panikher. He made his way back alone, in some pain and mostly unaware of all around him. Douglas and I were also suffering; he from a dose of Delhi ear and I from altitude which hit me with a vengeance as we groaned and geared our way noisily over the 4,500-metre Pensi La. The scenery was quite unbelievable but I remember acknowledging that skiing here in the winter was going to be not only sensational, but cold and remote.

With all our tasks complete in Zanskar, we enjoyed a warm walk in exciting scenery over the Kang La where summits of 6,300 metres, small by Himalayan standards, dominated every horizon. They seemed so invitingly close that we cursed ourselves for not having mountaineering paraphernalia with us. The descent from 5,468 metres to Udaipur at 2,800 metres over a distance of 65 kilometres was long and footsore but over carpets of edelweiss at the higher levels. It was surely not going to be so wearisome in the winter. The hazards of swollen glacial rivers, no map to tell us which side of the valley was best further down, and numerous and necessary dangerous crossings of the grey turbulent river delayed us a little until we reached Gumba. We had stayed in this village in 1970 when we were on Menthosa so from here on it was familiar ground. We passed by Karpat but only stopped to admire the North-West face of Phabrang and to point out the route that Ram and I had taken in 1976. Traces of avalanche debris deep in the bottom of the exit gorge of the Miyar Nulla were was ample evidence that this would be a dangerous place in winter.

A rickety, aged bus took us over the Rhotang La and down to Manali in a day. Quite how it managed, we shall never know. It was a dreadful, reckless journey and our only recourse to safety was to place ourselves beside the emergency exit of the overcrowded bus next to a Dogra herdsman and two of his sheep. The ascent towards and steeper descent from the Rhotang La were photographed in as much detail as the jerky movement of the bus would allow. It was extremely steep country and the road had to carve its way down the mountainside in short zig-zags. In one couloir, the bank of snow, still some 4 metres high even in midsummer on a south-facing slope, caused Douglas to comment that this could be considered to be an ambitious adventure. His comments did not go unheard and how to get over that particular pass remained one of the worries that irked me throughout the winter journey.

Two days later we were in Delhi, exchanging experiences with the Norwegians and enjoying last-minute hospitality from Tim and Kitty Wilson. Tim had organised a treat for us and announced that he had managed to obtain first class seats for us on an overcrowded BA flight to London. We felt distinctly unwell when we arrived at Heathrow, but very happy with what we had achieved. The skiing adventure was just around the corner, and the prospects were inviting even though Odd had declared that the two high passes that he and Knut had been over would be out of the question in winter.

In February 1981 and about two weeks before our departure for India, I hitched a lift with the Royal Air Force to Oslo. Having been desk-bound for the past five months I felt it wise to accumulate some distance skiing and thus be in a better position to keep up with Odd and Erik once we started. They of course had been on snow for three months by that time. In fact the two of them had a wager to attempt to ski 200 kilometres in a single 24-hour period. When Odd met the plane he casually announced that he was disappointed that he had only managed 181 kilometres. Erik had gone out with him the same day but retired, spent, at 132 kilometres. I was quick to tell him that I was in no condition to do any of his short tours, pleading for the break-in of idle muscles to be gentle. I knew that it would be futile but felt that it was necessary to provide a reminder that I was an office wallah after all! It didn't work. That very evening we skied 25 kilometres on the flood-lit track up at Holmenkollen.

Thankfully, Odd worked most of that week and I was able to be more leisurely in my skiing activities and keep the daily distances below three score kilometres. It was good preparation not only for India but for a weekend's skiing up at Hamar with Knut, which topped four score plus ten on the Saturday, returning to a mere three score on Sunday before the sleepy drive back on the E6 to Oslo. Considerable head-scratching poring over maps each evening that week produced an alternative way to those two high passes to get into Ladakh but it would mean leaving the food dump at Sokhniz uncollected. That would leave us a bit short of food but not seriously so—what was important was to traverse safely the Zoji La (3,500 metres) over which the summer road twists and climbs, and get down to Dras and gain entry to the magnificent Suru valley from there.

Swiss cousins of neighbours at home had kindly asked Erik and me to stay when we arrived in Delhi on our way to Srinagar, and by noon on 21st February Erik and I were there, lunching with John and Catherine Ray in the Tyndale Biscoe School. We had five days to kill before Odd's scheduled arrival so John directed us up to their school hut, nestling in the forest up at Gulmarg (2,400 metres), and once a very popular hill station during the Raj. A case of beer, four days' food, our sleeping bags and a change of clothes were all we took to the hut from which we ventured on skis daily up to 3,300 metres on perfect snow and in warm sunshine.

It was ideal acclimatisation for both of us and we made the most of it. On one day we skied up to the head of the Gulmarg bowl to the north west, and followed a route for 20 kilometres up to Batha Pattri parallel to the ceasefire line between India and Pakistan. We crossed one deep furrow in the snow which we followed and after two kilometres ventured upon a section of Indian Army infantrymen on their way up to relieve others in positions on the frontier. They were walking in waist-deep snow and making heavy weather of it.

'It's crazy' said Erik turning to look at me. 'Here they are in a place which gets snow without fail every year, and yet they don't ski!'

I couldn't disagree; it would undoubtedly make sense for the Indian Army to institute ski training for their Frontier Forces.

'Perhaps they should ask the Royal Marines to provide some instructors!' I said, and asked Erik to remind me of the incident when we returned to Delhi when I would mention it to the Military Adviser in the British High Commission.

During the morning of our meeting Odd's flight in Srinagar, Erik and I skied round the Circuit Road at Gulmarg to seek out a house called 'The Pines'. This example of late-Victorian, early-Edwardian colonial architecture had been the home of my grandmother after her marriage to Hugh Gordon, an Indian Army officer. She and my mother, then four years old, moved there in 1914, when my grandfather, then commanding a special detachment of the Maharajah of Kapurthalas Rifles went to East Africa to campaign against the German forces. It was there, too, that news of his death in action was cabled in September 1917. So, it was of particular significance for me to find their home, a sort of pilgrimage into the family past. To help me I had taken out from England three old sepia photographs. Two portrayed the view from the verandah and the third was taken from below looking up towards the house. The two with the view were the key, for in the middle and far distance were two mountain peaks exactly in line. Up and down we went, herring-boning up most of the steep slopes that ringed the bowl, visiting existing buildings, some ruined ones, and some which were snow-filled shells of their previous glory. We had almost run out of time when Erik called to me from a small snow platform above. I traversed and side-stepped up to join him.

'This is the place,' he said confidently. We lined up both photographs and everything seemed to confirm his confidence.

'Where's the house?', I asked looking about.

'Over there,' he said, pointing with his ski stick. 'There's a chimney brace.'

It was difficult to see it initially as its stonework was well hidden from where we stood but we pushed over to it in knee-deep snow and realigned the photographs.

'So this is where they lived.' A small lump grew in my throat. 'Sorry to bore you, Erik, with all this family sentimentality, but it means quite a lot for me to stand here.'

'It's been interesting for me,' he replied supportively.

As I stood there I thought back over the train of events that had brought me here. It had all begun in 1977 whilst staying with Odd and his family in Marangu, Tanzania. We had just romped up the Heim Route on Kibo and were on our journey back to his home, when at Moshi, we saw a sign saying 'Commonwealth War Graves Cemetery'. I asked Odd to pull off the road and we drove up a small avenue of flowering Jakaranda trees to the gate of the cemetery. We walked through the wrought iron gates and towards the centremost grave. As the inscriptions on the headstone came into focus, I stopped dead in my tracks.

'Odd, you're not going to believe this. That's my grandfather's grave!'

As I stood beside the remnant chimney and what existed of 'The Pines', now knee-deep in snow, I reflected on how removed from war-torn, disease-ridden, torrid German East Africa the situation here must have been in 1917. And how utterly incongruous the black-bordered telegram arriving on a peaceful warm September day 2,400 metres up on the very edge of the Himalayas must have been for a beautiful young wife and daughter waiting expectantly for his return. A tear welled and I tried to muzzle the slight shivery pursing of the lips. It was a sad reflection for me but how ghastly it must have been for the two of them that day.

'It's time to go', said Erik, pulling me back into the present.

'*Ja,* it's time to get on with our little adventure' I replied, and with that we pushed with our sticks, and schussed down the slope that had once been my grandmother's colourful garden and away from that humble spot in its lovely setting.

Odd arrived that afternoon and after packing and weighing our kit, we were entertained to a curry supper by John and Catherine in their home beside the school. John had booked a taxi for us to leave the next morning so now all that remained between us and Manali (the finishing point of our expedition) was a two-hour taxi drive and almost 800 kilometres of untrodden snow, in high valleys, over glaciated passes, through part of the greatest mountain range on the planet. We were excited, a little apprehensive but above all eager to get going.

The bumpy tarmac road ended at a wall of snow beside which was an Indian Army post at the village of Gangangir. A signpost marked 'Leh 459km' poked out of the snow and behind it some 10 kilometres away we could see the high sides of the valley converging to form the Sind river gorge. After unloading the taxi, we smeared red Klister wax on our skis and under a hot sun demolished the bottles of beer that had somehow found their way into our rucksacks. The sacks were heavy enough without the beer and bottles, and the first entry in my diary reveals just that:

Friday 27th Feb: *The packs are quite heavy—about 23kg and we only went about 9km before finding a camp site before entering the gorge. This was not far from another Army post where we were given a cup of tea and some greasy cake. The tent is comfy and my place is between the two Norwegians. Our cooking arrangements are simple—each day one of us will use the 24-hour food pack from his rucksack and the one to whom it belongs cooks as well. The next day that person washes up, and the day after it is idle day. The sky clouded over at dusk and it began to sleet at 21.00, not long after we had turned in. It's an early start tomorrow to get through the Sind river gorge in the coldest part of the morning.*

We had all seen the gorge in the summer but now it had been transformed into what seemed to be one enormous avalanche chute. In the murk of dawn we clambered awkwardly over great zones of debris, skis going in every direction over large frozen balls of snow, some as large as a table. It was snowing heavily and while we made our way laboriously forward, our worries were accentuated by the echoes of the crump and roar of avalanches all about us. It was a nasty place to be and we didn't loiter. It was difficult to comprehend how such a tranquil scene in the summer could be transformed unto an ugly dangerous cauldron, and it was with relief that we reached the end of the gorge. Here the valley swung north a little before opening out into the alpine meadows of Sonamarg.

Wet snow was bucketing down for the whole day and it obscured the mountains that we knew surrounded us. The wet snow was clogging badly under the skis and frequent frustrating stops were necessary to scrape it off in an attempt to remove the offending wax. We never got it all off in one but gradually through the day, numerous scraping sessions cleared most of it.

The village of Sonamarg was buried in two metres of snow and impossible to identify as the bustling little place full of tea and samosa shops that we had seen in the summer. A little man in sheepskins apeared out of one of the half-buried houses but the barriers of language kept our conversation short and we learned little from him.

We pushed on, changing the lead every ten minutes as the effort of trail breaking began to tell. We passed the last inhabited village in the valley, Nilgargar, at four o'clock in the afternoon when almost twelve hours of effort rang the bell to stop. We had covered 25 kilometres and Erik's altimeter was registering 2,850 metres. Wet through to the bone, we camped by the open river and were in bed before dusk. It had been an extremely hard day; we all felt it and we cursed the persistent snowfall.

It grew a little colder that night but there was no respite from the snow with 50 centimetres falling during the night and showing no signs of stopping. Our lonely campsite was only about 3 kilometres from Baltal, an uninhabited group of shacks used by pilgrims on summer excursions to the holy shrine in the Amarnath caves, and about 8 kilometres from the Zoji La. We lazed in the tent all morning discussing the dangers that would now face us if we crossed the pass too soon after such incessant heavy snowfall. The crump of yet another unseen avalanche nearby reinforced concern and it was only a delighted yell from Odd, who, in the early afternoon had shuffled out of the tent to fetch some water from the river, that broke the worried spell cast over us.

'The sun's coming through; a patch of blue sky!' he shouted. This was followed by a sudden shuddering of the tent as a hidden guy rope booby-trapped his progress although it served the useful purpose of shaking some snow off the tent.

'There's been a metre of snow,' he went on.

'A metre?' I repeated, thinking momentarily not of avalanches but of the toil of trail breaking.

'Ja—beautiful mountains all around.'

That got Erik and me out of our bags and outside. It was a staggering sight. Higher up the valley the sky was the clearest blue and the peaks a dazzling white; peaks up to 5,000 metres. There was the Zoji La looking rather insignificant but mantled in snow. It was just possible to see small portions of the sharp line where the terraced road zig-zagged up the steep slopes and on up towards the pass. Soon the sunshine reached us and its warmth rekindled our desire to get onto skis and have a closer look at the awesome obstacle ahead. The snow was colder and blue Swix wax provided good grip and glide as we furrowed our way towards Baltal, its ugly little shacks just visible as small roof triangles above the snow.

They seemed so close that we left the tent and rucksacks where they were. There was no question of crossing the pass that day anyway, probably not for another day and certainly not until all that snow had avalanched off it. As we neared Baltal we realised there were people there. Our proximity to them was detected by a dog whose defensive bark soon took on a more aggresive tone as we closed the gap. An Indian Army Signals lieutenant took charge of Tiger, the name given to the battle-scarred canine, and he welcomed us into his camp. I wondered what misdemeanour he had committed to earn a winter's sentence in Baltal. For him and his group of soldiers this posting must have been penal servitude because there were only two things to recommend Baltal in winter— masses of snow and magnificent scenery. But Lieutenant Rajan Probhakar was clearly enjoying his work and we joined him in his semi underground cosy quarters for tea and a chat. His job, he told us, was to maintain a telephone line that looped over the Zoji La and down to positions near Dras on the ceasefire line. He and his men walked everywhere in the snow but he and his Sergeant Major had a pair of skis each. He showed these to us and Odd agreed to give him some lessons after we had told him about our journey.

'The pass is dangerous at the moment', Rajan warned us.

'Yes, but do you know of another way?' Erik's concern equalled Odd's and mine.

'There's a gorge which the locals use and we have used it before. But it is only safe in the spring or after a long spell of good weather which allows all the avalanches to fall off the mountainside. Why don't you go up and look at it?'

Why not, we thought, and the following morning we did, skiing directly up from our tent beside the river. It was a lovely day and the view down the Sonamarg valley and up to Kolahoi, a beautiful 5,000-metre mountain, was quite wonderful; the higher we traversed up towards the Zoji La the better the view. We crossed the chute of one large powder snow avalanche and gained ground steeply, side-stepping and doing precarious kick turns, until we were able to ease gingerly to the very edge of the gorge. It was a gruesome sight. 'No way, *cabissa*' exclaimed Odd, using a Swahili word with every suggestion of finality about it. Even while we stood there, the roar of something descending into the gorge further up and out of sight confirmed Odd's opinion.

'*Ja*, a non starter, but what about a direct line to the ridge?' I said pointing upwards and across the steep slopes which still retained the last fall of snow. It looked evil and Erik said so too.

'It looks like a wait for a day or two and a crossed finger that the sun will trigger it all to fall away.'

The Zoji La was becoming a nuisance and one which generated much discussion for the next two days as we waited for the snow to fall off those long exposed slopes. We filled part of a day by skiing up towards the Amarnath Caves. On our return to Baltal we saw Tiger unattended and untethered near the shacks. He had already taken a chunk out of one of Odd's snow gaiters so he was an evil to be reckoned with. We put high ground between him and us and returned towards the Zoji La, wishfully hopeful that it had avalanched itself clean. With the clear skies came colder temperatures which parried the sun's warmth—indeed it was $-18°$ C that morning. All that deep snow was now locked in a cold embrace to those slopes, and it didn't look as though it was going to budge. That evening, our third in Baltal, we decided we shouldn't wait any more. We were consuming food and if we did get over the pass, we would be cutting it fairly fine before reaching our next depot.

Wednesday 4th March: *We decided last night to return the way we had come so wearily four days before. The Zoji La had defeated us and we were not prepared to risk forcing it. We shall fly over the wretched thing to Leh, get a bus or jeep to Kargil and carry on the journey from there. We will miss about 60km of our planned route but we were united in our decision to return to Srinagar. Better the devil we know than the devil we don't.*

My diary doesn't reveal our innermost feelings of disappointment when we turned our skis 180 degrees and made that first stride back the way we had come. We didn't talk much and we made fairly rapid progress down to Sonamarg and the head of the gorge. The gorge had worried us on the ascent a few days earlier but with such a heavy snowfall in between it now became an obstacle of much greater danger. Like the ascent, we decided to go through the gorge as late as possible (though before it became dark) to make use of the colder temperatures. We laid out sleeping mats beside a large boulder to rest awhile under a watery sun. Painted on the boulder, black lettering on a yellow background was the sign 'DO NOT HURRY—LIFE IS LONG'. A significant message both to reckless drivers in the summer and to skiers in the winter, though we doubted whether many of the latter had ever ventured up to this glorious valley.

We obeyed the suggestion on the sign for two hours before we entered the gorge and when we did set off, we were confronted by a scene of utter

105

confusion with enormous cones of debris that in places spanned the bottom of the gorge up to 50 metres deep. In one nasty place we skied through one at a time, nervous and reacting to the faintest sound echoing round the cliffs and steep slopes on either side. The open river had been blocked in several places, the older avalanches obvious by the tunnels carved out from beneath them by the river, the more recent ones creating small lakes upstream. In three days the gorge had transformed its character completely and we were thankful to get out into the open fields above Gangangir by nightfall. As we were putting up the tent, the heavens opened and it began to rain.

Thursday 5th March: *It was +2°C and raining but we were able to ski down the line of the road for 7km before having to walk the remaining 6km to Gund. It was a dismal grey day with snow settling down to 2,400m. It rained persistently while we walked and it was welcome relief to get into the bus at 11.30. Erik was having trouble with his back—an old recurrent injury—and when the bus stopped in Gund, I prevented it from leaving while Odd ran back to fetch Erik's rucksack. Erik could hardly walk and had to be assisted aboard the bus. It is worrying and he is very depressed about the prospects of his continuing the journey.*

Although we were not to know it, my diary entry heralded a problem which was to be with Erik for the rest of the trip. This new development was indeed a worry, not only for Odd and me but more so for Erik who had staked so much on this journey. He rested all the next day on a boarded bed in John Ray's home while Odd and I stood and fought with the queues of Ladakhis and Kashmiris to get our tickets for the flight to Leh. We killed time for two days before we got our flight, thoroughly feasting on a scenic shikara journey down the filthy canals of Srinagar. The reflections in the still water of the mountains encircling the Vale of Kashmir were adequate distractions from the plethora of flotsam and jetsam that characterise the network of canals.

We were impatient to get on because with only 24 days ahead to complete the journey (our return tickets had been booked) there was little or no flexibility to allow for delays en route. In the event we didn't get away until midday on 9th March, but at least the rest had been good for Erik's back.

We took off into thick cloud that obscured the view from the aircraft until we were well across Ladakh and over the deep defile of the Indus valley. To the north and on the horizon the peaks of the High Karakoram could be seen—probably Saser Kangri and the Rimo peaks. The approach to the airfield at Leh was spectacular. When we alighted on the tarmac, its altitude of 3,500 metres was noticeable as, breathlessly we gathered up our rucksacks and skis. Not a flake of snow was in sight save for the Zanskar range to the south and the Ladakh range to the north and then only above 5,000 metres. It was bitterly cold with a stiff penetrating wind coming from the direction of the highplateaux of Tibet, and we were thankful to move out of it into the dishevelled building that made do as a terminal. There we made contact with Fida Hussein, a friend of John Ray. He owned the Hotel 'Yak Tail' where we stayed.

Leh was delightfully peaceful after Srinagar and it was strange to walk around the quaint empty streets to witness the curious blend of western influence with the ancient ways of Buddhism. Thank goodness the flocks of trekkers were not there to clutter those empty streets. We walked up the steep hill behind the town to the ruined monastery from which fluttered long strands of gaily-coloured prayer flags. The altitude and an appetite signalled it was time to go back down to the town to visit a tea shop where we met Dave Mallon, an English biologist. He had come out to Leh with two friends, Simon Fraser and Ben Osborn (whom I'd met in England), to do some studies on the snow leopard and other wild life in Zanskar. Simon and Ben, he told us, had left a couple of days earlier by bus for Kargil. They had been unable to get over a pass to the Markla valley and had had to abandon their original plan and go the long way round through the Suru Valley.

'Are they walking?' queried Erik with a frown.

'No, they've got skis' replied Dave.

'When did you say they left?' My words almost interrupted Dave.

'Two days ago.'

I looked at Odd, who looked at Erik, who looked at me. We changed the subject, finished our tea and walked with a sense of purpose back to the Yak Tail. We were concerned that the locals with whom we'd left our food caches would mistake Simon and Ben for us and give them our food. We had to leave the next morning and our evening activity was geared to negotiating a price with Fida for the drive in his jeep to the Suru valley. Once that was agreed we lashed our skis to the roof of the jeep—where they looked totally out of place against the surrounding sun-bleached countryside—and arranged to leave at six o'clock the following morning.

The 11-hour drive in the jeep was a totally new experience. It had no heater and was doubtless built for small short-legged Indians. We crammed ourselves in with two in the front, knees pressed hard up against the dashboard, and the third in the back with the rucksacks. It was a squash and it was bitterly cold: − 15 °C on the freezer thermometer from home that was kept in my ditty bag—so cold that we changed round every hour to take a turn in the 'deep freeze' of the rear compartment. At least there was some warmth coming through the metal shield between the dashboard and the engine so, although joints and muscles were cramped, it was marginally more comfortable there than in the back.

Fida drove extremely well. The scenery was truly magnificent as we dropped down to the frozen Indus. It was difficult to believe that this was the river that provided the lifeblood of Pakistan and emerged into the Arabian Sea as a mighty delta. We passed the junction where the Zanskar river joins the Indus and could see the beginnings of the cleft that becomes the famous gorge which effectively bars easy access to the hidden kingdom. It is only in the winter that the more intrepid can use its frozen surface to gain the central Zanskar valley, and even then the ice often breaks up and people disappear. We drove up a massive series of zig-zags towards the Lamayaru pass leaving the frozen Indus below, which dwindled into a silver blue thread as we gained height. The road is a feat of military engineering for this is an all-season road built and kept open for strategic purposes.

We passed Lamayaru and we could see the monastery and village quite clearly; we now had no reason to wonder why this pretty, isolated group of houses and its dominating monastery featured on the itineraries of summer trekking parties. We roared through the gears up to 4,200 metres to gain the Fatu La. Here there were banks of snow beside the road and gangs of Indian Army Pioneers with long-handled shovels were keeping the road clear. This was the edge of the high mountain desert climate and from here on towards Kargil the snow cover gradually increased to a depth of about 75 centimetres.

The day was overcast, cold and grey without any welcome views of mountains to distract us from the discomfort of the jeep. However, we enthused over the amount of snow around because we didn't know that the winter precipitation on the Kashmir side of the great range would fall over this far to the north. We turned south some 10 kilometres short of Kargil and the road became distinctly more snowy with huge icy ruts which Fida nervously negotiated. We arrived in Sankho, 20 kilometres from Kargil at five o'clock in the afternoon, and it was as far as any vehicle could have gone. Within minutes we were surrounded by curious onlookers with more standing on the flat roofs of the houses grouped on either side of the road.

It was while we were unlashing the skis from the roof of the jeep that a figure dressed in the crimson robes of a Zanskari monk approached us. He was certainly no Zanskari; he was too tall and he bore a handsome beard.

'Hello Guy,' he said, but I recognised neither the voice nor the person. He must have sensed it.

'I'm Simon Fraser!'

'Of course! How's it going? Meet Odd and Erik,' I said introducing them.

'I hope you've got your passports with you' he said, pointing to a house nearby, where a grubby sign 'Police' was nailed to the wall.

'Why?'

'You won't get any further than here if you haven't. We left ours in Leh. Ben went back this morning by bus to collect them and he probably won't be back for 3 or 4 days.'

Simon looked closely at our skis and rucksacks with genuine interest. 'Aren't you using pulks?' he asked.

'We're travelling with everything on our backs, and picking up food at dumps on our route. Why—are you using them?'

Our convesation continued while Odd and Erik clambered up a rickety ladder into a dusty little room to sign the police registration book and have their passports scrutinised. Simon and Ben were travelling 'heavy'. Although we didn't see their equipment, they were using heavy alpine touring skis and as well as pulling pulks, they were carrying rucksacks. We wished Simon luck and, without any further delay, clipped on our skis and moved off and out of the village.

It was 10th March—exactly six days after we had turned back under the dangerous stare of the Zoji La—and we were enjoying that same feeling of excitement and apprehension for what lay ahead. It was wonderful to move under our own steam again. We camped with the altimeter reading 3,120 metres in failing light, in a dusting of snow, and talked about Simon and Ben while we tucked into our supper. All night the wind whistled through the guy ropes of the tent which were attached to our skis and sticks, anchored firmly in a metre of snow.

We skied 24 kilometres the next day, stopping for lunch between the villages of Partak and Damshura for a couple of hours. From that picnic spot, where the river was open, we had our first magnificent views of Nun and Kun (both spectacular peaks of 7,100 metres), which dominate the Himalayan skyline between Nanga Parbat to the north west and the Garwhal Himal to the south east. A great plume of snow swept out from the summit of Nun and we guessed the winter jet stream was running its course. The complete southern horizon was a stunningly beautiful scene, but it must have been cold to the extreme up there. For us, however, it was warm for our picnic; too warm really because the heat played havoc with the snow and frustrated our waxing efforts that afternoon. Tired and dehydrated, we arrived at the village of Panikher at half past four from where we could just see the Umba Pass over which we had planned to go if we had succeeded in getting past the Zoji La.

We stayed that night in a two-storeyed house that was arrogantly named the 'Snow Line Hotel'. The house was infested with rats at which we threw our ski boots and other objects that night. The stay brought back painful memories for Erik who had concussed himself on one of its low ceiling beams during our reconnaissance the previous summer, and there was no sadness whatsoever when we left early the next morning, having gathered up the 3 days' food and $4^{1}/_{2}$ litres of meths left with a Dr Habibollal.

Although we were gaining altitude, and Panikher lies at 3,320 metres, the gain had been gradual. When we left the dingy Snow Line Hotel before dawn, the valley was dark and cold (-13 °C) with the only sign of sunrise appearing as the deepest of red glows atop Nun and Kun. Gradually it turned to crimson, through the shades of red, to orange as the shadows marched relentlessly down the mountainside until the sun's first streak of warmth hit the valley floor—and us. And with its arrival began the ritual of stripping off quilted jackets and sweaters, sure in the knowledge that, if the sky remained clear, we probably wouldn't need to put them on again until sunset. We valued the outlook because not one of us had experienced skiing in such circumstances and surroundings before. To spite the radiant warmth of the sun, our greater altitude kept air and snow temperatures below freezing and blue wax was perfect.

As we approached the village of Tarangaz, an avalanche sprang from a hanging glacier below the summit of a nameless peak that was probably nudging on 6,000 metres. The crunch and crack of its first second of life alerted us but by then it had grown one hundredfold and had spread its awesome power for over 1 kilometre across the mountain's face. Simultaneously came the roar of its descent as it gathered momentum and size. We watched it all the way down wondering which way it would turn and where it would stop. Whilst we thought we were safe, I couldn't help remembering a remark made by André Roch at an Avalanche Symposium when after witnessing an avalanche in the Yukon, he'd said 'You're never safe from the wretched things.' But this time we were, because the mass of potential destruction came to rest on a ridge of moraine about 500 metres up the hill from where we stood.

We descended adjacent to Tarangaz and lost about 100 metres in height. It was a delight because it was the last downhill run until the descent from the Pensi La, still a good 120 kilometres away. We crossed a small metal girder bridge which spanned a deep dark crevice, and shortly afterwards turned the corner in the valley and started to traverse up the steep south-facing slopes. These were the slopes about which Ram had spoken on his return from Kang La in 1978: they were set about 35–40° and had recently avalanched. We took off our skis to cross one pile of debris lodging up against some rocks, and stumbled over great frozen blocks and balls of snow. Using skis like supporting walking sticks to steady balance, we cautiously moved across three large zones like that, very aware of the consequences of accidentally dropping a ski. Several hundred metres below was the Suru river, which was only frozen in places; if a ski went down there we would certainly be in trouble! Beyond those three zones of debris, we crossed a long exposed slope, also avalanched clear of loose snow. This was particularly unnerving and the silence between ourselves was indication enough that each of us was worried. The surface was hard névé and each step required a hefty bang with the foot to give any form of supporting edge for the ski on the 35° slope. Having metal edges only in the centre of the ski was some help but we were frighteningly conscious of the softer plastic edges at the tip and tail not having too much effect. At one point we heard a deep thud spread away beneath the slope as the weight of one of us, or perhaps all three, had upset the precarious frozen link between the surface and what was beneath it. We traversed in this fashion for nearly 4 kilometres and with aching ankles and tense calf muscles we were glad to gain easier flatter ground which led up to the village of Parkutse. I wondered how Simon and Ben would tackle such slopes with their pulks.

Parkutse is the last inhabited village in the Suru valley and it forms the demarcation between Mohammedan Kashmir and Buddhist Zanskar. A stark reminder of the Islamic influence were the silver domes of two mosques brightly reflecting the sunshine; out of harmony really with such a snowy mountainous scene but nonetheless an impressive sight. Beyond the village the valley turned again, narrowing to rocky cliffs on one side and on the other an outflung glacier that dropped into the valley bottom as a cold greenish-blue 30-metre ice cliff. Under an overhanging rocky spur the sun's warmth against the red rock had thawed the snow to reveal a flat sandy strip about 3 metres wide and 15 metres long. Odd saw it first and it became our site for the night. We lazed, stripped off to enjoy the late afternoon sun and stretched out upon our mats on the warm sand. One could almost reach out and touch the glacier on the other side, then in a shivery dark shadow. Before the sun dipped behind the bulk of Kun, Nun's more rocky neighbour, and cast us into the same cold shadow, we took some photographs of the tent and skis for our generous equipment sponsors, a task that is all too easy to overlook.

The glacier, at 3,560 metres, must be one of the lowest if not the lowest, in the Himalayas, and the following morning its ugly snout seemed to add extra chill to the $-15\,°C$ that registered at dawn. Although we woke at five o'clock we didn't get away until just after seven; how much longer it takes to get organised in a tent when it is cold! After following the line of the river for perhaps 4 kilometres, which was interesting as we crossed it by snow or ice bridges several times, we entered a narrow gorge where we were forced to escape upwards, removing skis to clamber up some avalanche debris to reach easier ground. We gained the line of the summer road which was just visible as a thin uniform indentation across steep slopes for 3 to 4 kilometres.

Further above it looked menacing and dangerous so after donning skis we slipped across it as quickly as we could, very conscious of some horrific drops down to the river below. At one point, when I was leading, the snow cracked right across the slope with a noise like a rifle shot but at least it wasn't as icy as the slopes we had traversed the previous day. When we reached the flatter part of the valley we were thankful that no harm had befallen us. My diary recalls that it was at this point that I had mentioned to Douglas in the summer that it would be best to take a line on the south side of the valley. It was too late to consider it at that point in time and anyway we overcame the problem without mishap.

The valley ahead rose very gradually, almost indiscernibly. This was the long approach to Ringdom Gompa, dominated either side by 6,000-metre peaks and numerous glaciers that were almost unnoticeable under their winter mantle. When we stopped that evening, we had covered about 25 kilometres and were at 3,940 metres. We were now high enough for the air temperature to remain below freezing all day although the sun still maintained its penetrating warmth.

We seemed to have fallen into a daily pattern of activity. We would try and be away each morning by 7.30, ski for 4 to 5 hours, then stop for lunch. This involved a two-hour rest around midday when, if there were no wind, it was possible to catnap in the sunshine. Lunch was no more than masses of sweet tea, packets of biscuits and chocolate and if there was water nearby, we would fetch it to save using valuable methylated spirit to melt snow. After lunch we would continue for 2 to 3 hours stopping early enough to pitch the tent while the sun was still up. Once the sun descended below the skyline, the temperature would drop so rapidly that it was almost possible to see the mercury falling in the thermometer. A drop of 15 °C in an hour was quite common but by that time we were almost certainly inside sleeping bags and down for the night.

The snow conditions at the greater altitudes were noticeably worse. Height and cold were competing with the warmth of sunshine. Further down the valley, the sun had won that little contest and the going had been good. The great golden orb was losing the battle now and there was no supportive layering of the snow. Instead, it was like coarse powder. A quote from my diary says it all:

Saturday 14th March: − *15 °C at 0600. Snow conditions are bad and it has* *meant changing round trail breaking every 1km. Occasionally the snow seems to be baseless and the poor fellow trail breaking up front goes in up to the thigh. All rhythm is lost and it is exhausting getting going again. Our daily average in these conditions is from 22–24km which is about 6–7 hours' skiing. These conditions don't help Erik's back and today Odd and I shared the trail breaking.*

Characteristically, Erik's sense of humour was unfailing although his back was clearly giving him a lot of pain and discomfort.

That afternoon we reached Zulidok, the first inhabited village of Zanskar and were invited to join a family in their house for tea. Tsering Nerbu, with his wife, mother and father, five children, and two monks, cleared up one part of their tiny living room for the three of us to sit around the smoky yak-dung fire. It took an age for the water to boil, but it did in the end and we were thankful for that—it would do no good for any of us to get some wretched stomach trouble or even diarrhoea. Tsering's wife and mother both wore the stunning Zanskari headdress, studded with turquoise stones, and bits of shiny brass and silver. Douglas and I had seen these in profusion the previous summer when all of Zanskar was in festival mood for the first visit in centuries of a Dalai Lama; we met him on the road between Seni and Padam and that indeed had been a privileged experience.

Tsering's house was large and it was surprisingly warm inside his living room. The smoky fire helped a bit but most of the background warmth came from his yaks and ponies which were stabled to provide insulation around the one living room. Consequently, there was a rich pungent farmyard smell. Their tea was a salty brew with a layer of molten, rancid yak's butter floating on the top. Although it doesn't sound appetising, it was pleasant to drink. Before we said farewell to these kind people we took a family photograph of them (which we managed to send to them via a friend the following summer) and skied off through the other half dozen houses that make up this remote village.

Ringdom Gompa was 7 kilometres from Zulidok and there was a well-trodden furrow in the snow between the monastery and the village. Provisions and loads of yak dung were undoubtedly transported to the Gompa, and visits to the village by the monks for other necessities of life probably kept the furrow firm and easy to follow over the flat plains. We skied in the furrow and made the best progress so far, getting to the Gompa in an hour, just as it was getting dark. A dog barked persistently as we got nearer and a dim light appeared at the back of the building. We traversed up towards this hoping that whoever was holding the lamp had also taken charge of the dog. A canine night attack would be difficult to foil on skis! We were welcomed into the monastery and followed a monk through the narrow, low passageways to the central courtyard, where we placed our skis in a pile of snow. We were led back up a short flight of steps into the main meditation room. There were two Bokharis, rather crude tin heating stoves, which were burning yak dung fiercely and the room was so warm that we were forced to remove sweaters and long johns to remain comfortable.

The head Lama, Tondup Sonam, appeared with our bag of food, fuel and waxes, clutching the one ski stick in the other hand. Behind him followed the fifteen Lamas that make up the complement of the Gompa. The three of us raised our hands together in pointed reverence and said 'Jule', bowing heads at the same time to each monk. They shuffled round to their designated places in the room, where each had a cushion, a small finger bowl, a bell and a book of Buddhist scriptures. From there they watched us as we prepared our supper on the hot Bokharis, silent in their fascination at three bearded foreigners in their midst. They watched us for over an hour before leaving, one by one to return to their cells. It was late by our standards, 8.30 pm, before we were able to spread our sleeping mats and get some sleep.

Our short stay in the Gompa is best reproduced directly from my diary.

Sunday 15th March: *− 13 °C at dawn outside although our room was warm at + 2 °C. It was a great privilege and experience to be so welcome in the monastery and to have been allowed to sleep in their main prayer room. We absorbed everything that was possible while this unique experience lasted. We deliberately got up early so that we could have ourselves sorted out by the time the monks came in. The day had dawned almost clear with a few clouds speckling the sky and covering the highest peaks. Erik's altimeter was down 30m from last night's reading and now stood at 4,020m which gave hope for another spell of good weather. There was about 3cm of new snow in the courtyard and the only things that had disturbed the dusting were the Gompa dog and a pair of Alpine chuffs. Soon a monk emerged and began swishing the snow away from the main thoroughfares with a twig broom. It wasn't long before all the monks came through to the prayer room and began to pray, totally oblivious of our presence. Little cymbals were clashed, there were murmurings of 'Om ne ha Padme Hum' and small marbles of tsampa were rolled between the palms of hands and put into the little silver bowls in front of the monks. Tea was passed around and we got Tondup Sonam's permission to take photographs. We were delighted, as I believe they were, and we promised to send our prints out with Dr Henry Osmaston. The monks seemed to be really enjoying seeing us in the middle of their winter. They put on our rucksacks, examined the skis and sticks and received a demonstration* *from Odd of how to clip them on. They gathered together for a photograph, dwarfed by the bearded viking figures standing behind.*

Erik, Odd and I carrying skis through the rocks; Burdem monastery set on a rocky outcrop beyond.

We were sorry to leave this most friendly of places. We decided to take 5 out of the 8 days' food with 4 litres of fuel and leave the remainder and the ski stick with the Lamas. We thought the stick may come in useful one day to ward off a Zanskari wolf or even the lorry loads of trekkers that pass this way in the summer! The monks lined up on the parapet outside the heavy double doors of the Gompa and watched, giggling with delight and amazement, as Odd and Erik pushed over the edge and swept down the slope to the plain below. I captured the unique scene with a photograph, before going over the edge to join them. I looked back momentarily, waved, lost my balance, crossed a ski and fell! Ignominy for me but comedy for them. And so we left Ringdom.

That night we camped at 4,190 metres, about 4 kilometres short of the slopes that rose up to the Pensi La, and 1¹/₂ kilometres beyond the entrance to the valley that led to the Chilung La. We relived the previous night's experience in Ringdom throughout the day, chattering as we clattered along on good hard snow. We felt fortunate to have had that opportunity to spend 12 hours in such a colourful place and we ended the day perfectly by cooking supper outside in warm sunshine and wondering whether we had been the first foreigners to have been in the privacy of the Gompa in midwinter. Probably so.

The night below the Pensi La was the coldest so far, −24 °C. The condensation inside the tent was fairly heavy and bobble hats came in useful to rub the thick ice crystals away from the liner before they melted and dripped into sleeping bags. It was Erik who unselfishly gathered in the cooker from the flap outside and started a brew.

The top of the Pensi La had registered 4,650 metres on Erik's altimeter and we were quite breathless getting there. The slopes that had looked to be so uniform from the tent turned out to be very foreshortened, and on two occasions we took skis off to walk up steep little stony ramps which had been burnt free of snow. A large cairn, which may once have been a chorten, marked the high point of the pass. It was festooned with prayer flags that fluttered violently in the stiff breeze, their edges tattered into thin linen filaments. The views were simply staggering and we could even see the Chilung La, the 5,000-metre pass that sits astride the southern approaches to Nun and Kun, at the far end of a twisting glacier.

The Pensi La was long and fairly level and near its eastern end was a frozen lake. We skied to the flank of this until, in difficult light, we skimmed its eastern tip and peered down onto the Durung Durung glacier. We had studied photographs of this at home and had decided there that the 500-metre loss of height was best achieved by getting onto the glacier and not following the descent line of the road which was very steep where it passed under some cliffs. Discerning the lie of the slope and its steepness down to the glacier was not easy in that sort of light where horizon and sky merged deceptively into one. Unperturbed, Odd slipped away and out of sight, followed more gingerly by Erik who was worried by the effect of a fall to his back, and myself in my traditional position for downhill excursions. We had hardly been going a minute before we saw Odd's tiny figure skimming over the glacier way below. We had his tracks to follow but we didn't take the same steep line. Odd's control at speed needs to be seen to be believed and it was not to be the last time we were to witness some phenomenal downhilling from him. In spite of the early ascent that morning, we made excellent distance and camped after 26 kilometres at a small ice-free spring. It was bitterly cold, and when the thermometer registered −18 °C at 7.30 pm, we knew we were in for a cracker that night.

And it was too! At −29 °C, we decided to wait until the sun eased its warmth into the valley before we made a move; it made all the difference to how quickly we packed and sorted ourselves out. We diverted through the village of Abran Kongma to deliver a letter to a brother of one of the

Lamas at Ringdom; a good first-class postal sevice, we thought! On the way we saw a silver-grey fox dash off up the mountainside away from the village. It was the first wild animal we had seen although tracks of many different species were plentiful. We wondered if any belonged to the Zanskari wolf!

That day, 17th March, was a day when the temperature range must easily have spanned 50 °C. At midday it was scorching, yet the air temperature in the shadows was still below freezing. Lips and noses split and became sore despite copious quantities of cream and Labisan. The snow softened up too and ski boots began to get wet. We had rubber overboots for them but snow creeping down through the top and condensation from within added to the damp. To help prevent them freezing solid during the night, we kept them in the hoods of our sleeping bags and used them as pillows. But in the temperatures we were experiencing, they were nearly always partially frozen in the morning and it was with discomfort that we pushed them down our bags and between sweater and shirt to thaw out a little while we ate breakfast. Once on and moving though, body heat did the rest, helped during our lunch spells, when we put everything out to air in the sun.

By the end of our eighth day out from Sankho we had skied almost 200 kilometres. Apart from one day near Ringdom, the weather had been marvellous and the warm sunny days more than compensated for the extreme chill of darkness. We had also dropped down to 3,740 metres, the gradual descent from the Pensi La enabling a steady 25 to 26 kilometres to be skied a day. We acted as postmen again and delivered three letters from another of the Lamas at Ringdom to a brother in Shagham whose delight turned into some emotive high spirits. It was nice to have been able to help even if our service could only have been geared to 'second class' speed.

We arrived in Padam shortly after noon the next day, 19th March. It had been our intention to rest there for two or three days and take the opportunity to ski across the wide Zanskar valley to visit Karsha monastery and some of the other villages that seemed to hang from the steep mountains to the north, but the days we had lost by being defeated at the Zoji La now made that impossible. We were saddened not to have the time for these deviations, because not only did we miss the experience of seeing these interesting places in mid winter, but we couldn't do justice to a programme of winter research which Dr Henry Osmaston had asked us to complete during our stay in Padam. A further disappointment lay in our inability to demolish a litre of malt whisky and other extra goodies I had left in the food cache in the summer, especially for such a period of rest.

We had previously calculated that we had about 275 kilometres to go to reach Manali and we needed to be there by nightfall on 28th March. This left no allowance for bad weather or any navigational difficulties we might encounter over the Kang La. We explained all this to Punchok Dawa, the son of the King of Pada, who fortuitously was over from Karsha for a holiday of three days. I gave him a letter from Henry in which Punchok was asked to give answers to some important questions linked to Henry's geographical studies. Leaving him to work them out, the three of us walked through the narrow muddy and filthy streets to the police station below the village. We had some hot, sweet tea with the Sikh signalman in the radio room and asked him to send a telegram to the British High Commission in Delhi, which would give Molly some idea of when we could be expected to arrive there. It cost 15 rupees. The telegram never arrived and I couldn't really blame the signalman if he did pocket the money!

Returning to Punchok's house, we sorted out food and fuel. We left four days' food, two litres of fuel and some spare socks and other bits and pieces for Henry's return in the summer. He could also have the pair of skis. A reappraisal of ski wax was called for and we decided to take all that we had left in the dump (see appendix A). We had got through quite a lot so far and we were pretty certain that once we had got over the Kang La we would experience Klister conditions for considerable distances. While Odd and Erik reshuffled food and fuel to get us to Karpat, I had a long talk with Punchok and wrote down in my diary all his answers to Henry's questions. As a final thank you to Punchok for looking after all our effects, we gave him 400 cigarettes (bought in Abu Dhabi the previous summer and taken to Padam specifically as a gift for this occasion), a surplus snow shovel and three litres of fuel. We sat in our sleeping bags chattering to Punchok until about nine o'clock that evening. About half of the whisky was consumed and finally washed down by some chang which Punchok had brought up from his room below. It was, however, insufficient anaesthetic to deaden the noise of barking dogs which continued through the night.

Morale was high when we left Padam at 7.30 on 20th March. Erik was feeling better now after a bout of fever which had given him a temperature. My left eye was hurting and watering profusely, and although we all suffered cracked lips, we were in pretty good shape. Keeping away from local food was certainly proving to be a wise policy. Ahead lay the highest pass on the journey and we couldn't have been better acclimatised to take it on. It was a rather mild − 5 °C and overcast when we started. We had no real difficulty until we were adjacent to Trakkur when, quite suddenly, snow conditions deteriorated, forcing us to drop down to the ice on the river. This was beginning to break up in places. One or two 'tiptoe' manoeuvres were necessary to skirt a rocky bluff and we removed skis to step over surging open water. A slip here would have resulted in being swept under the ice to certain death. From here, with the Burden Gompa monastery perched atop a 100-metre vertical rock above us, and a fast-flowing river below, there was no alternative but to gain the line of the summer path which hugged a precarious line through steep rocky buttresses. There was no room to ski, so off they came to be strapped high onto rucksacks. We ploughed our way delicately through the snowy rocks on foot, almost to the front door of the Gompa before we were able to don skis again.

We were breaking through a thick crust with every step, sinking up to thighs in snow that was akin to granulated sugar. To extract each ski was an enormous effort. It wasn't possible to push the ski through the snow because the crust would jar up against the leg and, like a doorstop, prevent any further advance. It was a matter of kicking with all our might to force the ski tip to break the crust from below and somehow shuffle it half a metre forward before sinking back to thigh level again. Our earlier high morale began to sink sharply, compounded by progressing only 800 metres in one hour.

Whilst our lunch break provided a rest from this purgatory, we surprised even ourselves by discussing alternative ways out of Zanskar if these conditions persisted. My left eye had now become a bore and was troubling me. Not one of us could understand what the problem was; we had worn snow glasses all the time so snow blindness was not even considered.

After lunch, Odd took a line directly up the slopes behind our lunch spot, powering his way up.

'Where the hell does he get his energy?' I asked, turning to Erik.

'He's a horse' was the reply. We heard Odd shouting down to us.

Det er fin snø her oppe—vind blåst.

'Thank God for that.' Our gradual gain in altitude had taken us on to a slight ridge where the wind had packed the snow. Odd was romping up in his indefatigable way. Heading for a shallow saddle, Erik and I followed up more sedately to find him resting on a rock admiring the view up the Tema Shah Nulla to the glacier below the Poat La at 5,490 metres. We camped 3 kilometres further on from the saddle at 4,160 metres. My eye was now painful and was keeping me awake at night, so in the morning, using black sticky tape from the repair kit, I taped up the whole of the left eye piece of my glasses to blot out all light. With that I lost my sense of judging distance so the others took the lead for a couple of days.

We were now getting into high country. We turned left, due south, at a rocky buttress that looked like the Buchaille Etive Mor in Glencoe, and gained the snout of the glacier. Douglas and I had camped almost at that spot in the summer. We went a fraction higher to 4,775 metres and in failing light and plummeting mercury we got the tent up in the lee of an enormous boulder. The morrow would see us over the Kang La and hopefully on some sensational downhill runs all the way to Udaipur, a descent of nearly 2,800 metres over a distance of 65 kilometres. For that thrill we could hardly wait.

The long, slow climb up to the pass took four hours. It was less arduous for Odd who just took it effortlessly in his stride. He was soon a speck on the smooth surface of the glacier. It was a breathless advance, forcing us to stop for rest every two hundred or so metres. I remember trying to make myself do two hundred paces before allowing a rest, and then it was a lurch of body weight onto ski sticks supported from the armpit, face staring at the snow to get going again. It would have been easy to shut my mind off from the surrounding scene, but I recall making a conscious effort to admire the hanging ice falls and peaks to the flanks of the glacier, and frequently seizing a longer rest on the excuse of taking a photograph. There was a broken area of crevasses just below the pass and to the right as we looked up, but they were well away from our route, the line of which was easy to see. Certainly, it was no place to be in bad weather but this day the gods were with us and provided hazy sunshine all the way to the top. As Erik and I shuffled our way over, we came across Odd sitting on some rocks to one side of the pass, waiting for us. He was shivering from the brisk wind that exaggerated the temperature of $-16\,°C$, and he was glad to see us. We stopped long enough for Erik to extract his altimeter to register 5,600 metres before descending slightly into the lee of a hollow for a brew. Getting there had made us dehydrated and we boiled masses of sweet 'Kang La' tea as we sat in that amphitheatre of peaks which had been so inviting in the summer. Alas, it was too cold to stay long in this beautiful place, so we gathered ourselves together, clapped our skis back and forth to remove clogging snow, gave a push and welcomed the force of gravity as a friend for once.

Below us spread the Miyar glacier. Where we were the glacier was 3–4 kilometres wide with tentacles of other glaciers flowing down to join the main glacier like branches of a tree. Further down it narrowed to about 2 kilometres and snaked away out of sight behind a precipitous spur of rock and ice. We kept reasonably close together as we traversed down some steep slopes which I remembered were crevassed further over to one side. The snow was quite deep and it allowed us to take a steep line down, under good control. With gravity working for us our inactivity was chilling and we were happy to reach the flatter surface below and get arms and legs moving once again. Although it seemed flat, each stride of a ski and push of a stick gained a metre or so; the snow was too deep to allow any more for the trail breaker, but it was fine for those behind.

It was extremely cold when we camped at 5,200 metres, 10 kilometres down the glacier and where it began to turn the corner. A nasty wind gusting to 30 knots made the impact of the temperature that much greater and it was with difficulty that we raised the tent. Both Erik and I were suffering nasty headaches and Odd had caught a dose of the dog, either from an over indulgence of chang or from some dirty water given to us in Padam. The medical kit was aired again but the pills didn't work fast enough to stop Odd taking hasty excursions at half hourly intervals outside. Each time he went out he shouted the temperature to us: just after 6.30 pm it was $-16\,°C$, at 7.00 it was $-20\,°C$ and a fraction before 7.30 on Odd's final foray it was $-24\,°C$.

Three days of a black patch over my left eye had eased the discomfort and now that the persistent watering had dwindled to almost nothing, I was able to assume my share of the trail breaking. The problem could only have been snow blindness caused, surprisingly, by the strong glare getting in through the side of my snow glasses.

We had seen the summit of Menthosa illuminated by a beautiful sunset the previous evening but now the wind, having strengthened during the night, had spun up the surface snow, blowing it along in a hazy white mass of spindrift to gust above head height. When we moved off we were grateful to have the gale behind us but it did spoil the view for much of the morning. The further we descended the less strong the wind became and when we reached the turbulent terminal moraine that had been the devil to negotiate in the summer, we found ourselves in clear still air and warm sunshine once again.

We took the moraine directly in the centre, with Odd forging ahead as route finder. This was really quite fantastic skiing with ups and downs and swooshes in deep snow. It demanded concentration beyond the norm because one second we would be traversing down on a north-facing slope with cold snow, and the next we would be turning a corner onto hard névé. What had been an ankle-breaking, boulder-hopping evolution in the summer had been transformed into the most exhilarating descent on skis that any of us had before experienced.

The short notes in my diary hardly do justice to the thrill of that $1^1/4$-hour descent, but for Odd and Erik to applaud it as one of the best said it all. We made 38 kilometres that day.

To the surprise of the local folk we entered the village of Khanjar, the highest in the Nulla. We had just skied down the line of the river, which provided some ecstatic manoeuvres similar to the terminal moraine of the

Miyar glacier, and apart from Odd's breaking a ski stick, we were in high spirits. A couple of days before, Odd had created for himself a face mask using some old food packaging to protect some very sore lips and a nose that was burnt raw. He attached this to his glasses with sticky tape and it hung down rather grotesquely over his face, so it wasn't surprising when our sudden arrival in Khanjar sent the folk into scuttling away to the safety of their houses. It seemed like an age before anyone had the courage to come out into the open. Slowly the doors creaked open, little by little, until whole faces peered out. We stood there watching this saga as one by one, they gained more confidence, and came out. Their fear was understandable: they couldn't possibly have seen skis before, or foreigners in winter time, and our dishevelled, roasted and bearded frames, one with a mask, one with a black patch, all three filthy dirty, would have raised eyebrows anywhere. We spent some time with them and departed the best of friends, speeding down through patchy juniper forest, away from the village to a rickety bridge over an open river. It was here that we displayed some totally irrational behaviour. We stripped and washed in the icy water! We were mad, yes, but wow was it refreshing!

We were in Karpat by one o'clock seeking out the house of Moti Singh with the help of David Nicholls' map. Phabrang loomed in the vee of the valley above and it confirmed yet again my opinion that it is one of the most beautiful mountains in this part of the Himalayas. The ski down from Khanjar, through Gumba, where the route to Menthosa branched out of the Miyar Nulla, had taken about an hour and it had been spectacular. The village seemed to expect us and after sticking skis and sticks into the snow, we were ushered directly to Moti Singh's house and upstairs into an empty room. Moti and his brothers and sons gathered around us and pumped an antique primus into life to boil some tea. These friendly people are Dogras and their woven greyish woollen baggy dungarees and jackets and small circular hats, with gaily-coloured bands around their rims, were an interesting contrast to the crimson textiles of Zanskar.

The room was cold and while we waited for the water to boil, someone went to fetch the *compouda*, the Urdu and Hindi term for a medical attendant, who arrived and announced himself in English. Our package of food and fuel was brought in by a couple of young boys, who stayed to join the many other onlookers who had gathered around the walls, some standing, some gaping, most chattering amongst themselves. A lot of laughter and noise was coming from outside and a glance through a tiny window gave the reason. Some of the village ladies, prohibited from entering the house, were trying out our skis, falling in the snow, legs in the air and thoroughly enjoying themselves until one got out of control and crashed into a stone wall. We called a halt at that point and the *compouda* shouted instructions below to stop. We still had 150 kilometres to go to Manali and the last thing we wanted to do was walk!

Tea had just begun to brew when Moti Singh left the room to re-enter two minutes later with two bottles of arak, a strong alcoholic beverage made from rice. Between the three of us, the *compouda*, Moti and two of his brothers, we demolished both bottles. We heard from Moti through the *compouda* all about Nicholls Sahib and his expedition and how he had been the chief cook at their advance base camp. Before the arak began to have its full effect we established that the west side of the valley was better to ski down than the summer path on the steeper eastern slopes. We should therefore get an unrestricted run down to Shakoli, the final village before the exit gorge.

The arak thwarted that unrestricted run but we somehow managed to extract ourselves before more bottles appeared. We hiccupped through our 'thank you's, paid Moti a handsome retainer for looking after our food, and lurched out of the house. Giggling amongst ourselves, we skied rather clumsily over a bridge and away through rocks and junipers on the other side, being forced to take skis off at one point to negotiate one boulder field where it was easier to walk. It was here that I tripped and accidentally dropped one of my skis. It slid forward gaining momentum rapidly, heading for the Miyar river below.

'Come back you bastard!' was the only reaction I could manage, thinking of the long walk ahead if it were lost in the river. Divine intervention, invisible forces or whatever, the ski did a complete somersault and speared into the snow not 15 metres down the slope, from where I retrieved it. It was with greater sobriety that we advanced thereafter. We camped early, the arak having taken its toll.

We arrived in Udaipur at noon the next day. We had walked through the 8-kilometre gorge which, on its west side, was snow-free. In several places the summer path had disappeared with a landslide or avalanche which meant some quite delicate moves to get around. Colossal cones of avalanche debris filled the gorge almost everywhere and it was obvious that once winter had set in, the people of the Miyar Nulla were trapped in their valley until about this time each year. It was a narrower version of the Sind river gorge, altogether more menacing and we were happy to reach the open valley and snow-covered fields that perched precariously above the banks of the Chandra Bagha river. Udaipur was very familiar to me as I had visited the village three times before: in 1970, 1976 and the previous summer with Douglas. So it was direct to the attractive little PWD rest house that we skied.

Apart from a coat of paint and the lack of hollyhocks and

chrysanthemums that I remembered had added colour to the unkempt garden on previous visits, the rest house had changed little. We hadn't planned to stay long there, maybe an hour or two to have lunch and enjoy a nap in the sunshine, but when two Indians, one an Army officer, came out of the front door and greeted us with a bottle of beer, our resistance was too low to refuse.

Mr. Bilwa, a road engineer, and Captain Ranjbir Singh, an Army doctor, had wintered in Udaipur and were occupying one half of the rest house. They were responsible for a couple of platoons of Indian sappers who were building a new road downstream and beyond Udaipur. They had also cleared about 5 kilometres of snow from the road towards Manali and they explained that eventually they would work towards the Rhotang La and meet up with other engineers coming up from Manali, probably in mid-June. They asked us to spend the night and join them for dinner, an invitation we didn't refuse. We ate tender meat from an ibex, shot some days before by the Indians, and washed it down with Diplomat Indian Malt Whisky and a seven-year-old rum which Odd and Erik much enjoyed. We were getting closer to civilisation and not one of us cared for that particularly.

At six o'clock in the morning of 26th March, Molly should have been arriving in Delhi. At the same time we were woken with tea, fried eggs and chipolatas by two Gurkha orderlies. The two Indians were still in bed when we left the rest house in a battered old TATA lorry that took us 5 kilometres up to the limit of the cleared road. Then we were on our own.

The snow was patchy and quite rotten when we left the lorry—it was not surprising at the lower altitude of 2,620 metres—and our progression up the valley saw us on and off skis for most of the morning. It was extremely hot at lunch time, warm enough to strip down to underpants to sunbathe on the side of the road. Snow conditions became better as we gradually gained height to Kirting, a small village where we spent the night. Manali was 90 kilometres away and we reckoned our arrival there would be spot on time.

We opted for a different routine the next day so that we could maximise our use of colder conditions of early morning. By doing this we were able to make 7–8 kilometres an hour. We didn't bother to cook breakfast until about nine or ten o'clock, after 2–3 hours' skiing, when we arrived at the bridge at Tandi. This small village on a hillside stands above an important crossroads. The main road goes north here and it leads eventually to the Barralach La, one of the highest road passes on the planet, and further on to Leh. We sat in the ruins of a small stone building to have breakfast and while it was cooking, Odd carried out a repair task on his ski stick, using fibreglass tape and one of the spare fibreglass tent poles. While he did this

I recalled that in the summer there had been a roadside circus performing here, tea shops, open air stalls and hundreds of people waiting to crowd into whatever transport there was going either to Manali, Darcha or Leh. But now there wasn't a soul to be seen and the only evidence of people having passed by were footprints in the snow.

While we were eating our porridge a couple of well-dressed Indians came round the corner. They were wearing suits with their trousers tucked into their socks and just ordinary shoes. They stopped and we chatted for a few minutes. They had crossed the Rhotang La earlier that week and told us that they had been in the first group of people to cross the pass on foot that winter. Warm spring sunshine was obviously triggering the movement of folk from the Kulu Valley up to the highlands to prepare for the short summer season ahead. Our timing was about right and that was vital, because these people told us that the snow was melting rapidly above Manali. The arrival of these two strengthened our confidence that the extremely steep descent from the Rhotang would be reasonably safe, although until we got there we wouldn't know for sure as the sun could have had a deteriorating effect on conditions. This concern was heightened as we were funnelled between the open river and an escarpment to our left. Above some cliffs were steep scree slopes, topped by more lines of cliffs and huge boulders. The slopes angled at 40–45 degrees and faced directly into the midday sun. That they were relatively free of snow was some consolation because we would be safe from avalanches but there was the other danger of stonefall to contend with. As we skied through that zone we were bombarded by stones, some the size of ping-pong balls, others as large as card tables. They would ricochet through the lower scarp and with a whine like a bullet would drop into the accumulations of wet snow beneath with a loud thud and a splash. Terminal velocity absorbed in a fraction of a second! It was an unnerving business to weave our way through this alley and we felt more like skittles than skiers. The uneven surface of avalanche debris, with frozen blocks and balls of snow, was an anchor to our speed, and like everything unpleasant, it was nice when it was over.

The terrain was much more amenable after that, even though the snow was soupy and we had to resort to trail-breaking again. The rewards of early morning skiing on a hard crusty surface were only too clear to us. If there had been a moon at night I am sure we would have done some of our distance in its light. Certainly we talked about it although we would have missed a lot of the scenery if we had. There was plenty of that to impress us during a long lunch break.

That evening we passed Sissu, a small village that boasted a pretty little PWD rest house (alas locked) and using the colder evening temperatures to our advantage we sped on, skating on the refrozen soup to clock up about 39 kilometres before we camped.

My diary records our final day with greater clarity than my memory allows.

Saturday 28th March: *−11°C and we had decided to follow the same routine as yesterday, merely a cup of tea and a biscuit at 5.30am to make use of the excellent conditions of the early morning. We were on our way by 6.30am and at Khoksar by 8.30am. There must have been 3 metres of snow here and the dilapidated huts of this shanty place were hardly visible. There were three policemen in residence who had moved in only 3 days before to check the human traffic which was beginning to cross the Rhotang. There was also a wide-smiling friendly chokidar who provided hot water for our porridge. We asked how long it would take to get to the pass and each gave conflicting times. We had asked about the time it would take so that we could assess the best time to descend to Manali. We knew that the descent would be extremely steep and had reasoned between ourselves that while to descend on bone hard névé would be fast and fun, a fall would almost certainly result in an unstoppable slide and a crunch over cliffs or rocks! It would be better to go down in late afternoon when the snow would be softer although probably more prone to avalanches.*

We were able to ski, away from Khoksar, on a diagonal incline upwards but this soon gave way to steeper ground where it was physically uneconomical to continue on skis. So we removed them, strapped them onto rucksacks and continued on foot. We were up on the pass in 2¹/2 hours with Odd getting up there about 15 minutes ahead of Erik and me. Erik's back was troubling him and he was making a hard effort of the climb and it was with a thankful gasp that we lurched over the top. There were 15 locals on the top who were resting before descending to Khoksar, having spent 10 hours climbing up from Manali. We waited on top, basking in the still air for two hours, setting off for the descent at 3 o'clock. The pass is about 1¹/2km wide and flat but it wasn't long before gravity was doing its work. It wasn't easy to pick a natural line down onto the steep convex slope, so, with Odd leading, we eventually reached the top of a large avalanche run. We took a calculated risk and descended on shallow, narrow but very steep traverses, kick-turning on the end of each, occasionally sideslipping and sidestepping over steep bumps. This went on for a drop of 500m as nervously we cast our eyes frequently up and around for safe havens if something were to come down. The shute was enormous and penetrated further down than we thought. Odd got way ahead, with me in my traditional position, and certainly I had never experienced such steep skiing before. It was hairy but exhilarating.

We paused for a short while in Murree, tea shops looking dirty, deserted

126

and forlorn and decided to ignore the line of the road. Instead we followed the line of some footprints, steeply down into the edge of the juniper forest. 25–30 zig-zags in soupy snow saw us eventually in a snowy glade by a bridge. It was nearing 5 o'clock but we decided to push down to Manali all the same. We were able to ski within 1km of the Kothi rest house from where we were forced to walk down the road, now clear of snow. A PWD lorry came rumbling towards us and we hitched a lift to Manali where we arrived at 6 o'clock. Three happy men were we.

That was the penultimate entry in my diary. It had been a long hard day: 55 kilometres and a fabulous end to a fantastic journey. The descent from 4,050 metres to 2,000 metres where the snow petered out had been more of a sensation I thought than the Vallée Blanche descent from the Aiguille du Midi.

We walked up the hill, past the circuit judge's bungalow to the Mayflower Guest House, a comfy colonial-style bungalow where Molly, Ram and I had stayed in 1976 and which Douglas and I had also used in 1980. We ordered a dozen bottles of beer, ate rather a tough chicken for dinner, washed ourselves in buckets of hot water and collapsed into bed feeling very contented, me now longing for the Delhi reunion with Molly.

We tarted up the skis, cleaning the paintwork with meths and scraping the wax off the soles. The tails of each had delaminated badly—the result of being used as pegs for the main guys of the tent.

'Ingen problem' Odd declared, rooting for the repair kit in his rucksack.

The master carpenter from Oslo provided the remedy. In a matter of seconds 210-centimetre skis became 190s. A touch of rapid araldite compressed by the weight of a bed for two hours and they were like new. The final entry in my diary was short and sweet.

Sold the skis, sticks and boots for 2,000 rupees.

Appendix: Equipment and Stores

Whilst it has not been my intention to include long detailed lists of equipment and spares taken on our longer journeys, I thought it would provide a useful guide to anyone considering completing similar ski tours in remote parts of the world if I gave a brief outline of what we had in the Himalayas:

Ski Waxes
In Srinager: 3 violet, 3 blue, 3 red Swix tubes of Klister; 2 blue, 3 green, 3 violet, 2 blue Extra Swix stick waxes; 2 yellow stick Klister.

In Padam: 3 violet, 3 blue, 1 red Swix tubes of Klister; 2 blue, 1 green, 1 violet, 1 red special, 1 blue Extra Swix stick waxes; 1 red, 1 yellow stick Klister.

Ski Accessories
Carried: 3 pairs spare ski stick over-baskets (extra large), 10 pairs small baskets, 2 spare ski tips.

In Padam: 1 pair ski bindings, 4 pairs ski stick over-baskets, 1 pair skis.

In Ringdom: 1 ski stick.

In Sokhniz: 1 ski stick

Footwear Accessories
Carried: 6 pairs rubber oversocks (2 pairs each), 3 tubes Dubbin.

In Padam: 3 pairs rubber oversocks, 3 tubes Dubbin.

Tool Kit Carried
Rapid Araldite, spare bindings, ski screws, ski boot heel caps, heavy-duty needle, horse-hair thread, screwdrivers, sewing kit, insulation tape, fibreglass tape and thin nylon cord.

First Aid Pack Carried
1 heavy shell dressing, 1 4″ crepe bandange, 1 2¹/₂″ crepe bandage, 2 pkts Steri Strip skin closures, assorted plasters, 25gm cotton wool, tube Dequadin lozenges, 2 thermometers, Lamotil (for diarrhoea), DF118 (for pain), Anthisan tablets, Septron antibiotic tablets, 30 Codis headache pills, Brulidin antiseptic cream, Lasonal cream, Anthisan cream, 12 Streptatoid tablets, 1 Cavit Kit for tooth filling, Diazepan tablets (for anxiety), Senakot tablets (for constipation), Piriton tablets, water sterilising tablets.

The commitment of high mountain skiing at 4,100 metres.

Above: Erik Boehlke reaching the Kang La, at 5,600 metres the highest point of the Indian journey.
Below: Descending the Miyar Nulla above Gumba.

Above: The winning military patrol ski team from 45 Commando Royal Marines at the British Nordic Ski Championships, Bavaria 1987.
Below: The author competing in the South Norway Biathlon Championships, 1970.

Above left: A young Bakhtiari boy on his home-made skis.
Above right: All that remained of the author's grandparents' home at Gulmarg, Kashmir.
Below: Erik Boehlke and Odd Eliassen, Odin and Thor in the Jotunheim mountains.

Above: Odd Eliassen and Erik Boehlke examine a fumerole in Iceland.

Below: The author in Bodie Town.

Above: The deserted mining camp at Howard's Pass.

Below: 2,800 metres up on the Spanish Andorran frontier, looking west.

Above: The Scottish mountains at their best. Lochnagar's southern slopes in the far background.
Below: Henry Beverley approaches the summit cairn of Claise.

Above: Odd Eliassen enjoying June snow on Langskarvel, high over lake Bygdin in Norway.
Below: The author 3,000 metres up on day one of the Zagros ski journey.

Iceland: Hot Rivers, Mud Baths and Good Skiing

Not long after 42 Commando Royal Marines had moved over to Norway in January 1983, and the Regimental Headquarters had taken over use of the Fossheim Hotel in Lom, I was beckoned to the telephone at the hotel reception offices which had now become the domain of the commanding officer, Lieutenant Colonel Nick Vaux, his adjutant and the chief clerk.

'You're wanted on the 'phone, Sir.'

The duty clerk occupied the chair which would normally have been the preserve of a pretty Norwegian receptionist. It was a very different scene from that to which the Norwegian salesman leaning against the desk was accustomed. He was trying to book into the hotel for the night and the duty clerk was attempting to tell him that he was wasting his time.

'Sorry, no room here, mate! The British Government's rented this place. No room at all.'

The clerk turned to me. 'There's a Norwegian on the 'phone for you. From Oslo I think. Fellow called Odd or something like that!'

'Thanks.'

It was indeed Odd Eliassen and he asked whether I could get away the following weekend. There were a couple of points to discuss. Could I join him and Erik and two other Norwegians on a ski trip to Iceland at the end of March? The other topic was more important but the detail for both could be sorted out at the weekend. As a parting shot before he rang off Odd said 'Don't forget your skis. We'll do a short tour.'

When I put the phone down, the poor salesman was still trying to book into the hotel and understand the clerk's colloquial English. I interrupted them and in Norwegian explained what we were doing there and apologised for any inconvenience. He went on his way no doubt frustrated by the apparent occupation of his country by the Royal Marines.

Lom is a crossroads village nestling in the junction of two deep valleys in the Eastern Jotunheim, the central and highest mountains in Norway. The Fossheim Hotel is the largest, and most traditional hotel in the village and

129

Odd, Erik, Ram and I breakfasted there in April 1980 on our way back to Oslo after testing and checking our food and equipment for our ski journey across the Western Himalayas. Little did I expect then that three years later I would be the chief administrator of a Commando and ultimately responsible for the care of the Fossheim, one other hotel in Lom, and three others in Sjødalen. It was not a job I relished at all but it was in a beautiful part of Norway and the prospect of $2^{1}/_2$ months' skiing and living in this fabulous mountain area more than made up for that.

It was high time to break away from a six-year attachment to a pair of glassfibre Landsem skis which had probably accumulated 7–8,000 kilometres of use; their soles ample evidence that not all of those had been on immaculately prepared ski tracks. So I boldly dipped into my pocket for a new pair of Blå Skia racing skis, which were discounted through a friend of Erik. They were an example of the complete revolution in ski manufacture, started in the mid 1970s when wooden types were either cast into the fire or elevated as wall displays. Featherweight at $1^{1}/_2$ kilos, they would be a joy to use although quite a handful to control on speedy downhill runs.

The weekend revealed all. Odd's short tour on the Saturday turned out to be another of those 90-kilometre treks he was so fond of. Suitably waxed up, we set off on those wonderfully-prepared ski tracks that vein the forests to the north of Oslo. As we gaited along, pushed down the hills, skated round the corners, increased the tempo of our feet on the hills, so Erik explained the plans for Iceland. Neither he nor Odd ever seemed to lose their breath. Listening was quite enough for me; just to keep abreast of them on the double track took all my breath and any questions would have to wait until we stopped; Odd had promised a break at a café.

Four hours after we set out we reached the café and I sat down for a well-earned rest. Erik fished out a large-scale map of Iceland from his rucksack and traced a circular route with his finger from Burfell over Myrdalsjøkull and down to Porsmark. He had been there the previous summer on a walking tour and he now enthused over the possibilities of a good 10-day ski tour. He had enlisted two other friends, Torbjørn Eggen and Bjorn Halvorsen so there would be five in the group. Both had been with him and Odd on a 400-kilometre ski tour of the Atlas Mountains in Morocco a few years before.

The short January day at Oslo's latitude prompted an agitated glance at the clock. It was all of four hours back to the car for Odd and me, and Erik had a bit further to go back to Frognersaeter in the northern suburbs of Olso. Before we rose wearily from the table, Odd asked if I could do anything to get him attached to 42 Commando in March because he had received a 'call up' letter to complete three weeks' mandatory military training, 'repetition service' as it is unaffectionately known to Norwegian menfolk. It was the 12th Infantry Regiment to which he had been summoned and it was coincidentally with that formation that 42 Commando were going to work. I told him I would see what I could do and would be in touch.

'Quite soon, I hope' he said.

'*Ja*. If I ever complete this short ski tour.'

Sarcasm couldn't hide my unspoken concern about the return journey to Vestmarka; I wasn't really ready for such a long ski trip so soon. Erik disappeared down the hill with a wave and a shout of 'See you in Reykjavik' and I stumbled stiffly into some sort of rhythmical gait behind Odd. It was almost dark when we reached the village of Sollihøgda and I was completely done in. I told Odd I would catch a bus for the rest of the way back.

'There's no bus from here' he declared smugly!

Fait accompli! I knew it was 22 kilometres back to the car and I knew that it was by no means flat or downhill all the way. Memory cannot recall the final score of kilometres but my body and soul needed no reminder from Odd that we had skied just over 90 kilometres that day. The new Blå Skia skis were superlative.

'Another one of your damned short tours', I complained to Odd.

But once over, the discomfort was soon forgotten and I was satisfied with achieving such a distance, although from the warmth of Odd's sitting room in his cosy little house in Asker I was extremely thankful I hadn't gone with Erik—he had another 20 kilometres further to go and wouldn't be home till well after dark.

The Iceland trip took on greater meaning as we pored over more detailed maps and searched out a line to take through this barren land of lava and mountains. They revealed an interesting variety of active volcanoes, hot springs, lava flows resembling glaciers in their tongue-like shapes, massive icefields and mountains galore. And all so remote. Unlike the Indian Himalayan journey there would be no hot sun and no lunch breaks spent basking and snoozing on sleeping mats; the weather was sure to be diabolical. In Iceland there would be new challenges and I was looking forward to it.

The person with whom I had to clear Odd's request for attachment to 42 Commando was Nick Vaux. Nick and I had long been good friends and he knew of my travels with Odd and Erik over the years. An enthusiastic cross-country skier himself, he agreed to the proposal and felt the unit would benefit from Odd's wealth of mountain and skiing experience. So for the duration of the ten-day exercise, Odd worked with a Reconnaisance Section, ahead of the Commando and mostly operating at night.

Much later Odd was to tell me how impressed he was with the professional skills of the four-man team he was with and how much he had learned from the attachment. By the same token, the team leader expressed to Nick how he admired Odd's skill in mountain and snow craft, and his ability to ski with a heavy rucksack. Both seemed to have benefited from the attachment.

At the end of March, I flew with Iceland Air from London to Reykjavik. It was one of those clear, crisp days that heralds the coming of spring and the views of the Pennines and Scottish mountains, their tops still under snow, were remarkable. I remember thinking it a pity that Great Britain didn't receive the consistent good snow cover of other countries at a similar latitude, because if it did, the British landscape would provide sensational cross-country skiing terrain, comparable to the best anywhere else. As we approached the coast of Iceland we were told by the Captain to fasten seat belts, since bad weather was expected for the last part of the flight. Iceland's weather was living up to its reputation.

Odd and Erik had arrived three or four days before me and had already tasted the fickleness of Iceland's weather. They were waiting for me in the airport terminal in Reykjavik, and eagerly chatted about a three-day trip they had done north from Geysir, taking in the spectacular waterfalls at Gullfoss where the Hvita river plunges over a cliff into a gorge. The falls were frozen and Odd had slipped on a mushroom of icy snow on the cliff edge and, but for some swift assistance from Erik, would have plunged into the abyss below. The weather had been foul with blowing wet snow, yet on their second night the skies had cleared and the mercury had plummeted to −20 °C. The colder weather had given some spectacular skiing conditions on their way to Hlodufell, Skridutindur and down to Laugarvatn before it broke yet again and they found themselves walking 40 kilometres down to Selfoss to catch the bus back to Reykjavik and their rendezvous with me. Their enthusiasm was infectious and inverted weather patterns were not going to dampen it.

Erik had booked us all into the Salvation Army Hostel in Kirkjustraeti, almost in the centre of Reykjavik. It was warm, comfortable and extremely good value. I was introduced to Oona, the owner, who called us 'her boys'. She was of Norwegian birth, with the most charming welcoming smile and her warmth and friendliness made such an impression that we still talk fondly of her.

We sorted out our food and equipment in the bedroom using our well-practised systems of the Himalayan journey as our guide. Communal kit was virtually the same apart from the medical box from which the tropical medicines had been removed. With ten day's food for the tour, we reckoned we could accomplish a 300-kilometre line without pushing ourselves excessively. As usual, Erik unselfishly opted to carry the tent and I drew the short straw for the extra day's food. While we were doing all this late into the evening, Tobben and Bjørn, the last two of our party, arrived and Erik booked a taxi and trailer for the three-hour drive out to Burfell the next morning. Before going to sleep we toasted our unusual ski tour with a giant tot of duty-free whisky, and suitably comatose, fell into the land of nod.

The taxi was a huge American car and well it needed to be for the five of us to squeeze in. Rucksacks and skis were loaded into the trailer and we drove out of Reykjavik in the murky grey light of dawn with a nasty tail wind and driving snow to accompany us for most of the 150 kilometres to the dam at Burfell which marked the end of the road. The weather obliterated the view throughout the drive and at a few exposed places, the road as well. The car charged the snow drifts and somehow we got through without recourse to shovelling and pushing.

The three of us were using Åsnes skis, waxable with metal edges under the centre, and Tobben and Bjørn were on waxable ones as well but bearing a different label. The weather, although by now improving, had been full of that infuriating wet snow. This fact alone generated discussion on which wax to use, because we would begin to climb after about 8 kilometres and as that crucial height was gained so the snow would become colder. Too soft a wax and we would be clogging up and carrying half of Iceland around under our skis! The inevitable compromise was reached and a colder wax applied, with an irksome acceptance of some backslip for those early kilometres. We got away shortly after noon.

Our route followed the line of a summer road called the Landmannaleid. It passed close to the snout of a large lavafield that flowed north from the summit of Hekla, a 1,491 metre high volcano which had last provided a spectacular display of fireworks in 1980. Regrettably, as we ascended towards this lavafield, mist and cloud hid this impressive mountain from view. We didn't obtain a sighting until late that afternoon when we camped for the night in a small col called Klofningar.

The weather remained unsettled and too mild for really pleasurable skiing the next day. Although it was $-3\,°C$ when we packed up our tents, patches of sunshine and a mild westerly air stream soon had the temperature hovering around zero. A climb up a long slope to the 600-metre contour line did nothing to ease our frustration over waxing. Aggravating backslip with all the weight of rucksack and body centreing down onto our triceps which were drawn with effort from pushing hard on the ski sticks behind, made this rather hard work. We paused for a few minutes to talk to a couple of Icelanders who appeared out of the mist on noisy snowscooters. It was a welcome break to catch our breath and apply some more wax. While scooters obviously had their uses, the noise and pullution were ugly intrusions into the silence of the snowy environment. Our remoteness had disappeared in a blink and I remember hoping that we would not see any more.

We skied on upwards, using a herring-bone occasionally to help compensate for backslip and weary arms, and went over the brim onto the flank of a lavafield. Great black shapes of pumice, distorted and ugly, reached for the sky out of the smooth surface of the snow. They were like menacing seracs on a glacier but without their translucent beauty and associated dangers. Instead they were evidence of a past natural phenomenon which had released its destructive power; now they were frozen into weird shapes, each with a cap of snow. Our ski tracks weaved through the lavafield, up a valley and onto a flat plain bordered by the steep hills of Sandleysur to the north. A *kofi* (Icelandic for a hut), was visible snuggling under Hellisfjall about 5 kilometres away, and the small black dot that was Odd was still visible for a few minutes before it disappeared from our view. The four of us couldn't keep up with the Horse, the name that Erik had given to Odd. He was indefatigable and quite impervious to the heavy-going conditions which made us stop for a break and some hot tea.

We were heading for Landmannalaugar, now a more appealing 15 kilometres away than the 35 kilometres it was at the previous night's campsite. The sun revealed itself for a lengthy hour and when we caught up with Odd, we found him resting in the lee of a rock reading a book and soaking up what warmth there was from the sunshine. A good schuss, all too short and brief, deposited us on the frozen, wind-rippled snowy surface of Frostastadavatn, a large crater about 2 kilometres in diameter. A steep climb on the other side, taken rather quickly in a zig-zag traverse by Odd and Erik, but with less speed and longer pauses by Tobben, Bjørn and myself, was the last bit of a long day's effort before we slipped round the corner of a rocky bluff and came within sight of the Laugar.

Landmannalaugar is a popular tourist attraction in the summer because here, out of the snout of a lavafield, flows a hot river which is deep enough in places for swimming. As the three of us rounded the final corner there were Odd and Erik already stripped, skis, sticks and clothes piled untidily upon rucksacks, stepping down a clumsy-looking step ladder that protruded through a metre of snow into the water.

'Come on in, the water's fine!' they shouted.

We were in there, the five of us, for almost three hours until wrinkled skin on feet and hands, now white from immersion, told us it was time to brave the cold and get out. The sensation was startling. There we were, one moment very tired after skiing 35 kilometres with rucksacks at their heaviest, the next moment totally revitalised by the incongruity of a bath in a hot river surrounded by snow and in temperatures of $-5\,°C$. Behind the river was a hut, and once inside the hut little else was talked about for a few minutes until appetites drove us to the chore of preparing supper. We were unanimous in our decision to do a day tour from the Laugar the next day and enjoy again the delights of the river, before pushing on southwards towards Myrdalsjøkull.

On the other side of the hut was a French party of four, two men and women who had come out on the snowscooters the previous day. Their plan was to do daily ski tours returning every evening to the hut for its comfort and proximity to the river. I remember thinking rather arrogantly that the difference between us was that we were the purists: the difference between 'aided' and 'free' in the climbing world! The bubbling of a meat stew and the smell of near burning on the Trangia cooker produced the alarm to bring me back from thoughts of elitism. So I gave up the mental comparison and called in the others for *mat,* the Norwegian for food.

The steep slope behind the Laugar was, in fact, the snout of an extensive lavafield with more numerous and seemingly more grotesque towers of black lava and pumice dotted all over it. The lava had flowed from a deep scar which was just visible through the mist as the next morning we skied up through the maze of towers. Gradually we climbed to the large, steaming, snow-free patch of ochre-coloured ground packed with boulders where once had flowed that great tongue of molten lava. We reached its edge and were able to remove our skis and explore the scene on foot. It was a different world in a frozen white mountainous landscape because here was a microcosmic tropical humid garden of mosses, small plants and grass. Upon it all existed trillions of insects, gorging themselves on the succulent warm vegetation, and as we walked around, we disturbed small colonies of birds which by rights should have migrated south four or five months before. There was food the year round for them here, food even for a brace of ptarmigan, brilliant white in their winter camouflage, but clearly oblivious to their conspicuousness as they pecked away on their murky dining table.

We ventured up the steeper slopes behind, herring-boning initially until the angle forced us into sidestepping in deep snow for the final few metres to the crest. Tobben and Bjørn had decided to ski eastwards to a series of hot springs while Odd, Erik and I went off in search of the hot springs beneath Hrafntinnusker, some 10 kilometres away to the south-west. It was a delight to be without heavy rucksacks, and we made good speed, climbing up to the 1,000-metre contour level. Up there the snow was firm and windpacked, and we followed a series of marker posts placed at infrequent intervals, some with only 30 centimetres sticking out of the

135

snow. The terrain was undulating and although the weather was hazy, close to whiteout—conditions where horizons, bumps and dips merge into one with simply no distinction between them—we found a steam vent, not by good navigation, but by its roaring sound. The noise emerging from the plate-sized vent was probably the sole factor which alerted us to be careful. Without it we may well have skied straight into the enormous hole that the high-pressure steam, which billowed into the grey sky, had melted in the snow. The hole was about 6 metres deep with an accessible trough leading into one part of it: otherwise it was circular as though a giant plug had been carved out and removed from within. We skied with trepidation into the trough and sidestepped carefully down to the fringe of the hot rock. Down in the bottom, the roar of steam was amplified tenfold by the near vertical walls of snow that represented that winter's snowfall. If we'd had our cooking pots with us we would have been able to brew some tea in a matter of seconds over the jet of steam. We lingered only to satisfy our curiosity before clambering out and pushing on to where there was a hot spring with a hut nearby.

The hut was a small refuge and it didn't take Odd more than a few minutes with the shovel to dig away the drifts piled up at the door. We enjoyed our biscuits and chocolate inside, protected from the wind, but it wasn't long before the cold interior penetrated through our woollen underwear, damp from the exertions of fast skiing. The weather had been worsening slowly throughout the morning and when the wind suddenly increased it reminded us that it was time to leave the relative warmth of the hut and return to the Laugar and the hot river before the worsening weather caught us out without proper clothing and equipment.

Erik took the lead on the return because he had the map. Expertly he navigated us 10 kilometres back to the steep slope above the lavafield. Our outward tracks had long been obliterated and with visibility at virtually zero, and a mild blizzard blowing fortunately at our backs, his was a skilful and timely display of navigation. The patch of steaming ochre-coloured ground was a welcome sight as we groped our way down in clumsy snow-plough turns towards the thick towers of black lava. Once there we were almost home, but I couldn't help noticing that the two ptarmigan were still on their patch of moss, pecking away at whatever they fancied and caring not a bit for the storm that now raged about them. Half an hour later we joined Tobben and Bjørn, a young Icelandic couple, Tord and Brenna and three friends in the river.

'Fantastic!' said Erik, and he was fully justified in his utterance. The snow was falling thickly and without the wind it was soon settling in quantity on top of everyone's head. Odd clambered out of the river, squelched through ankle-deep mud and disappeared from view. A few minutes later he emerged covered in thick brown mud from head to toe.

'A hot mud bath, *utrolig!*' he shouted, looking down at the six of us sitting up to our necks in the river.

I didn't venture out to try the mud and I don't remember whether the others did but Odd really was enjoying himself. We had found a point where a small tributary and a much hotter stream joined the main river. Like a hot water tap, this stream blended nicely to provide the ideal temperature; if too hot you moved outstream a little and back in again when you felt the water was getting too cold. Not one of us had experienced this sort of pleasure before although in 1977 Molly and I and some Swiss friends had taken a swim in a violently smelly and sulphurous pool high upon the slopes of Iran's second-highest mountain, Kuh-e-Sabalan, near the Russian-Iranian border.

Two nights at the Laugar were all we could afford, otherwise our stocks of food would not see out our plans for the next part of the trip. We set off after an early breakfast the next day. Our rucksacks were slightly lighter but it was still an effort to surmount those steep slopes above the lavafield. The weather was holding up to its traditional Icelandic form and it was being unkind. As we topped the crest above the lavafield we were hit by the full strength of a Force 9 gale which was whipping up the snow and ice particles and spinning them along, seemingly all at head height. They bit into and stung the exposed parts of our faces as heads down, we forced our way on and up into the teeth of the gale. Gusts frequently blew us off balance and only a quick move by a ski to one side or other, edging it fiercely into the hard icy surface, prevented a slip and a rasping slide down the steep slope. Behind us, the rocky volcanic pinnacle of Brennisteinsalda slowly retreated into the grey murk as we clattered and banged our weary way up. The higher we went the worse it became, until the moment came when even Odd, usually tireless, stopped. The four of us behind struggled up to huddle round him and we had a small soviet, each of us shouting his views to be heard over the roar of the wind.

'Shall we go on?' Odd opened the batting.

'What do you think, Tobben?'

'Va?'

'Shall we go down?'

'Ja!'

'Bjørn, Erik, Guy?'

'Ja Ja Ja!'

'Okay. Back for a swim, *Ja?'*

'Ja!'

Thank God for unanimity and common sense!

Descending with the gale pushing us from behind was tricky and my inferior downhilling skills soon revealed themselves yet again as I took up my traditional position in the rear. Within the hour we were back in the river, totally removed from the serious situation that faced us 600 metres higher up on the mountain; now it was as though it had never happened at all. We hogged the favourite spot by the small tributary and decided that we really had to move on the next day.

Move up and on we did, and on a cloudless, windless cold day, we sidestepped up those same steep slopes above the lavafield, the third time for Odd, Erik and myself. It was nice to see the sun and everything around us for once and as we gained those undulating slopes we glimpsed Hecla's summit some 30 kilometres distant. We passed the small *kofi,* its door back in a deep drift again. Keeping Reykjafjøll to our left we descended gently onto an open plain some 4 kilometres long. The gales of the previous few days had hardened the snow surface and we were able to push and skate across most of it at a handsome speed.

Dotted across the plain were several small plumes of steam, places to avoid in bad visibility because each emitted its noisy jet from circular holes in the snow, some deeper than 6 metres.

'Fall into one of those and you'll be there until summer', jibed Tobben.

Beyond were the uniform slopes of a small icefield descending from Kaldaklofsfjøll. It would have been nice to have made a detour to get to its 1,278 metre summit because a descent down those slopes would have been worth the effort. Time precluded it, however and we traversed around its western flank, at one point crossing a mini canyon where delicate sidestepping and slipping were necessary to get to the bottom and out at the other side. There was a group of four hot springs just beyond the canyon, each with its associated plume of steam blowing eastwards in the gentle breeze. Beyond was a crest from which we had a remarkable view over to the mass of the Myrdalsjøkull, whose crevassed and broken northern edge was about 15 kilometres away. Between were numerous mountains, all around 800 metres high and all with steep escarpments scarfed around their summits. It was a spectacular scene, framed to the south by the round icecap of Myrdalsjøkull and the steeper broken icefields of Eyjafjalljøkull. The sun shone throughout and it was warm with no wind. A glance high up to the west revealed a slight opaqueness in the sky, too distant to be meaningful at that moment, but it was obvious that we could expect a change of weather in the next couple of days.

Seven kilometres down and about 600 metres below our crest was a small lake, Alftavatn. It nestled between two steeply-scarped peaks, Torfatindur and Bratthals. There was a *kofi* on its northern shore and we all thought that if there was no-one there we would stay for the night. The descent from where we stood was a good test for control. Not so for my four friends who, with shouts of delight, launched themselves off and away. They were out of sight before I had given myself a tentative shove with my sticks and taken off on a much shallower angle. The route down was on the line of a ridge, the Svartihryggur, and by keeping to its eastern side it was possible to link some turns, pausing occasionally to stop and rest aching thigh muscles, and on the steeper sections to do a precarious kick-turn before taking a new traverse line.

The others were specks far below me by the time I had passed half way down the ridge, and lower down still the hard dry snow of the higher altitude changed abruptly into hard sun-glistening névé. As speed increased, thankfully the angle of descent lessened and in a matter of a couple of minutes I rattled to a stop above a wind scoop beside a rocky bluff in which the others were already establishing a lunchtime rest place, the cooker out and a pot full of snow perched on top. It was a warm spot, mostly out of the little eddies of wind that now and again gently swirled around the scoop.

We spent that night in the *kofi* and we weren't alone. Soon after arrival at the lake, the noise of snow scooters preceded their riders' arrival about half an hour before they came into sight. There were seven of them, all teenagers bedecked in thick sheepskin coats, dewliners and enormous motorcycle helmets with visors that swivelled down to protect their eyes. We had no right to complain because it was their country and they were obviously enjoying their chosen sport but their presence was obtrusive and spoiled the silence and beauty of Iceland at its winter's best. Just before darkness fell Tord and Brenna, the Icelandic couple we had met in Landmannalaugar, and three others also arrived at the *kofi*. They had skied over to us pulling their gear on pulks but they'd found the descent down the ridge too steep so had walked down, their skis strapped to their pulks.

We were glad to leave the next morning but arranged to meet Tord and Brenna in Reykjavik at the end of the trip. We skied due south to the edge of Maelifellssandur, a pancake-flat area spanning the gap between the edge of Myrdalsjøkull's ice and the subsidiary peaks of Torfajøkull, 10 kilometres to the north. A short discussion produced agreement to put our tents up there, dump our rucksacks, and ski over the long plain to go and visit a hot river under the south-eastern flank of Torfajøkull. It was about 15 kilometres away and would take about $1^1/2$ hours to get there.

In the summer the open plain of Maelifellssandur, a 600-metre high mountain desert, was very obviously extremely exposed to the atrocious westerly storms that fling their might at Iceland. In winter its surface is a bumpy, uneven mass of *sastrugi,* an ugly word for the curious snowy formations carved and formed by the wind. *Sastrugi* are dreadful to ski over; often up to half a metre high, skis slide off their crests and slip to the sides at any angle, and concentration and fast reactions are the only recipe for remaining on your feet. It is exhausting too, and after about 10 kilometres of silently cursing these snowy phenomena, we reached rising ground where the surface became more amenable. At that point we had another soviet and reach an amicable agreement: Tobben, Bjørn and I would return to the tents and prepare supper while Odd and Erik would ski the remaining distance to the river, have a swim and return in about two hours.

They returned a little earlier than expected, disappointed that the river was a mere trickle in comparison to the Laugar, not deep enough even to paddle. The weather had surprised us all by holding good for two days but the ominous signs of a change on its way from the west were still there. We only needed a couple of days of good weather to traverse Myrdalsjøkull and Eyjafjalljøkull, a total distance of about 60 kilometres and it would be a prerequisite for safe navigation once we were on the featureless white expanse of these huge icecaps. In the light of a candle, we studied the map and fingered a probable line up onto the ice avoiding the worst of the crevasse zones near its edge and, before drifting off to sleep, I prayed for that ominous break heralding itself in the western sky to keep away.

The seventh dawn broke cold and clear with a red sky throwing its crimson glow on to the icecap that filled the southern horizon. It looked settled enough to give the icecap a go, so we devoured our breakfast with haste, packed and departed. We couldn't help looking to the west as we skied towards the edge of the ice, Odd in the lead. It was Tobben who yelled for everyone to stop. To the west, the sky looked more ominous than the day before and now faint patches of mackerel-patterned cirrus could be seen.

I remember we all stood in a circle, ski tips inwards and almost touching. Then we began the 'shall we?' 'If we do what happens if the weather breaks?' 'If not what shall we do instead?' routine. We talked through each question and attempted to gain consensus. We were after all without an appointed leader and utterly reliant on our interdependence and companionship to help us reason out any differences of opinion in a mature and amicable fashion. That discussion was no exception and although it may have been more disappointing for one or two of us, our consensus was not to get onto the ice with a threat of bad weather in the next few hours. It would be better to head for Tindfjalljøkull which was a much smaller massif than its southern neighbours and would probably be a lot easier to cope with if we got caught out in a storm. So it was to the west, towards the threat, that we turned and skied on much the same sort of *sastrugi* as the previous day in the direction of a very prominent peak called Hattfell. It reminded me of Hattavarri, a peak of similar shape and size, that dominates the skyline near Skjøld in north Norway.

It was an icy traverse, quite steep too, that we took round the northern slopes of Hattfell. Below was a deep cleft, eroded away by a tributary of the Markarfljot river, and although the river in the cleft was frozen I certainly was very conscious of the iciness of the slope and the drop beneath it into the dark murky depths of this mini canyon. Each step needed a hearty slap into the ice with the ski to ensure a good purchase with the metal edge. We had been on similar and often much steeper ground in India but here it was the drop into the cleft that seemed to make it different. The other four took the slope head-on as if on a Sunday stroll, showing not a flicker of apprehension.

Once past the slope, it was a doddle down to another small *kofi*, perched on a little knoll where, on the southern side the sun had burnt away the snow to reveal some bedraggled yellow grass. Nearby were two small, semi-underground byres with turf roofs and they indicated that in the summer this place was probably a pasture for sheep. We had lunch outside, leaning against the wall of the *kofi*, and draped out our damp sleeping bags to get whatever warmth and drying power there was out of a very watery sun. The hut had bunks for eight and to our delight there was a propane gas bottle with a burner on the floor in a corner.

Consensus suggested a night stop at this *kofi* with a quick dash up the glacier of Tindfjalljøkull over the summit at 1,448 metres and down to the high plateau of Hraun above Fljotsdalur the next day. There was still time to do something that afternoon so, leaving Bjørn in the hut, four of us set off up the hill to the west to a col to view the snout of the glacier and check if it was heavily crevassed. It began to snow lightly before we got to the col and by the time we reached the smooth surface of the glacier, snow was falling heavily and the wind was increasing. Tobben and I turned and followed our fast disappearing tracks back to the hut while Erik and Odd went on further up the glacier for a few hundred metres. By the time they had returned, a blizzard was raging and the wind whistled and whined through the heavy-duty wires that anchored the hut to the ground.

The hut was given a thorough battering that night, the whole of the next day and the next night. We dozed away most of the time, relieving the long hours with copious quantities of tea, taking it in turns to keep the hut door free from drifting snow. We were all extremely glad to be in the hut during the storm and not surviving it up on the exposed ice of Myrdalsjøkull, because certainly that would have been survival in its literal sense. There were no regrets at the decision not to go and we were rather pleased with ourselves for getting it right.

The weather abated early the second morning and as it had successfully destroyed our plans for the last two days of the trip, we were now eager to leave and reach the nearest road. It was a good 35 to 40 kilometres to an isolated farm at Fljotsdalur where there was a jeep track marked on the map. If we were to get to Reykjavik on time to catch our flights back to Oslo and London, we had to use the break in the storm to get out of the mountains.

Overcoming the lethargy that thirty-six hours of inactivity in the hut had generated, we gathered up our gear and packed hastily, waxed up with blue Swix under the middle of the skis and launched off down the hill. Tobben and Bjørn were not so speedy in their packing manoeuvres and we reckoned that they may have missed the two-hour window of calm weather that allowed us to get abreast of an ugly volcanic peak called Einhyrningur where the descent into the Porsmork valley began. Then the storm returned but with less ferocity. At the lower altitude the temperature rose and the wind blew sticky wet snow through every seam in our clothes. Soon we were wet through but not too unhappy to enjoy the last swinging descent to the head of the flat wide flood plain of the Markarfljot river.

The flood plain is a mass of small tributaries of the main river between which are extensive boulder fields, dumped there as a result of centuries of shifting river activity. There were occasional patches of snow which slowly reduced in size and quantity as we progressed until it was impossible to ski. Our lot was then less pleasing, because we hadn't come to Iceland to walk. But walk we did, for about 12 kilometres, wading through icy rivers cursing the weather and feeling very disgruntled, our skis and sticks strapped high up on our rucksacks.

We knocked on the door of the new farmhouse at Flojtsdalur as the light was fading and to our surprise an English lady opened the door. We were offered the use of a turf-roofed former farmhouse not far away which turned out to belong to an Englishman called Dick Phillips. He used it in the summer months as a base for trekking parties. It was cold and damp but a haven in the storm and very welcome in our wet bedraggled condition. We were given some eggs and a portable gas burner and the little sitting room was soon home from home. We were dry and grateful and slept well that night.

The farmer gave us a lift in his Land Rover to Hvolsvollur, a small town about 50 kilometres away, stopping on the way to visit the ancient church at Hlidarendi. This fertile area of Iceland is known as Fljøtshlid and was the scene of the Njøls saga, an old Viking family feud, when human butchery and suffering was almost a daily occurrence. From Hvolsvollur we were given a lift in a converted lorry to Hveragerdi where there is a profusion of greenhouses, hot and humid from the limitless water piped from the hot springs on the hillsides above. Even a grove of banana trees was visible through the glass of one greenhouse. We didn't have to wait long there before we were given yet another lift to Reykjavik, our skis sticking out of the boot of the car. When we reached the crest of the high ground half way to the capital, I realised my camera was missing. Our kind driver turned the car and we drove back to the spot on the roadside where he had picked us up but it had gone and with it was lost a unique record of our trip.

Oona welcomed 'her boys' in the entrance lobby of the Salvation Army Hostel as though we were long lost relatives, and from beneath the reception desk, she produced a camera.

'I think this belongs to one of you,' she said, her eyes sparkling.

'Yes, it's mine!' I said, hardly believing my luck. 'But how did you find it?'

'The police saw you standing by the side of the road and when someone handed in the camera they telephoned a few hotels to ask if they were expecting three people with skis and rucksacks.' Oona relished telling the story. 'We were the first they contacted and they came in only a few minutes before you arrived. Well my boys, did you have a nice time?'

'Yes, it was a great trip,' replied Erik, speaking for us all. And it had been. Iceland had given us a huge variety of adventure and fun. The desire to return had been kindled and as we were discussing where we were going to eat, Tobben and Bjorn arrived, damp but in good spirits. They'd left the hut two hours after us but had to go back for another 24 hours when the storm returned to release its fury.

Our interest in Iceland during winter remains. Odd and Erik with another Norwegian friend returned and traversed the centre of the island from Myvatn to Geysir, a distance of about 400 kilometres, in March 1984 and our future plans extend to a traverse from Egilsstadir in the far eastern fjord area, to Reykjavik. When, we are not sure, but what is certain is that Landmannalaugar will be on the itinerary as a watering stop.

Nevada and California

Neither Hans-Arne Vikan nor I could believe the invitation was true. Both of us had been asked to be Technical Advisors for the production of a NATO film on Cold Weather Operations. We met for the first time in Leiden, Holland in September 1984, to discuss the filming sequences that were due to be shot during the forthcoming winter and by the end of the week we were living and dreaming those aspects of the film for which we would be technically responsible. Scripts had been adjusted from their original rather 'New World' style to take a more realistic line appropriate to the ways the British and Norwegians did things, and we had sorted out the requirements of each scene and the sort of location in which they would need to be shot. This enabled us to finalise the programme of location shooting to fill the winter as best we could. November and December were allocated to location reconnaissance in Norway—visits that took us from the Jotunheim mountains to the Lyngen peninsula at 70 °N. January was to include three weeks' shooting in the Sierra Nevada mountains of California, returning to Norway for the main filming in February and March. It looked like a 'Cooks Winter Tour' and certainly when Hans and I left Amsterdam at the end of that week, we blessed our good fortune at having been selected to do this job and with it have the opportunity of skiing in the American Sunshine State.

Hans Vikan is a 6ft 5-inch major in the Norwegian Infantry with many years' experience of soldiering in winter conditions. We flew to San Francisco via Washington where we spent a solitary New Year's Eve in a bachelor quarter on the edge of a sprawling Air Force base. It was not the way we should have wished to start the New Year although we were able to 'Skål' 1985 with a healthy tot of duty-free before jet lag overtook us. For the flight to San Francisco we were crammed into the centre of a packed Jumbo and saw nothing of the landscape as we passed from east to west of that vast country. We were better off, however, for the flight from San Francisco to Reno as we were both given window seats. It was

144

possible to see as far over the Sierras as Mount Whitney, at 4,400 metres, one of the highest peaks on the American mainland. We descended steeply into Reno to land in the gambling capital of the State of Nevada. Round every corner in the airport and lining the side of the long passageways to the main hall of the airport terminal were rows and rows of fruit machines each with someone cranking the arm.

I gathered up our skis and baggage while Hans and an American Marine Colonel went off to hire a car. They came back with an enormous Dodge whose boot easily swallowed Hans' 215-cm long skis. There were a few patches of snow lingering in the shadows of the airport building, evidence that even at this latitude, Reno did not escape the occasional snowstorm. At an altitide of 1,500 metres the air was bone dry, crisp and fresh.

We wiggled through the cluttered streets of Reno in the half light of dusk, the flashing neon lights of this gambling city making it difficult to distinguish the traffic lights. We were heading for Carson City on the 385 and the Californian border near Coleville. From there the road began to climb and weave up deep, forested valleys with snow banked up high on cither side. Frost was beginning to form on the inside of the car windows as we drove into Bridgeport at nine o'clock in the evening. It was −20 °C, the moon was almost full, casting a shimmering silvery glow on the rim of the Sierra Nevadas that filled the western horizon.

The American Colonel had booked us all into a motel on the outskirts of the small town. It was comfortable and warm and above the reception building there loomed an enormous satellite dish which gave us a choice of 24 programmes on the TV in each room. This was the America I had seen so often on celluloid! If you cared for it you could pay for a 25th channel which was continuous pornography, but you would need to have won the jackpot in Reno first. Even if we had cared for it our wallets did not extend that far.

Some 18 miles from Bridgeport there is a delightful valley called Pickle Meadow and it was here, in the early 1950s, that the US Marines built a hutted encampment to train their men in cold weather before drafting them to fight in the Korean War. A summer road, No 108 takes a line through the centre of the Meadow before it disappears into the forest beside Leavitt Meadow and zig-zags steeply up following the line of Leavitt Creek then Sardine Creek to Sonora Pass at 2,935 metres. The US Marine Corps Mountain Warfare Training Centre overlooks Pickle Meadow, and its utility buildings clutter around Silver Creek, one of the many rivers that drain the summits of Wells Peak (3,320 metres) and Lost Cannon Peak (3,338 metres). The West Walker River meanders across the level Meadow fed further upstream by creeks large and small, and boasting imaginative names like Wolf, Cloudburst, Poison and Cowcamp. When we drove up to the camp at nine o'clock the sun was already high enough to provide sufficient warmth to begin to melt the thick frost that had smitten the needles and branches of the fir trees during the night. A trillion sparkling crystals winked at us from the level ground by the West Walker River and we guessed, in the $-25\,°C$ of that dawn, that it would take some time before the sun caused those sparkles to lose their vigour down there in the valley.

By the time we returned to Bridgeport that evening, Hans had already obtained two 1:50,000 maps of the Leavitt Peak area. This was where most of the film would be shot. The peak (3,527 metres) was at least 20 kilometres from the camp and beneath its uniform summit and nestling in a corrie was Leavitt Lake at 2,913 metres. A tented camp had already been established quite near its frozen shore to house the platoon of Marines which would supply the actors and also to provide shelter for the film crew if the weather became bad. Our next twenty days in the Sierras was beginning to look very good indeed, and we spent a deal of time poring over the map searching out ski route possibilities. At the end of the first day, the Colonel announced that we would be flying by helicopter daily from Pickle Meadow to Leavitt Lake. I glanced over to Hans and our eyes met in silent acknowledgement that this was going to open the door to some golden skiing opportunities.

I unpacked most of my kit that night and in a drawer of the dressing table I found the remains of a brochure for Bodie State Historic Park. Its front page was dominated by an oval photograph of a church, typical of a Wild-West style of overlapping wood plank construction. I turned the page and, below a street map cluttered with numbered buildings, was an explanation:

> Bodie State Historic Park is best visited during the summer. At other times the weather is unpredictable, and off season visitors are cautioned to check at Bridgeport, Mono County Seat, for road and weather conditions before making the trip. The park is on Bodie Road 13 miles east of its junction with State Highway 395, 7 miles south of Bridgeport.

It ended there. The remaining pages of the brochure were missing and undoubtedly had been cast into the waste paper basket long ago. It didn't matter because that first paragraph was enough to whet the appetite and I trotted along to Hans' room to propose that we should ski to this old relic of the Wild West.

'*Ja*' he agreed, 'But not tomorrow!'

'No! No! Let's get used to the altitude first.'

'Thank God for that', he sighed.

It was at my insistence that Hans brought his skis with him so that we could do a few short tours together while we were in America. He knew that I was preparing for a long journey in the Yukon with Erik Boehlke and Tobben Eggen (Odd would have been coming along too if he had not been a member of the Norwegian Everest Expedition of 1985), and he was well aware of the ski training I was planning to do to get on top form for the trip. I was not sure, however, how much enthusiasm he would show in joining an English ski crank pursuing his ideals. He dispelled that doubt the next day when we were flown in a Huey helicopter to Leavitt Lake. In spite of the altitude, he was off like a bullet, over a low ridge and the start of the 20 kilometre descent to Pickle Meadow, leaving me to say a few pacifying words to the Colonel before I too launched off in hot pursuit. I was unable to catch him until the last 2 kilometres along the snowy road into the camp. It was a sensational introduction to Sierra skiing and all those posters advertising the game in the Sunshine State now made sense. The sun had been hot at midday, not quite so hot as we found it in Zanskar but warm enough to roll sleeves up yet, surprisingly, the altitude had preserved a crispness to the snow. Even Hans, who did not normally display his feelings about things, now enthused quite openly. We were both fairly well hooked.

Later on in the first week we used the same helicopter to ferry us to a shallow col 3,100 metres up on the flank of Mount Emma (3,208 metres) the most prominent peak in a group due south of Pickle Meadow. The helicopter crew thought we were mad and they said so as they throttled back to let us jump out into the snow. Skis and sticks followed the rucksacks and with a thumbs-up the crewman gave the pilot the nod to take off. We sat astride the untidy bundle of skis and rucksacks, cupping our heads under our arms as a great whirlwind of snow was whisked up by the rotor blades. Ice crystals and hard snow stung what flesh remained uncovered and before the maelstrom had subsided, the chopper had nose-dived over the precipice to the west.

Only the gentle pitter-patter of snow falling out of the whirlwind broke the silence that suddenly encompassed us. Then the scene about us for 360 degrees revealed itself. The views were phenomenal. To the north some 50 miles distant were the mountains that rim the crater of Lake Tahoe. Leavitt Peak did not look anything like its 3,578 metres from where we stood, and to the south we could just see Mount Whitney in the far distance, peeping above the peaks of Yosemite. In between the summits were wide valleys with thick forest in places and many interlocking open snowy alpine meadows. I thought that the Sierras could be put on the list of ski tours for the future and made a mental note to let Erik and Odd know of the potential.

Our plan that day was to ski over the watershed of Poison Creek, and drop 700 metres to the Little Walker River Valley before turning towards the west for the last 8 kilometres to Pickle Meadow. With a total distance of about 30 kilometres we had plenty of time to enjoy the descent and have a lunch break in the sunshine on the way. The snow was impeccable along the watershed and it provided that perfect balance of sufficient powder lying on top of hard crust to maintain good control at speed. We cruised along for 4 kilometres to a round summit at 2,957 metres where we had planned to begin the descent. Our 1:50,000 map indicated a forest-free spur and we were able to verify that that was so. However the map's contour interval was 40 metres, and the spur was very much steeper than we had thought from our earlier interpretation. We agreed to stick to the crest of it and with a push, slipped away down the slope. It was magical.

'*Utrolig!*' said Hans.

But it was not to last. When we reached 2,700 metres the snow deepened, our speed dramatically reduced and our only recourse was to push hard on our sticks through the sugar to get any movement at all. It was a struggle all the way down to 2,300 metres and even more so when we arrived at the relatively level area adjacent to the Little Walker River. We were sweating profusely in the hot sunshine and with what little assistance there had been from gravity now gone, it was a slow step-by-step plod up to the knees, changing the lead every few minutes until we reached the frozen surface of Kirman Lake above Pickle Meadow. I remember wondering whether I should remove the Sierras from that list. At least January was not the time to contemplate such a tour. Later February or early March would almost certainly see a consolidation of the snow and ease travel on skis a bit. As we gained the crest of the lip of land overlooking Pickle Meadow, I gave the possibility of a long ski tour in California no more thought. Gravity did little to help us down the final slopes to the West Walker River, where we tiptoed warily across a fragile-looking ice bridge and reached a ski track that took us direct into the camp. It had been a long day but the scenery had more than compensated for the toil and sweat. This certainly was big country; we had not seen another soul all day, and what a spectacular but idle way to reach to the start of a day's ski tour!

Our opportunity to go to Bodie, the ghost gold town, arose the following week, on a day which dawned grey and overcast. There had been a good snowfall two days before and although not much had settled at Bridgeport, we had been down the road towards the turn off, to Bodie where the snow had settled well. On the roadside was a sign which warned people who dared to venture up in a car that the road was blocked. Tyre marks in the snow revealed that someone had not been deterred by the

148

sign and whilst that gave us the urge to proceed as far as we could by car, we were secretly hoping that no other people were doing the same. We swung into the corner skidding a little in the Dodge which was most unsuitable for driving in snowy conditions, and drove slowly up the road, gaining altitude as we went. We did not have to drive far before a deep drift across the road brought us to a sliding halt. We U-turned the car with panache to park on the correct side of the road. We were quite content that we were unable to move any further along the road because this guaranteed a longer ski tour and we were even happier that there was no evidence of earlier traffic getting this far with other skiers.

The surrounding countryside reminded me of the high country around Dasht-e-Arzan in Iran with abundant thorn bushes and reddish rocks more used to the searing heat of the sun than the mantle of white that now smothered them. There were no lizards basking on the rocks nor any sign of the rattlesnakes that throng this high desert in summer. Of other wild life only the tracks in the snow were evidence that anything lived in this remote place: coyotes, foxes, and no doubt a cougar or two. We had passed the carcase of a mountain sheep further down the road, its ribs curving into the sky and bare of flesh. It had clearly been the scene of a ravenous free-for-all judging by the maze of tracks converging on the grotesque skeleton. Only tufts of wool littering the hard-packed snow had been rejected by whatever those starving creatures were.

We left the car in a flurry of snow, whisked into a tiny whirl by a stiff breeze. Fortunately, it was behind us at that moment, but nonetheless it had a chilly impact. This kept the snow crisp enough for Blue Extra wax which would suit the snow temperature range of $-7\,°C$ to $0\,°C$ that we could expect that morning. The wax worked well as we struck out following the line of the road, visible through the treeless scene as a clean white thread that weaved its way up and down until it disappeared from view hugging a south-facing slope. High desert grass protruded through the snow at the road's edges and beyond were stunted desert thorn bushes and an isolated cactus that looked totally incongruous. Behind each bush was a sculptured *sastrugi* that indicated in which direction the last storm had passed.

The unpredictability of the weather was running true to form. The motel proprietor had repeated the wireless forecast for the day before we left. The predicted grey overcast day was giving way to a thin line of blue which advanced upon us gradually as we skied along. With it came sunshine and views that extended up to 100 miles or more to the south; and with the sun came warmth, the shedding of bobble hats and jerseys, and the rolling up of sleeves.

We passed a sign which indicated the altitude to be 2,553 metres and, just beyond, the road swung away to the left to descend in a long sweep to cross a river bed and gain height on the other side. Hans was ahead and took a straight line down as a short cut—steeper and more exciting than the road. I followed in his tracks with increasing velocity and without the brake action of blazing a trail in new snow. I did not hear Hans' warning shout and suddenly found myself over the steep bank of the snowy river and facing a group of prickly cacti ahead. Alas my braking skill was insufficient, and I took the line of least resistance and sat down, fervently hoping that I had done it in time. I shuddered to a halt in a shower of snow with my skis abreast a large cactus with frighteningly long spikes all over its base. Hans' downhill skill had just got him past the unwelcome desert flora—but a miss is as good as a mile in those circumstances. For me, however, the indignity of a funk's way out of a crisis was voiced grumpily with a Norwegian expletive, and acknowledged by a chuckle from Hans!

We passed a sign on the other side of the valley which warned motor vehicles to engage low gear. Glancing back we could see that our return would be much steeper and I made a mental note to take the longer way and follow the road. We crossed a shoulder and began a gentle descent, double-poling idly for about 2 kilometres until we rounded a corner and went through an open gate in a barbed wire fence.

'Bodie Historic National Park' was emblazoned on a sign by the gate. We were getting close but there was nothing of this Wild-West ghost town to be seen. A line of power pylons cut a straight path across a slope a few kilometres ahead and we guessed we should follow them. As we step-turned round the next corner on the road a large corrugated-iron complex came into view. It was on the other side of a shallow valley about 3 kilometres away. Circular galvanised chimney stacks with anchoring hawsers projected out of the ruin of what must have been one of the separation plants. Great drifts of snow filled the doorways and covered the steep piles of quarried rubble on either side and below. Above were the scars of the workings, visible as small cliffs each rising out of a level platform. But where was the town? I did not know quite what to expect and my imagination was conjuring up a vision of Grytviken, a deserted whaling station in South Georgia that I had visited during a military operation in 1982.

We were soon rewarded. We topped a small rise and there below us was the town. To our left there was a fenced-off area with the tops of gravestones protruding from the snow. The road went straight down to a small group of wooden buildings, passing a sign to Lee Vising where there were numerous tracks of an oversnow vehicle. We followed these to the centre of what was left of the town. The tracks turned left and at the top of the street we could see an orange vehicle parked up outside a house. We skied up to it.

'Anybody at home?'

A curtain parted in a ground floor window and a few seconds later the door creaked open. A bearded fellow with a cowboy hat emerged.

'Whadda yer doin' here? Bodie's closed.'

'Good morning', I chirped, attempting to break the ice after that unwelcome introduction. 'What do you mean Bodie's closed?'

The man turned out to be the resident warden of Bodie and his main job was to prevent visitors from souvenir hunting. He told us a little about the town which in its heyday had a population of 10,000. That was in 1878 when there was a gold rush which brought with it all the trimmings of whores, bars, gamblers and every sort of entrepreneur. The town earned a reputation as second to none for wickedness, badmen and the worst climate out of doors.

'The people who come here are reputed to have said "Goodbye to God, I'm going to Bodie" when they left the security of Carson City or San Francisco', the warden said, warming to his topic. 'Killings occurred every day and the fire bell tolled the ages of the dead when they were buried.'

We were being given the visitor spiel but it was interesting and we did not interrupt.

'Robberies, stage coach hold-ups and street fights provided a little variety. And there was an awful lot of drinking in the town's 65 saloons.' He told us a lot more about this curious place and while we tucked into some sandwiches and flasks of coffee which we had brought with us, he said that we were the first visitors to come out on skis that winter. Only a handful of people came out in the winter and most were on snow scooters. One lot, he said, even came in by helicopter.

'Do you ski?' I asked.

'Nope, perhaps I should.'

'It's a cross-country skier's paradise here, you ought to get yourself a pair.'

'Yeah, I oughta', he said unconvincingly.

After our picnic lunch we said goodbye to the lonely warden and skied off down into what used to be the centre of the town. A sign said this was Green Street. We christied to a stop to look through the windows of Bodie Stores where goods of every variety of the period were still on the shelves; no doubt partly the reason for the full-time warden.

On the opposite side of the street was the morgue and in the gap between it and the next building which had a brick facade, an old four-wheeled wagon lay up to its axles in snow. The metal hoops that once supported the canvas cover were now bare and rusty. I shut my eyes and tried to imagine the frenzied activity that would have been going on in Bodie a hundred years before, and I wondered what the people of those times would have done throughout the winter. The clatter of a sheet of corrugated iron banging in a gust of wind broke the silence and I heard Hans bellowing to me from an old barn further up the street. He was looking at his watch.

The sun was high and warm as we returned to the car in a couple of hours under a cloudless sky. The Sierras were stark against the western sky and our view of them untarnished. Bodie had been an interesting destination for an unusual day's skiing across high desert. A near miss with a cactus and being overtaken by some tumbleweed blowing along in the wind had provided just the right sort of props to remind us that this was the true Wild West!

We were able to utilise the helicopters again the following week. One day we came close to accepting an offer to go up in a huge Sikorsky SH 53 but we were prevented from doing so by an unscheduled conference in the camp. As the helicopter was heading up towards the top of Wolf Creek it lost its tail rotor and the aircraft crashed into the snow, fortunately without injury to crew or passengers. Thereafter, our preference was to go up in the Hueys in which it was possible to see much more of what was going on in the driver's seat and also attain greater peace of mind!

There were two small ski tours left to do which simply begged for action. I wanted to ski up to Leavitt Lake from Pickle Meadow and use the effort as a training session. It was about 20 kilometres with a height gain of almost 1,000 metres. Hans declined the offer to go with me so he flew up instead. The route took me an hour and 31 minutes to complete, with the altitude, latterly, beginning to take its toll. It was a good hard session which was useful preparation for one of those 'short' tours in Nordmarka in Oslo scheduled for the following week with Erik and Odd. I was too whacked to ski down with Hans so, I grasped the chance to descend in a Huey!

The other tour which unfortunately we were unable to experience was to ascend to the Sonora Pass and return via Wells and Lost Cannon Peaks to Pickle Meadow. Time precluded that lengthy tour so we settled for a shorter day and cut west some 2 kilometres short of Sonora and contoured for several kilometres into the centre of Wolf Creek. There we chanced upon a US Marine Corps Company on a ski exercise. Their skis looked good but their boots and bindings were those outsized rubber things called Vapour Barriers. Their bindings reminded me of those step-in cups with leather straps that you often see Scandinavian children using. All in all they looked very cumbersome but the men seemed to be getting along quite well.

'Det er lit rart' said Hans.

'A little strange, yes, almost verging on the comical!' My comment fell unheard on snowy ground. Hans had slipped away while I was watching the Marines walking through the forest. A kick-turn and a push and I was after him on the long fast descent to the camp, the last part of which had been burnt free of snow by the sun. A sliding, slipping walk in sticky mud using our ski sticks for balance ended the day and our short stay in the Sierras. We returned to Reno the next day via Lake Tahoe. The lake's surface reflected the rim of mountains and around its shore, in 2-metre deep snow, were the apartments, huts and burger stalls of a wealthy society. Shops displaying downhill skis and signposts to the ski lifts were everywhere but of a cross-country skier there was no sign. Squaw Valley lay on the other side of the lake and I remembered that this was where Henry Hermansen, our Biathlon Team trainer all those years ago, had raced for Norway in the 1960 Olympics. We took the road to Reno from the northern end of the lake and stopped for coffee at Rose Mountain ski centre. The ski lifts were clanking away and there were a few people on the slopes. We sat out on the open-air patio in the warm sunshine and talked to an ageing Austrian who had emigrated to the States after the Second World War. His was a simple answer to our question of why people did not cross-country ski here.

'I suppose the Americans prefer the lazy way', he said.

He was probably right! California certainly offers the widest possible scope to enjoy some of the best ski touring available in the Northern Hemisphere. We had taken the opportunity to do some and had tucked away some interesting experiences.

That afternoon we descended into the fog of Reno to wait for our flight to San Francisco. To pass the time we visited one of the huge casinos with some of the lads from the Canadian film team who had been with us in Bridgeport. The sound recordist put a dime into a machine and cranked the handle. We watched idly as the wheels spun until suddenly a buzzer rang and lights began flashing. He'd hit the jackpot! The commotion brought a nylon-coated official over and he opened up the back, checked that there had been no fraudulent workings and, presumably satisfied, issued a note to the smiling disbelieving young man. Our sound recordist had won 1,000 dollars.

He bought champagne and we toasted farewell to California and Nevada.

* * *

153

Yukon: A Remote Experience

There's land where the mountains are nameless,
And the rivers all flow God knows where.
(Robert W. Service, *'The Spell Of the Yukon'*)

The Selwyn Mountains were named in 1901 by Joseph Keele, a noted northern explorer and geologist, after Dr Alfred Richard Cecil Selwyn, who was one of the most distinguished geologists of his time. The mountains parallel the Yukon and North-West Territories border from 62° to 65°N and run north-west from the Nahanni Range for about 800 kilometres to the Dempster Highway where they merge into the Ogilvies. Within the Selwyns are three major ranges, namely, the Logan, Hess and Wernecke Mountains. Straddling the territorial border for much of the same latitude are the Mackenzies, a range from whose snows flow the Nahanni, Keele and Red rivers. A closer look in *The Times Atlas* reveals an area the size of Norway and Sweden together, mountains that peak to just under 3,000 metres, and rivers that have played important roles throughout the history of the exploration of the remote Canadian North and whose names ring with the tales of legendary gold prospectors, adventurers, trappers and the Mounties. The atlas does not indicate that there are only 23,000 inhabitants of this vast territory, over half of whom live in the capital, Whitehorse. A cursory glance at the scale at the foot of the page clearly illustrates the remote and extensive character of these mountain ranges.

That atlas was spread out on a table in Asker near Oslo one evening in March 1984, and those present were Dr Peter Steele, Erik Boehlke, Odd Eliassen and myself. Peter had been in the Yukon for ten years and was no stranger to Nordic ski touring. He was describing the possibilities of a ski journey in the Yukon and answering the many questions that we raised. Having returned that same week from completing the Finlandia 75-kilometre ski race, Peter was departing the following day to try his

154

hand in the 86-kilometre Vasaloppet in Sweden. He and Odd were old chums and had met on the International Everest Expedition in 1971. Before he left he gave us two pieces of advice—to watch out for the grizzlies which comprised half the Yukon population, and to 'Think big!' And we did! Our fingers lurched along the red filament of the Alaska Highway on plate 101 of the *Times Atlas*. The further north that red line went, the more remote it seemed. That was just what we were after and the prospect of doing something up there in the far north became more magnetic. We noticed another thin red thread heading north out of Watson Lake, and after 100 kilometres it divided, in one direction going east-north-east to Tungsten. This we decided was going to be our start point. From there we could go over the Mackenzie and Selwyn mountain ranges to Dawson City. Erik's thumb went to the scale at the foot of the page and using this as a ruler, he leap-frogged across the Yukon and announced '1,500 kilometres!' Watching curiously as he journeyed in seconds across the Mackenzie Mountains, I wondered just how many obstacles there would be on the ground and how we would overcome the problems of logistics for such a trip.

The following week I attended a military exercise in North Norway as the senior umpire to the 1st Battalion, The Parachute Regiment. Although the soldiering was boring, it was enlivened by one of the other umpires, a character called Paul Ream, a Captain in the Royal Tank Regiment who, quite unsolicited, began to talk of a trip to Western Canada that he was organising in late April. No doubt he wondered why I was showing more interest than our short-lived acquaintance should have warranted, but a plan had formed in my mind.

'When are you going?' I asked.

'Mid-May', Paul replied.

'Where are you actually going?' I quizzed.

'Edmonton, then to the mountains and hopefully over to Vancouver.'

'Could you do me a favour?'

'Sure', he said amiably. And that was how I solved the major problem of getting six-weeks' food out to the Yukon! Paul agreed to take it out to Edmonton with his party and despatch the lot up to Peter at Whitehorse by Greyhound Bus.

On 17th April Erik wrote from Oslo and enclosed a map of the Yukon that Peter had sent to him. Peter had marked several route possibilities but of the two Erik had highlighted, I favoured the one from Tungsten to the MacMillan Pass, thence a long curving sweep through the Selwyn mountains to Dawson City in the Klondike. It looked good with reasonable access every 200–250 kilometres to place food dumps and I replied enthusiastically, reaffirming my commitment to the journey by telling him about our stroke of good luck with the food and that it was already on its way to Whitehorse.

Neither Erik nor I could believe that things had moved so fast. Our experience of bureaucracy in India rang warning bells that perhaps some vital piece of the planning process had been forgotten or ill conceived, but try as we might we could not detect a flaw in what had been arranged. Odd wasn't able to join us on this trip, but in late May, Erik recruited Tobben to the team. Also by then a friend in Ottawa had obtained two sets of 1:50,000 maps that covered the complete route. There were 61 sheets to each set, one of which was kept in Devon, the other sent to Erik. Erik wrote to say that he had to clear his whole flat of furniture to look at them and he was quite exhausted after having walked from Tungsten to Dawson through his living room! He confirmed that he was happy with the route I had highlighted but insisted that we must take a set of 1:250,000 maps to enable us to 'escape' if we encountered problems. The need for those sets was magnified by the reality that once we were nearing our first depot 260 kilometres out from Tungsten, it would be easier and quicker to seek help by skiing westwards. Our friend in Ottawa, Hector Gullan, drew another trump card and managed to get a set of those as well.

The food boxes sent up to Whitehorse by Paul had been there about a month when I applied to the Mount Everest Foundation for a grant to go towards our expenses. I was not summoned to the Royal Geographical Society in London to appear before the Screening Committee until October—well after my return from a six-day 12,000-mile round trip sprint to Whitehorse at the end of August. The 48 hours that I had spent in the capital city of Yukon had been remarkably productive so when I was asked to go through our plans and explain our objectives to the Committee, I was able to do so with much greater confidence and commitment than if that short visit had not been made. The Committee seemed no different to that which I had faced in 1980 before the Indian ski journey. The centre group dressed in smart London suits was flanked by four members of the younger generation of mountaineers whose faces were familiar but whose names were not known to me. There was one, however, who sat at the end of the table and asked me which skis and bindings we would be using.

'Rottefella, 3-pin Nordic norm on Åsnes no-wax skis,' I replied.

'But the 3-pin Nordic norm bindings are no good, they are known to break', he said.

I was astonished to hear such a statement and parried it quickly by asking where he had experienced such a calamity. He did not answer immediately.

'Oh, I heard that they were no good', he said after a pause.

156

'Well, we used them on a 600-kilometre journey through the Western Himalayas in 1981 and found them to be quite excellent, and we have used them on all our ski trips so far.'

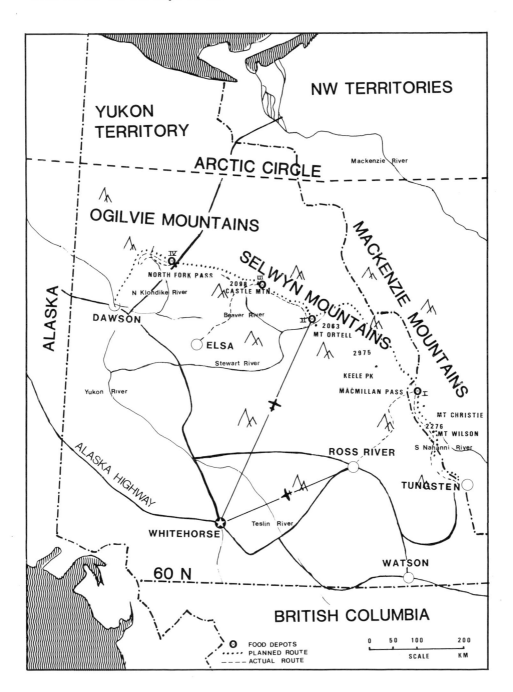

The Chairman intervened at that point. Perhaps he sensed that the exchange of words was about to become more heated, and he changed the subject, asking about our plans for food. I explained about the depots and pointed them out on the map.

'Depot 1 is on the MacMillan Pass in a broken-down hut 250 kilometres from our start point. The box is already out. Each depot contains 8 days' food, spare socks, some nylon rope and 3 litres of meths. Depot 2 at Ortell Lake is with a trapper 280 kilometres from the MacMillan Pass. The box will be sent out with the trapper when he goes out early in the winter. Depot 3 at Elliott Lake is with a trapper and only 200 kilometres from Depot 2. It will be put out in the same way. Depot 4 is at the North Fork Pass on the Dempster Highway, 250 kilometres from Depot 3. Dr Peter Steele will arrange for the box to go out to the snow-plough base near the pass where we can collect it. The highway is kept open in winter. That's it!'

'What about animals?' asked someone further down the table. I told them that we hoped to see bears, wolves and caribou but that we'd decided against taking a gun as it was an unecessary burden.

'Bears are asleep—so we are told!' I said and went on to tell them how I had been reassured by the people in Whitehorse where not one person said we need worry about bears, though they had qualified this by saying there was just an outside chance we might either encounter a sick bear which was not hibernating or stumble on one in its den in which case we would have a problem.

I remember Peter Steele's solution to the bear problem which he passed on from one of his patients, a hunter called Joe Martin. 'I was out hunting beaver,' Joe had told him, 'when a grizzly bear ran after me. So I shoot him. I kill that one, but I don't want to shoot him, y'know. So next time I see a bear I say "Hey Mr Bear, you go that way and I go this way," he do it and he go away. He don't bother me. I don't want to kill no animal for nothing, only if I need meat. Always talk nice to a bear.' I didn't think the Committee would be too impressed by this though and didn't mention it to them.

The MEF forwarded a cheque for £200 and with it their endorsement of our adventure. We never knew who it was that claimed the 75-mm Nordic norm bindings were hopeless but we did believe that if he or someone else had had an unfortunate experience it must have been unique. Later on we mentioned this to the Rottefella Company in Oslo and they declared that to the best of their knowledge no complaints or evidence of broken bindings had ever been documented.

In February Peter wrote to tell us that our Ortell box was dropped into the Boivins hut by a helicopter on the 11th of that month and also that the Elliott Lake depot had gone in with a trapper, Claire Briand, to a hut at

Braine Creek. He told us not to worry about Depot 4 as we could make the arrangements for that to go out when we arrived in March. As a postscript to his letter, Peter suggested he join us for the last leg, North Fork to Dawson. All this was excellent news and apart from the long road journey from Whitehorse to Tungsten, a distance of 800 kilometres, there was little else to organise.

Hundreds of kilometres of weekend training on the ski tracks around Vågåmo and Heidal, Hedmark and Oslo got us into pretty good shape throughout February, and on one occasion I experienced the treat of training with Odd and his two dogs called Thor and Odin. After securing their chest harnesses and rigging the long elastic bungees to hook onto a belt around our waists, we were off at 20 kilometres an hour. It seemed effortless until the first long uphill when the reality of there being much more to it made its impression on arms and legs. It was harder work to keep up with the dog than if he were not attached to one's waist at all. Downhill stretches required lightning reactions to avoid being tripped by the slack bungee as one's skiing speed increased to overtake the beast at full gallop. Yelps were ample evidence that Thor didn't like being left behind. It was never more than a 50-metre lead and all too soon the situation reversed when it was only a patient command that slowed him to a halt with time enough to grasp the flailing bungee, hook on, and push off again. It was great fun and Thor and Odin enjoyed it with equal enthusiasm. Little did we know that there would be many occasions when we wished we had the company of Thor and Odin to pull us around the Yukon!

Two weeks before we left, Peter raised the question of whether we should consider taking snow shoes with us. Friends of his who were familiar with snow conditions in the Selwyns had told him that the 'depth hoar' that was a feature of the stable cold of the Yukon interior was quite different to the 'layering' of snow in Northern Europe that was caused by the fluctuations in temperatures imposed by the Gulf Stream. It would, they claimed, be extremely laborious and slow to ski through such deep snow, especially over the distances between our food depots. But hadn't we experienced deep snow elsewhere in the world? Surely it couldn't be too different to the deep snow we had ploughed through in Zanskar, or for that matter in Norway? Anyway, could we afford to carry the extra weight? After much debate we decided that snow shoes were unnecessary, particularly as most of our route was to be above the tree line, but in deciding this we knew we were taking a risk in going against local advice.

At the end of February Erik collected our new Åsnes MT54 no-wax skis. Our boots had been donated by Alfa, an established Norwegian ski boot manufacturer. There was no argument over the skis because of our

159

long experience with them in Iceland and we knew that during the six weeks of the tour we would encounter huge variations in snow conditions. Gone were the worries and difficulties of applying wax, scraping it off, heating Klister into a pliable paste and gone was the daily threat of clogging skis or tiresome backslip.

Tobben and Erik arrived at Heathrow on the evening of 5 March, and we took them back to David and Anne Barraclough's house in Egham which was soon filled with skis, sticks and assortments of clothing; just as it was before the India journey. A Kransekaker, a rich marzipan-flavoured cake resembling a helter-skelter in its coil-like shape, graced the centre of the dinner table with small Norwegian and Union Jack flags dotted about it. Ice cold aquavit helped to wash it down and helped to anaesthetise a sore throat that had been with me for three days and which was about to erupt. I was not in the best of health to start the three-day journey to Whitehorse, two days of which were spent in joint-stiffening contortions in the uncomfortable Greyhound bus. By the time we arrived there, however, Erik had contracted the same irritating bug, leaving Tobben totally undisturbed to reach the end of a gruesome book on true grizzly-bear stories. Of the three of us Tobben had been the one most strongly in favour of taking a rifle, and the book only strengthened his belief—but it was too late now.

At Whitehorse, the Steeles were wonderfully patient and kind hosts and we were very untidy guests; but Peter knew the form only too well and gave us space in his basement to strew our gear. A sketch map of Depot 1 on the MacMillan Pass was drawn for us by Gavin Johnstone who had placed it out in September. Steve Goodlet, the helicopter pilot who dropped Depot 2 off at Ortell described exactly where it was. He knew this huge wilderness pretty well from the air and was able to mark the exact sites of isolated trapper huts on our 1:250,000 maps should we need to get to some sort of fixed shelter in an emergency. A latitude and longitude fix on the Braine Creek Depot was given to us by Claire Briand. Major Dick Fawcett, the boss of the Canadian Forces Detachment in Whitehorse, agreed to drive us in one of his pick-ups to Tungsten if I sang for our supper and agreed to give a talk to an audience of cadets in Watson Lake about South Georgia and the Falklands War. The debate about snow shoes continued as we met and talked to people who had skied near Watson Lake and into the Ragged Range west of Tungsten. To our delight Peter confirmed he would join us on the North Fork Pass and we arranged our rendezvous through Ray Magnusson, who gave permission for us to use the Dempster Highway Camp radio telephone to tell him of our arrival there. In between the rushing around we skied with Peter on the World Cup courses near the town (yes, we did take our racing skis with us).

160

Our farewell to Peter and Sarah was followed by a reminder of the potentially hazardous nature of our little venture when we collected an Emergency Locator Beacon from Trans North Air down at the airport. This satellite actuating beacon was to sit in the bottom of Tobben's rucksack providing psychological comfort for each of us just in case we should become another chapter to be added to Tobben's grizzly book!

It is 486 kilometres from Whitehorse to Watson Lake and mostly through rolling forests, thick with lodge pole pines, and another 300 or so to the small mining community of Cantun, (the local Canadian name for Tungsten). It was a pristine cold day and the last part of the drive was through increasingly spectacular mountains rising to 2,300 metres. We tracked down a contact in Cantun, a pilot, whose knowledge of the area between there and the MacMillan Pass was second to none and he described an alternative route to the upper reaches of the South Nahanni River over Howard's Pass where there was a deserted mining camp. Before leaving civilisation we clocked out with the small Mountie detachment where Corporal O'Brien wished us good luck and as we clambered into the pick-up he shouted over to us 'Don't forget there's a stocked kitchen, gas and all, up in Howard's Pass.' With that and a wave, we drove 8 kilometres back up the road, sorted ourselves out, thanked Captain Dennis Frenette for the drive and after sidestepping up the steep snow back on the roadside, slipped away into the flat river valley and the wilderness. At last we were on our way and in the two hours before the setting sun induced some urgency to find a camp site, we covered 13 kilometres.

We found a hut beside a lake. It was pretty spartan but it had a stove and as we searched for wood in the patchy surrounding forest, a small aircraft buzzed us. It must have been Dwight Herbison, the Cantun pilot, out to see how we were getting on. We waved, he dipped his wings, and when he'd disappeared to the south silence returned to crown this great wilderness. My diary reminds me of those first few days.

14th March, −6 °C: *Dawn. A good day's distance, 28km, and it was a weary trio that slipped into sleeping bags as the mercury dropped to −18 °C.*

15th March, −19 °C: *Deep snow and hard going. We change the lead every 10 minutes. The front man dumps his rucksack to forge the trail up to the knees and ski sticks half submerged, to return and collect his rucksack, for the weary trudge back to join the others. 19km in this fashion was the gain for the day, but we know we have each skied half as much again.*

16th March, −9 °C: *Same procedure as yesterday. We cheerfully tell each other that things couldn't get much worse. Continuous heavy snowfall for second day running; only 17.5km but we are gradually climbing. There is*

161

plenty of collectable dead wood to make a fire upon which to brew tea and dry away some dampness.

17th March $-6\,°C$: *There must be a huge area of low pressure over us—surely a rare phenomenon so far inland. Almost 50cm of new snow has fallen in three days. We gained height all day, up to 1,700m and well above the tree line where the snow was marginally better. Howard's Pass loomed out of the murk of whiteout and the dilapidated remains of a hut became a cold retreat for the night. No sign of the stocked kitchen, claimed to be here by the Mountie Corporal. A miserly 19km today.*

18th March, $-9\,°C$: *We are nearing the halfway point to Mac Pass. A frightful night with painful eyes makes me suspect mild snow blindness despite use of glasses. A blizzard was blowing and the hut kept us more sheltered than a tent although a tent is so much warmer. Erik and Tobben went hunting for the kitchen, to no avail!*

The bad conditions that plagued us for the first 100 kilometres dominated the daily entries in my diary. The going certainly had been heavy but the gradual reduction of weight on our backs compensated a little for the effort of pushing skis and sticks through such deep new snow. We were disappointed by the hut at Howard's Pass which the Mountie has said was well stocked. The hut itself was in poor repair and part of the corrugated iron roof was banging in the wind. Inside, the washbasins, pipes and water heaters were barely discernible in the drift snow that filled the building. Another hut just visible in a huge drift was alas too small to be a kitchen.

The blizzard had eased by midday so it was time to go on and forget about well-stocked kitchens. While packing up my sleeping bag and other bits and pieces in the hut something in the corner buried under dust and rubbish caught my eye. A brush with a ski boot revealed an Indian necklace of turquoise, bone and ebony beads. 'Finders keepers', I said proudly holding my prize aloft. 'Extra weight in the sack!'

'*Ja. Hva er det?*' Erik quizzed.

'A present for Molly, all the way from Howard's Pass.'

We departed on a compass bearing in a white whirlwind, conscious that ahead lay a steep descent into the head of Don Creek valley, one of the tributaries of Pelly River. Our bearing took us towards the eastern side where the descent would be gradual and not so avalanche-prone. We had hardly been going 15 minutes when Erik, who was leading, stopped suddenly and turned and shouted something through his hooded anorak and balaclava. Tobben and I shuffled up alongside him to hear what he was saying.

162

'There's the kitchen!' Erik yelled into the wind and snow, pointing ahead with his ski stick.

A hundred metres ahead were a number of portacabins grouped in a hollow square. They were barely visible save the small patches of bright yellow and green walls on two of them. Snow was banked high up to their roof tops and colossal drifts had been created between them as the wind eddied furiously. We skied down to them and circled inquisitively until we came to one with a notice 'Kitchen Staff Only' above the door. Using the snow shovel we dug the hard drift snow away from the door, turned the handle and entered.

Inside was quite a mess. On the wall opposite the door was a poster, in bright red, depicting a marauding grizzly: 'Know your bears' it warned us. A large 1981 calendar hung beside it, and 18th October had been ringed by a blue pen. Soft porn magazines littered the floor and the dining room was a shambles. The larder was well stocked but mainly with dry commodities—flour, oats and others—but we did find two small jars of cranberry jam, two three-litre cans of orange juice and a pot of honey—all frozen solid.

While Erik and I dug away at the snowdrift obliterating the door of one of the accommodation cabins, Tobben rooted about in the kitchen to emerge with an axe and some odd bits of timber. He dug a hole in the snow and using the blocks as a windbreak made a fire and melted the frozen orange juice. Once inside the cabin we realised that we would be foolish not to stay there the night so we chose the smallest room, shifted two mattresses in and started cooking our supper. We ate in the warm luxury of 0 °C and had cranberry jam with our dehydrated mutton! We had done nothing to deserve such a feast as it was only 1 kilometre from that derelict hut where we had spent the previous night, but what a feast it was and we slept soundly upon it as well!

When we had left Tungsten, we had set off with 12 days' food. Two days' rations were reserved to supplement the 8 days' worth in the depot on the MacMillan Pass, which was insufficient for the 250-kilometre leg to Ortell. We reappraised our stocks at Howard's Pass and found there was no cause for concern over the amount of food consumed for the ridiculous distance we had covered that day. For the 150 kilometres ahead to Depot 2, we had six days' food. It would be tight but just adequate if the weather behaved itself. We were sure, too, that the snow conditions could only get better after those first four days of exhausting trail breaking.

And they did. The sun came out as well and with its warming glow came rejuvenation and energy. It was a glorious morning when we left Howard's Pass and it was really the first day we had seen anything of a view. Whoever selected the site for the mining camp deserved an Oscar for stage management. It was a sensational spot with views northwards towards the Pelly River and the Itshi Mountains. We left the camp as we found it, leaving our few bits of rubbish in a dustbin in the kitchen, and made a short steep descent in cold crisp air to the head of Don Creek. The snow was so deep descending that we could take the steepest line without fear of excessive speed. Tobben, ever eager to see a bear, stopped to look through his small binoculars at a set of deep tracks on the other side of the valley and about a kilometre away. Whatever it was had come and gone during the night. That evening Tobben absorbed himself in setting snares around the camp site to catch some ptarmigan for the pot.

Our camp routine seemed pretty well established by now and camp tasks had evolved happily. Erik took on the job of erecting the tent and while this was happening Tobben and I would forage for dead wood. Once there was sufficient fuel to start a fire I would begin the cooking while Tobben gathered in more to feed the flames. By the time snow had been melted, soup and the main ingredient of supper rehydrated and cooked, Erik had the tent up with all the kit for the night inside. More often than not, hot soup was consumed outside but without exception we went into the tent to have our main course in the warmth provided by the Trangia cooker.

Before the final retreat into the tent our 3 thermos flasks and 3 plastic water bottles were filled with boiling water. The water bottles went straight into sleeping bags to warm up cold feet and the flasks remained near the tent flap ready for breakfast. The sole reason to leave the tent thereafter would be as a result of individual forgetfulness. The disturbance caused to all, not least the muffled cursing from beneath tightly drawn sleeping bags, ensured that a nighttime excursion only happened once!

We crossed the border from Yukon into the North-West Territories and entered the South Nahanni River valley the next afternoon after traversing dangerously steep loose snow for 2 kilometres above a steep gorge. We were enjoying the second day of good sunny weather and Erik's altimeter indicated that a large ridge of high pressure was above us for a few days. But with the good weather came the cold which looked as though it would persist for several days. The sharp darkness of each night provided the stage for that spectacle of the north:

> "And the Northern Lights in the crystal nights, came forth with a mystic gleam
> They danced and they danced the devil dance over the naked snow;
> And soft they rolled like a tide upshoaled with a ceaseless ebb and flow
> They rippled green with a wondrous sheen they fluttered out like a fan
> They spread with a blaze of rose pink rays never yet seen of man
> They writhed like a brood of angry snakes, hissing and sulphur pale;

164

Then swift they changed to a dragon vast, lashing a cloven tail
It seemed to us, as we gazed aloft with an everlasting stare
The sky was a pit of bale and dread and a monster revelled there."
(Robert W. Service, *'The Ballad of the Northern Lights'*)

It was too cold to stand outside the shelter of the tent to watch them any longer than it takes to read those few lines. Yet the magic of the displays seemed to be more startling and mysterious than those I have watched for hours during endless nights of many a uniformed exercise in Norway.

The extreme cold in the South Nahanni sharpened up our routines considerably. Like exertion at high altitude, everything done in that cold was a slow deliberate process. The unseen enemy pierced finger tips, nose and ears like red hot needles; it solidified damp boots; it penetrated from beneath the centimetre-thick sleeping mat and it coated everything in a thick hoar frost. The search in the dark of each morning's dawn for the cooker and the fumbling for the zip to the inner flap sent ripples through the fabric of the tent and centimetre-long crystals would deluge down. We tried to remove what frost there was on the inside but what was left behind melted with the warmth of simmering breakfast porridge and dripped, infuriatingly, wherever it cared. The morning ritual torture of putting ski boots inside bags and under jerseys drew deep breaths but was worth it when the time came to put them on! And God bless Tobben; he always had that extra pile of wood beside the remains of the fire outside. It would soon be ablaze, kindling our enthusiasm to get going and reducing our rubbish to harmless unspoiling ash.

We passed under the massive east face of Mount Wilson. What a plum it would be for someone to climb the 1,200-metre face of this spectacular 2,042-metre summit. We did 20-minute spells at trail breaking and made good speed towards Mount Christie and its pass beyond. Camping that night under the bulk of Mount Christie, and in the comparative warmth and safety of the tent, Tobben gleefully related the origin of its name. It was here, he said, that James Christie, while prospecting in 1909, was attacked by a grizzly bear which fractured his skull and jaw, broke one of his arms and mauled one of his legs. His companion managed to get him to camp some 15 kilometres away and patch him up with the help of some whisky before finding some local Indians to help get him to Lansing on the Stewart River, not far downstream from our Depot 2 at Ortell. After hearing that tale, the three of us agreed that winter travel, in spite of the cold, was far safer. Let sleeping bears lie!

A huge avalanche had crashed unseen and unheard down the west face of Mount Christie and we had to negotiate large frozen slabs of packed debris—a fine test of balance and patience—in order to get out of the menacing area and its bitter wind. Once past that, it was reasonable but cold skiing for 50 kilometres in a day and a half to the Tsichu River, 25 kilometres from the MacMillan Pass. There were patches of buckbrush, the characteristic scrub that usually surrounds bog and marsh in low lying areas, and we experienced tiresome deep crustless snow when we crossed these. Whilst we were floundering through one, a snowy owl circled low above us before silently disappearing to the east. Apart from ptarmigan, it was the only other living thing we had seen so far and as it floated effortlessly away I remember thinking how pleasant it would be to be able to hoist oneself out of the buckbrush to do the same. There were tracks of fox and wolf everywhere on the last stretch before Tsichu, seemingly heading north and, we assumed, to the winter grounds of the caribou in the top of the Selwyn Valley.

It was somewhere between Mount Christie and our depot at Tsichu river that Tobben began to notice something going wrong with his left ski boot. He had made a passing comment about it one lunch break but had said no more about it. My concern was directed towards the Depot and as we slipped nicely down a long gentle hill towards a group of derelict huts beside the river, my thoughts were quite irrational. I began to worry that the box of food might not be there. Why at that particular point, after 240 kilometres and nine days, and not before, I did not know. But for some reason I felt it necessary to search for the box and what is more, search for it on my own. So while Erik and Tobben began stretching the tent and their sleeping bags out to air in the sun, I slipped away on my skis to the other derelict hut about 200 metres away.

The first derelict hut had an open space where once had been a window. I unclipped my skis and levered myself up to look inside. The box was not there. I skied over to the next, kicked my skis off, and with a sweep of the foot removed some snow banked up against a thick plywood door, and prised it open. Relief! There was the blue box sitting in splendid isolation in the middle of the floor. I yelled over to the others and Erik skied over to help me carry it back to the hut.

Tobben was sitting on his sleeping mat removing one of his boots. He held the other aloft when we approached.

'Jeg har problemer' he said waggling his boot in the air.

'What sort of problem?' I asked.

Before I had taken my skis off, Erik had darted over and was studying the boot while Tobben continued to remove the other. Alarm spread over Erik's face, then Tobben's and finally mine as we watched Erik bend the sole to reveal a split behind the 3-pin holes for the Nordic norm bindings which had extended either side completely through the welt and into the leather upper. He bent the sole over even further and through the gap in the split, we could see the insole. Tobben's other boot was beginning to

166

split but was not so impaired. A hasty inspection of my own revealed a similar, emergent problem yet Erik's seemed to be sound. A well-known Norwegian boot breaking up after a mere 242 kilometres surely was impossible? Admittedly it had been extremely cold for four days ($-38\,°C$, $-40\,°C$, $-35\,°C$ and $-30\,°C$) and our boots had been frozen in the morning but they get similar temperatures in Scandinavia where the same boots enjoy widespread use. We could only surmise that we had uncovered a major design fault in the manufacture of the boot.

'Let's stay here the night!' Erik suggested, breaking into our thoughts. Through the frosty window of the large hut we could see a stove, a couple of chairs and a mattress. 'Let's discuss the issue in there tonight.'

Tobben armed himself with the shovel and began to dig through the enormous snow drift that jammed up against the door. Erik and I donned skis and pushed down to the frozen Tsichu river 400 metres away where we could see a number of dead scrubby trees. Within an hour we had collected enough wood for about six hours' burning and Tobben had dug his way through to the door and had already shifted the rucksacks inside. Soon a curl of smoke emerged from the rusty tin stack, the hut began to warm up and we started to discuss the situation which now faced us.

The dilemma was quite straightforward. The factors influencing our discussions, and ultimately our decisions, were largely focused on whether or not we should risk going further into the wilderness with one pair of boots already broken and another pair beginning to break. We were 250 kilometres from Tungsten and our next leg would take us another 100 kilometres into the back of beyond and further away from help if we needed it. We believed that the nearest human being to us was a trapper, Bill Carson, at Jeff's Corner on the Canol Trail. Steve Goodlet had marked his hut on our 1:250,000 map. That spot was some 80–90 kilometres away. Beyond his hut and somewhere down the Canol Trail was the settlement of Ross River, but exactly how many kilometres away we were not sure because our large scale 'escape' map cover didn't go that far west. Erik's altimeter still registered a high pressure zone upon us and the daunting temperatures we were experiencing were a sign that it was going to remain stationary for a few more days. Such cold with broken boots was a far from attractive combination. While we chatted away over our evening meal, Tobben manufactured jury-rig bindings for his left boot using some 5-mm nylon rope from the food box. This was soon completed to replace the spring clip which no longer functioned to hold the boot to the ski.

The three of us knew what the sensible solution had to be but we were reluctant to agree to it without persuading ourselves that we were doing the right thing, especially after so much had gone into the venture. So we

167

tossed all the options into the arena, trying to avoid the main issue. Perhaps the straw that broke the camel's back was the certain embarrassment we would face if we had to use the satellite beacon and call for help. The bill that would follow any rescue would be an equal embarrassment, and so we accepted our fate and disappointedly acknowledged that we must ski out to Jeff's Corner and seek the help of the trapper who we were pretty sure would have a snow scooter or a span of dogs. If the trapper was not at home then we would push on to Ross River and although we had no idea how far it was, with 10 days' food we reckoned we were good for 300–350 kilometres. My diary reveals further anxiety on the day we left Depot 1.

25th March, −25 °C: *Very cold again. Our fingers are crossed that the trapper is at home but we must plan on the worst. On the Mac Pass, where we arrived at lunchtime after 25 kilometres of fair going, we saw a sign sticking out of the snow. The figures 464 were printed on the top. 2km further on and every 2 km thereafter was another—462 and so on. We are worried that we will not have sufficient food for this distance to Ross—and we assume the signs imply it is Ross. Damn this suspense! Our only hope is for good conditions and an average of 50km a day. Tobben's rig is working well but for how long?—so Erik and I share the trail breaking.*

Erik, Tobben and I approaching the steam packet at Dawson city.

26th March, −15 °C: *Slightly warmer. No trapper at Jeff's Corner, his hut locked and forlorn, but evidence of snow-scooter tracks indicate his departure 6–8 weeks before. Damn, damn, damnn! It is to Ross River we must ski. Just around the corner on the Canol Trail we see a sign. Ross River*

200. Thank God—what a relief and we discuss what we are going to do when we get there. We agreed that we charter a plane from Ross, if we can, fly to Whitehorse, buy three pairs of new boots, charter the same plane to fly us to Ortell, and continue our route from there. A wolverine came within 5 metres to investigate our rude intrusion in his territory. It was a unique close-up of an animal that is rarely seen.

Tobben's jury-rig held all the way to Ross River where we arrived on 1st April. We were quite relieved to have covered the 260 kilometres from Depot 1 without more serious deterioration of our boots, but scrutiny of my own pair revealed that now they had become as damaged as Tobben's. Both he and I had to tolerate very cold feet because of the split and the gap which opened up at each stride of the ski. In spite of our disappointment at having to turn for Ross River we believed our decision to abandon Leg 2 was the correct one. We called Peter on the radio telephone from a small inn where we had a scrummy breakfast. 'It must be April Fool', he insisted. Joe Muff of Alcan Air sent one of his pilots over from Whitehorse and the noise of the tiny Cessna 206 circling to prepare to land at the small strip had us skiing and skating as fast as we could along the ice-covered tracks; Joe had warned of bad weather and insisted we were ready to go at a moment's notice so we skied like racers across the apron right up to the wheels of the aircraft.

Peter had advised a sports shop in Whitehorse that we were after some boots and Sarah met us when we landed. On the drive up to their house she asked us to open all the windows of the car. We, of course, were unaware of our 17-day-old aroma, but it must have been overpowering to warrant a −10 °C wind swirling around the inside! We bought three pairs of Czechoslovakian boots that evening and over the next two days prepared ourselves for the flight to Ortell. We passed some of the time sharpening Erik's legal sabres for the confrontation between him and the Alfa Company on his return to Oslo. The least we thought they could do was to pay for the charter flight out of Ross and into Ortell. Tobben ceremoniously buried his jury bindings which had done so well to sustain the effort of the escape to Ross—a fine example of the ingenuity of an Oxford-qualified architect!

Joe Muff called us the next day and asked whether we could wait two days for our flight to Ortell. If we were able to we could jump on a plane that was going to overfly Ortell on its way up to the Wind River to look for a trapper whom the Mounties wanted to interview. It would be cheaper for us and it was a kind gesture but one we declined. We had itchy feet, were very conscious of overstaying our welcome with the Steeles, and were worried about rivers and lakes breaking up at the end of April if we did not get started. Early on the morning of 5th April we loaded up and took off for the 450-kilometre flight to Ortell. We flew for 1 hour 45 minutes over wilderness and mountains with the weather improving the further north we went.

The pilot confirmed that he did not care much for the short flat strip of ice on the Stewart River upon which he had to land. The Boivin's hut was up in the trees above the river with a patch of open water reflecting the sunshine under the steep bank. We circled three times, completing touch landings in the snow on the first two. On the third I heard the pilot sigh into his microphone and say to himself 'here goes' with a resignation that did not exactly bristle with confidence. We turned tightly and dipped quickly until I saw the skid beneath the front door touch the surface. Suddenly, and most alarmingly, the aircraft ploughed into thigh-deep snow, visibility disappeared as snow cascaded through the propeller and obliterated our views. For what seemed a lifetime we were in an opaque and noisy cocoon and I remember wondering if being in an avalanche was similar. I looked at the pilot, then at Erik and Tobben sitting in the back seat, and back to the pilot who uttered another sigh and said 'Have you got room for another one in the hut?'

We had arrived in style at Depot 3! However the pilot was not to be a guest for the night. Somehow he bucked his craft back and forth and extracted it from its snowy blanket and after three trial runs, finally took off, almost clipping some pine trees before disappearing to the north west. We were alone again, back in the familiar silence of the wilderness and overlooked only by the beauty of Mount Ortell.

The next few days were cold and we struggled with frequent patches of deep snow. Perhaps this was the depth hoar about which people had warned us earlier in Whitehorse. Apart from the first two days out of the Boivin's hut at Ortell when we made 27 kilometres and 21 kilometres respectively, our daily distances were disappointing; 15, 15, 17 and 19 kilometres, and our passage past the Nadaleen range and into the East Reckla river valley seemed agonisingly slow. It was not until we reached the overgrown remains of the Proctor trail after 7 days' skiing and 140 kilometres, that we came across a snow scooter track. The week had been exhausting, draining our enthusiasm, and if the scenery had not been as good as it was, the majority of Leg 3 would have been purgatory. The scooter track was quite recent and we guessed that it was made by Claire Briand or her husband taking our box of food in from Elsa, a mining community some 100 kilometres to the south. A good hard track to ski upon renewed our vigour after a week's wanting and we relished the diagonal gait, and sometimes even the occasional skate, to cover 40 kilometres to their hut on Braine Creek where our box was safely stored.

After fixing the doors and windows of the hut to their frames (these are usually left off their hinges so that bears can wander in freely without breaking them down—food, loose furniture etc is stored or locked in a loft suspended from the roof and well out of reach of the tallest bear), we lit the wood stove and discussed the next leg to North Fork Pass, 250 kilometres away. To say we were not worried about the snow conditions which we believed would prevail until we got well above the tree line would be to belittle our concern whether or not we had sufficient food for the distance to North Fork. It was the familiar equation as old as time itself. The effort of skiing through the East Rakla river valley and across Kathleen Lake had certainly dulled my enthusiasm. Through my knowledge of Norwegian, I could tell that Tobben had begun to discuss with Erik the possibility of skiing 150 kilometres to Elsa and foregoing the long leg to North Fork. I could tell Erik was keen to go on as planned although even he acknowledged that the stretch we had just skied had been wearisome. Our discussions went on well into the night reasoning the pros and cons until eventually we agreed that we would forsake the next leg, ski to Elsa, reach Dawson City somehow so as to rendezvous with Peter Steele, and then ski from North Fork through the Tombstone mountains.

That is exactly what we did. It is never easy to accept defeat, least of all when strength and health had no influence on our decision. We shall never know whether the snow was as deep as we had found it in the Rakla valley and while we missed seeing a part of the Yukon which is enshrined in history (the Mad Trapper of Rat River and the story of the Lost Patrol are synonymous with this part of the Territory) we enjoyed some very fine skiing on the way to Elsa—small compensation perhaps. Anyway, we would never have met Keith and Sonya Hepner if we had pursued our original track.

We met this delightful young couple in unusual circumstances. Two days out from the Wagners' hut and still some 80-90 kilometres short of Elsa, we stopped for lunch on the trail, and in our usual fashion, gathered in some dead wood which was soon ablaze, to melt snow for a good brew of tea. The pot was just about to come to the boil when, quite unheralded, two snow scooters came whizzing round the corner and were forced to brake rapidly if they were not to run one of us down or end up in the fire. This arrival caught us totally by surprise, and as silence settled on the wilderness once again, the tea boiled. The timing could not have been better. I filled two thermos cups and walked over to our two bemused visitors.

'Would you like a cup of tea—milk and sugar?'

'You have to be English,' Keith said looking at me. 'Only a Brit would do that.'

We all laughed, brewed more tea and exchanged stories. They were on their way to collect tools and stoves from their trap before the ice began to break up, and bar the extended use of snow scooters. Their main home was beyond the end of Lake McQuesten some 30 kilometres away and it was to that we were invited for the night. They left saying that they would see us on the track on their return to McQuesten later in the evening.

We were almost there when we heard the motorised patter of the returning scooters. We had achieved the best distance in a single day so far (43 kilometres) and in perfect conditions of warm sun. The hard scooter track had inspired us to use some more technique and Tobben had raced ahead with a surge of speed as though he were starting in the competition. A shadow of his former self (Tobben had lost much weight since we had set out from Tungsten), that day he evidently enjoyed a surplus of strength. Erik and I advanced more sedately 2–3 kilometres behind him most of the day but we were all more than happy to be helped over the final 5 kilometres of the frozen surface of Lake McQuesten—two of us on the back of Sonya's scooter and the other riding piggy back on top of the rucksacks piled high on a sledge behind Keith's.

Our descent into the warm hospitality of the Hepners' hexagonal home was a luxury and the night we spent with them in their hand-hewn house endorsed the innovative and industrious stamina this young couple possessed to survive the rigours of the Yukon year. The skin and head of an enormous grizzly pinned to one wall amply illustrated that danger was never very far away. The beast had been shot outside the front door of their home, 'just as in one of those stories', remarked Tobben! The next day they drove us to Elsa and onto Stewart Crossing where eventually we secured a lift to Dawson City.

Although we were joined by Peter for a three-day ski into the dramatic scenery of the Tombstones from North Fork, our adventure through the Yukon had culminated at the Hepners' cabin which was a fitting way to end a ski journey with a difference.

Before we returned to Whitehorse, Peter showed us the Klondyke and we visited the log cabin where that doyen of scribes of the north, Robert Service, composed his writing. He epitomised the ambience when he wrote:

> You may recall that sweep of savage splendour,
> That land that measures each man at his worth
> And feel in memory, half fierce, half tender,
> The brotherhood of men that know the North.

We had skied through that savage splendour and had joined that bond of brotherhood, that interdependence so necessary in such daunting remoteness and cold. We had been tested, often to extremes, and in the end we had been defeated by the spell of the Yukon.

We were better men and surer friends for the adventure done.

*   *   *

Closer to Home

At 8.00 am on the 6th May 1986 I drove up to the Cheviots with Bill Wright for a day's skiing. One thing I have learned about skiing in England is to regard a good snowfall as a gift-horse and never to look it in the mouth. The north of England and Scotland had been in the grip of a very snowy winter and here we were, still enjoying the legacy of it well into May. Spring was hardly evident with farmers and market gardeners cursing the hard frosts that persisted to bite into vulnerable new shoots and buds and destroy hopes of bumper yields.

Ten years ago it was rare to see cross-country skiers heading off into the hills but today the conversion of frustrated downhillers to the freedom of skiing in the hills without the aggravating competition for space, let alone the expense, is growing apace. Newcastle like many other cities in the country has a thriving club, Tyneside Loipers, and I have often seen club members making their weekend pilgrimages to the hills on the Scottish borders, to the forests of Kielder or the high moorland of Hexham Common. Further to the west, family groups launch up in to the Pennines from Kirkby Steven, Appleby, Alston and other places in Cumbria. To the north in Scotland, the clubs are thriving and skiers are now able to enjoy prepared ski tracks in the forests of Glen Isla, Clashandarroch and the Queen's Forest in Glenmore.

Bill Wright and I were entirely alone on our skis as we went over the peat hags, up past Windy Gyle to the steeper slopes that lead up to the summit tableland of Cheviot (815 metres). It was sunny and the wind was cold although it was at our backs as we followed the line of a stone wall to the top. During the long ski over to the summit cairn we passed the remains of a crashed aeroplane that protruded from the snow—just the skeleton of an undercarriage and a riveted piece of aluminium. Nearby was a lone hiker, tent and sleeping mat atop his rucksack and we skied over to him.

'Where are you heading?' asked Bill.

'Derbyshire,' the lad replied. 'Wish I had those things you are wearing!'

The lad was standing up to his knees in old snow and his deep footprints behind were ample evidence that it was hard going for him.

'Yeah, its a lot easier—you ought to get yourself a pair!'

'Yes I should' he acknowledged looking enviously towards Bill who had started to skate off up towards the summit cairn.

The descent from Cheviot was good skiing, as good as you would get anywhere, and like all descents it did not seem long enough. When we reached the car for the return to Newcastle the weather was already turning. The next day a mild south-westerly dumped an inch of rain over the north-east of England and when it blew itself out over the North Sea towards Norway there only remained small white streaks on Cheviot. It was as well we had seized the opportunity whilst conditions were good.

Most of my adventures so far have been dependent upon detailed planning, consultation, negotiation and teamwork often over a period of two or three years. Now I will illustrate some adventures that can be enjoyed closer to home and done more spontaneously. They are, however, adventures which by definition assume a level of experience in both skiing and mountain craft in winter-time.

The chance of good skiing in rural England is so rare that when it does come, it has to be seized quickly. I can recall the blizzard that struck the south-west of England in February 1978 and plunged the counties of Devon, Dorset and Somerset into a State of Emergency. Opportunism ruled completely and in their enthusiasm to get to work many people unearthed aged skis from the cobwebs of attics, cellars and cupboards under the stairs, whilst for me the blizzard provided that once-in-a-decade chance to get up on to Dartmoor and to do something more personally satisfying than delivering bales of hay to starving sheep! With the moor deep in snow I launched out on my own that weekend to try and traverse it from north to south. The Marines' 50-kilometre endurance test on the commando course was the obvious line to follow and apart from one or two variations to keep to high ground, it would take me to the edge of the south moor between Ivybridge and South Brent and within walking distance of the A38 Plymouth road.

At dawn a Land Rover dropped me at the cattle grid on the eastern edge of Okehampton Army camp after a circuitous journey down empty roads; empty because the state of emergency declared by the local authorities had urged people to stay at home while the chaos caused by the blizzard could be sorted out. I decided to use the old pair of Karhu racing skis with 3-pin bindings that I had bought in Finland before the 1975 World Ski Orienteering Championships, and I kept some cold fingers crossed that the

175

snow would be hard packed. On my shoulders I carried a small rucksack with a thermos and some food which I estimated would be adequate nourishment for a tour I reckoned would take 5–6 hours. Into it also went a selection of waxes. The weather was fine when I started with below freezing temperatures and very little wind, but a change was looming from the south-west.

The snow was hard packed and it was possible to diagonal gait along the line of the thin asphalted road that formed the access to the Army ranges. Within the hour I had reached the southernmost point on the road at Okement Hill where it turned west before heading north under High Willhays and Yes Tor to return to the Camp. From this point on it was wild moorland which, under nearly a metre of snow, was not unlike the countryside around Nordsaeter and Hornsjøen in Norway. Gone were the soggy, spongy bogs that characterise the centre part of the north moor; gone too was the thick heather that clung to the better-drained slopes. Apart from the black mass of Fernworthy Forest silhouetted against the sky to the south-east, the few things that broke the white landscape were the occasional stone walls that mark the borders of someone's grazing right, and the look-out huts atop Hangingstone and Whitehorse Hills.

Towards the end of the hour the wind increased, whipping up surface snow in small eddies. Behind, cloud had already enveloped High Willhays (621 metres), and Yes Tor. That familiar silent debate whether or not to turn back began as I grappled with equations of time, distance and conditions, and only ended when the southern horizon merged into a grey menacing sky. I turned and followed the circuit road back to Okehampton, disappointed at missing the opportunity of traversing the moor.

Dartmoor has not seen the same cover since that blizzard although it has been possible to do shorter tours on the higher parts of the north moor around the head-waters of the Rivers Teign and Taw. A circuit of Fernworthy Forest provided a good 15-kilometre trip two years later when Molly and I returned from a party up at Old Langworthy in the early hours of the morning. Thirty centimetres of new snow was lying on the ground and I scooped up a handful and threw it into the air. It floated down to earth as a light cascade of crystals sharpened by a temperature of at least $-3\,°C$. That confirmed that the opportunity was there. After arriving home in Bovey Tracey, I telephoned Andrew Higginson and asked if he would like to join me for a ski tour at dawn up at Fernworthy.

'For Christ's sake Sheridan, do you know what the time is?'

'Yes, are you coming or not?'

'Okay.'

'I'll pick you up at five o'clock—bye!'

Andy is no dwarf and I expected a cool reception from him when I rolled up to his front door before dawn. He had captained the Royal Navy Rugby XV for a couple of years in the mid-70s and his bulky frame was already dressed for the occasion, skis and sticks fastened together. We were unable to drive all the way up to the forest because the road was blocked. But that did not matter. After we had waxed up the skis we slid off up the road, over the final cattle grid by Yardworthy and onto open moorland.

In the half light of dawn we passed a small group of Dartmoor ponies huddled together in the lee of the wall and started climbing up towards White Ridge (504 metres) and beyond the stone circles of Grey Wethers which were protruding from the snow. There was little wind and we watched the sun rise as a great red orb which cast a crimson glow over the tors to our west and north. We must have skied for about three hours before returning to the car and we were home for lunch. It rained later the same afternoon and there was no sign of any snow at all the next day. It had been one of those days over which we were to enthuse for many a moon (and still do) but few people, save two long-suffering wives, would believe how good the conditions had been.

In total contrast to the nature of Dartmoor and the buffeting it gets in the winter from mild south-westerlies, and where escape in bad weather is relatively simple, are the Scottish mountains. Almost 7 degrees latitude further north, the game of ski touring there enters a different set of rules. But even if greater caution has to be exercised, it remains a paradise for the opportunist. Those who live and work in the Highlands couldn't be better placed to seize those opportunities as they arise. For most, however, it is through luck or coincidence that a chance becomes a fine thing.

One such chance arose in February 1987. High pressure was holding firm over central Scotland after a liberal coating of snow earlier in that week. At the time I was working in Ballater and my boss, a Major General, had been up to see us with one of his staff. Included in the General's itinerary was a day's relaxation at the weekend during which he wanted to do a ski tour. I gave Douglas Keelan a call and he and his wife, Sue, agreed to rendezvous with us at the Glenshee car park at eight o'clock in the morning. It was a Saturday and the vital thing, according to Douglas, was to get up there before the downhillers.

The queues for the ski lift up to Glas Maol (1,068 metres), had already begun to form when we arrived. We had a bit of a struggle to put Douglas' nine-month-old cocker spaniel into his rucksack for the ride up the final button lift, but once on the top we skied away and out of sight of the 'cesspit', as Douglas contemptuously called the downhill scene. It was a perfect day with the only cloud visible lying somewhere down over Blairgowrie to the south. The temperature was −3 °C, the sun was warming and with 4–5 centimetres of new snow on top of wind pack, conditions could not have been better.

The General had told us firmly that he was reversing his commanding role and the day's tour was between Douglas and myself to decide. So we agreed to ski the 5 kilometres over to Cairn of Claise (1,064 metres), use it as a warm-up, assess the conditions and work something out from there. (It is easier to agree than to disagree in these circumstances!) With a push we descended quickly to the col at the head of Caendochan Glen and then followed the ridge, alongside a wall and the remains of a fence, up to the Cairn. Sleeves had been rolled up, and sweat was beading off foreheads as we discussed 'where next'. We had lunch sitting in warm sunshine, but not entirely out of a chilly little wind, on the very edge of the Canness Burn, where it carved a deep cleft through the head wall of the Glen itself. It was a sheer drop to the floor of the Glen from the edge of the plateau that characterises the high land between Canness, at the top of Glen Isla, and Glen Doll to the east. I had neither seen nor experienced such fine conditions in Scotland although Douglas, Sue and I had completed the Cairngorm circuit six years before when we found good snow cover down to the 400-metre contour level as late as early April. (Sue had only been on cross-country skis once before that trip.)

After lunch we struck up over wide open snow fields to the small col between Ca Whims (905 metres), and Tom Buidhe (957 metres), to reach the summit of Tolmount (958 metres). Up there we met an alpine ski tourer and we discussed the merits of his and our ways of touring. There was no doubt that he had the edge over us on steeper downhill stretches but thereafter the heavy nature of his boots and alpine skis with touring bindings caused his single advantage to disappear.

We sped over the Knaps of Fafernie and up to Broad Cairn, with its splendid view to Loch Muick and the southern gentle slopes of Lochnagar (1,150 metres). We encountered several parties out for a stroll in the mountains and from each, received stares that seemed to acknowledge that there were better ways of getting around than on foot.

We returned to Tolmount contouring around its southern flank before skiing round the head wall buttresses of Glen Callater. We gained height a little as we topped the steep cliffs hanging over Loch Kander to reach the long flat summit of Cairn an Tuirc (1,019 metres) and the start of the descent to the Glen Shee–Braemar road. Here we tacked north-east on a gentle sloping spur before turning almost 180 degrees to reach the top of a long open slope broken only by the hulk of an old ski tow motor protruding from the snow. Below that, fast progress was hindered by breaking through the snow to the heather and a river crossing that turned into a balancing act on ice mushroomed rocks. This evolution was the last straw for the spaniel who was happy to retreat into the relative warmth of Douglas' rucksack for the final 3 kilometres to the road. It had been a wonderful day with Scotland at its best and as good as if not better than any 30-kilometre mountain ski tour in Scandinavia. Apart from the lone alpine ski tourer we had not encountered another cross-country skier throughout our highland wander. The weather changed during the night and reinforced, perhaps, the notion that occasionally a chance does become a very fine thing.

In contrast to the opportunism of the United Kingdom there exist those rather special parts of France, Switzerland and Germany where neither steepness of terrain nor the dangers of glaciers are a hindrance to the ski tourer. I am of course referring to the Massif Central, the Jura, the Black Forest, the Eiffel, the Bavarian Wald, the Hartz mountains, the Pyrenees (Spanish and French) and the Ardennes. All these, unlike Scotland, are guaranteed snow cover each winter and if careful analysis is made, are hardly more expensive to get to than Scotland is from the south of England. At the risk of opening the flood gates to a lesser known part of the Pyrenees the next few pages describe a six-day ski tour which required little effort to organise and only fitness to complete. It was based on our practice of going light and, in so doing, collecting a dump of food midway. That essential ingredient of enjoying the skiing and scenery without being under the burden of an overweight sack was forever in the forefront of our planning.

The few colour transparencies that I sent over to Erik Bochlke in Oslo towards the end of 1985 had encouraged him to gather up the support of Tobben Eggen and before long another two had joined the party—Tobben's 17-year-old son Kyrre and an old climbing friend of Erik's called Dag Dawes. I had met Dag several times in Oslo and earlier that winter on my way to north Norway for an exercise, had joined him and Erik for a night ski through Nordmarka. That particular 40-kilometre experience using halogen head torches was a new one for me and, according to Erik, was purely a warm-up for a 75-kilometre tour the next morning and a slightly shorter one of 60 kilometres the day after that. 175 kilometres within 40 hours couldn't have been better preparation he said, although my triceps and thigh muscles took a week to recover from the exertion.

The four Norwegians arrived in Toulouse having visibly enjoyed some complimentary Côtes du Rousillon on the flight down from Oslo. It did not take us long to pass through the centre of capitalism that is down-town Andorra and into the wild and empty mountain countryside of Sierra du Boumort in Spain. The Peugeot clattered up the steep twisting road sounding more like a Norwegian fishing boat than a 305 diesel car. Behind, a well-used Citroen Visa driven by François Remy, strained on its 1100-cc engine to draw Tobben and son up the hill and maintain some sort of station on us ahead.

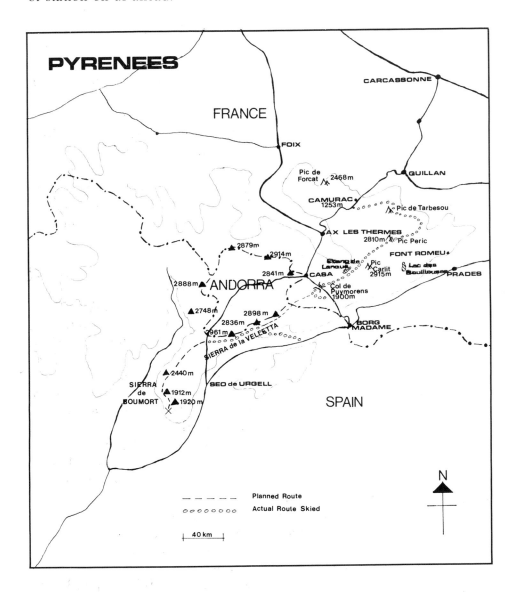

As we gained height that sunny frosty morning it wasn't difficult to notice that the snow that had been here at Christmas had disappeared.

'There's a lot more height to gain—there's sure to be some snow round the corner on the northern side', I said without the slightest confidence.

There was not a single glistening snow crystal visible in the sharp early morning sun as we pulled up onto our planned drop off place, 1,800 metres up on the south side of Sierra de Boumort, some 60 kilometres south-west of Seu d'Urgell. I feared the reaction of my Norwegian chums who had come a long way for this trip. But I had no reason to because a five-minute conference poring over a map spread over the bonnet of the car produced the answer.

We returned to Seu d'Urgell and drove to Arcabell, 1,142 metres up a twisting road on the Spanish side of the Andorran frontier. A short burst on foot for an hour soon found us on snow and we were away to follow the frontier ridge over Pic Negre (2,602 metres), and Pic Monturull (2,761 metres). The views across Andorra were wonderful and to the west the peaks of the Aigues Tortes National Park were overlooked beyond by the Maladeta (3,404 metres). The views were also a welcome diversion from the strain of trying to gain purchase on bone-hard snow. The effort was worth it because with waxable skies we would have been plagued by the problems of frequent reapplication of ice Klister. Once again our Åsnes no-wax skis were doing a good job.

From Pic Monturull we were unable to ski down the interconnecting ridge to Pic Peralita so we back-packed skis to scramble 50 metres down near-vertical rocks to gain steep snow fields at the head of the cwm to the Etangs de la Pera. After descending steeply, we had lunch in the sun beside the refuge and were rather horrified by the piles of rubbish and broken glass that the warm spring sunshine had revealed in profusion around the hut. We moved on and up to camp high just below Pic des Estanyons (2,836 metres), feeling the exertions of a long day unused to the thinner air.

The fickleness of that winter's precipitation in this part of the Pyrenees revealed itself for the second time the next morning. As we topped Pic des Estanyons and skied down towards the Portella de Setut, the snow disappeared and there was virtually no cover over on the Pic de la Portelleta (2,898 metres), where the frontier turned northwards. The decision was made for us; we had to descend south and move towards Bourge Madame and up to Porta, near the Col du Puymorens, to continue the line. Our frustration was heightened when we were stopped by gun-toting Spanish border police in the most unexpected place!

'Rien à déclarer!' 'Pas de problem!'

The next morning, after camping in a snowy field on the outskirts of Puymorens, we were off early to escape the hurly burly of thousands of downhillers. We collected our dump of food placed in the hotel on the Col du Puymorens by Molly and François on their return to Quillan after dropping us off at Arcabell. From there we had a chance to glance up the valley to the west of Porta down which we would have come had there been sufficient snow and it confirmed that the route from the frontier to the Col de Vall Civera and La Porteille Blanche would have been perfect.

From the Col du Puymorens we followed the line of a cart track that traverses the steep southern slopes of Serre des Lluuzes (2,618 metres), to the Col de Lanoux (2,468 metres). The bulk of Pic Carlit (2,921 metres) loomed above us and overlooked a glorious long descent to the Etang de Lanoux. The dam at its southern end stood clear and our own experience of regulated lakes in Norway told us to keep off the ice and take the longer way about its eastern shore before traversing up to the Porteille de la Grave at 2,420 metres. Descending, steep at first, then easing to that angle where again one was able to maintain balance and control without reducing speed, we dropped into the Val de la Grave where we camped beside a trickle of a stream.

It snowed during the night, but the dawn was cold and clear, the fifth day of sunny weather! Our progress up the slopes to the Etang de la Llose (2,238 metres), was watched by a couple of French Army helicopters which then buzzed off to do touch-point landings on the ridge of Pic Péric far above. Otherwise we were alone all day, through terrain reminiscent of parts of Sjødalen in the Jotunheim of Norway, to skirt the slopes of Pic de Terrès (2,540 metres), and descend into the top of the Val de Galbe.

The Porteille de Laurenti (2,410 metres), was too steep on its north side to attempt without ice axes, so we traversed down into the Val and camped early in warm sunshine. A steep climb the next morning, through forest initially and then open mountain, took us straight across the top of the ski runs of Puyvalador, a new resort near Les Angles. A damp mist shrouded our descent through pines draped in long lichen to the forest workers' refuge of Laurenti; it was a descent that was a test of our skill and required fast reactions to execute quick turns with little room to manoeuvre. The occasional four-letter expletive, Nordic and English, echoing through the mist was testimony that some reactions were not skilful enough.

That night we were camped in an idyllic meadow under Pic de Tarbésou (2,340 metres), with a black sky gathering from the west. It passed during the night, leaving behind a dusting of snow and a clear dawn with a sharp frost. The descent from the Col du Paillhères for the last 15 kilometres to Camurac went far beyond our expectations for a wonderful last day. We just missed Molly at Camurac where she and my daughter Peta had been enjoying some gentle pottering all day. It mattered little because there was plenty of cheap wine in the cafe and at the equivalent of 50p a litre, time passed rapidly until her return. We had skied about 180 kilometres in six days and had enjoyed warm sunny days on all but one of them. Also we had had the mountains to ourselves which was all the more remarkable in this most accessible part of the Pyrenees.

It is fair to assume that most British people who ski in Norway actually travel to that fabulous country to experience for themselves all the variety it offers. Whether on the high glaciers of the Jotunheim, in the forests of Hedmark, or the birch scrub of Lappland, the variety in the weather, which can change dramatically in minutes, demands that little extra bit of planning, and adds that extra bit of spice. It is not uncommon to be delayed by the weather or to find a bitterly cold easterly wind descending which sends overnight temperatures plumetting to $-30\,°C$, even in April. These and many other factors will influence the scope and nature of a ski tour, and can easily cause disappointment, as well as frustration.

I recall one January visit to the Jostedalsbraen with Doctor Ken Hedges in 1971 which ended in just such a disappointment. Ken, a doctor in the Army at the time who two years before had been with Wally Herbert's trans North Pole expedition, had agreed to travel up from Germany to join me for a ski ascent of Lodalskåpå (2,083 metres). This involved surmounting the Jostedalsbraen, crossing the icecap towards its eastern end and ascending the peak to return the way we had come. When we arrived in Jostedalen and checked into a small *pensjonat*, which boasted devastating views up to the Nygårdsbraen, Ken had a raw throat and a temperature. We reckoned the virus that gripped him would be clear in two or three days but in the meantime we agreed that I would ferry all the kit and food up to the snout of Fabergstolsbraen. I had been on this glacier the summer before and knew it to be a reasonably safe one for our approach onto the icecap itself. The ferrying task was leisurely and the 30-kilometre round trip was enjoyable on each of the two days that Ken sweated and shivered through his fever. On the third day Ken rose weakly from his bed and together we skied to the snout of the glacier only to find the weather turning against us when we arrived at the small tent. We waited in the tent for two days, time ran out and we retreated to the *pensjonat* for the long drive back to Oslo—disappointed yes, and certainly frustrated with everything having gone against us. But that is the name of the game for mountaineer or mountain ski-tourer alike and it is experiences such as these which make one appreciate, all the more, those excursions that go as planned.

If the notion of camping and all that is associated with camping does not appeal, then Norway has a unique alternative. Dotted throughout the mountains from north to south exist well-stocked and apportioned huts. Some are small and have no guardian. Others are more like hotels with staff to see to the needs of guests. Most of the huts are owned and run by the Norwegian Tourist Association or Local County Tourist organisations. However, some are privately owned and are run as commercial enterprises in the high skiing season and throughout the summer. (The cost of a bed reflects that.) Access to the unguarded huts is gained through membership of the Tourist Association which will provide a key that is common to all their doors. Possession of that key enables the ski tourer to pursue his own adventure in greater style and comfort. He is unlikely to have a hut to himself, however, especially in the latter part of the winter when late arrival may preclude his finding a bed. However, if he does he may have to spend three or four hours digging through drifts to reach the door and while there is certain to be a wood fire and fuel inside, it takes a long time for a half buried hut to heat up. My own preference is for a tent. Instantly warm when the cooker is lit, it provides that peace, freshness and solitude with a guarantee that you will enjoy a better night's rest than in a crowded hut where people are coming and going at all hours. Few will disagree that the mountains are at their best when they are empty so put up with the extra 3 kilos, get a tent and ski into those hills to see them as God made them.

Even at the height of the season, it is still possible to go to Norway, ski a healthy distance and not see another soul for days. And contrary to the belief of many, it is not so expensive to get there. Apex air fares, group discounts on trains, and use of public buses kept the travel cost of a 8-day excursion in April 1987 to a remoter part of Norway down to under £200. It was a long ski tour, 282 kilometres to be exact, and took no more than a few jottings on the back of a large envelope to organise. A telephone call to an isolated farm in a valley midway confirmed the arrival of a food parcel sent by post from Oslo and enabled us to enjoy our proven concept of fast and lightweight travel. From Umbukta on the Arctic Circle and on the Swedish/Norwegian border, we followed the frontier down to Nordli. We were in Børgerfjell National Park for three days which is a wild and spectacularly beautiful place with 1,700-metre peaks, glaciers hanging from their northern precipices, where the only company one is likely to have are small herds of reindeer. It was cold at night to be sure, $-20\,°C$, and that has to be expected at 66 °N, but some lunch stops saw chests and legs bared to the warm sun. We saw no other skiers and encountered only two groups of ice fishermen transported to their lonely patient vigil by snow scooters.

And so another winter passed by. A warning that it may be the last for two or three years was provided on the telephone when I returned home after that Easter ski tour.

'You can hang your skis up, you're off to Zimbabwe.' The Military Secretary in the Ministry said it with a finality that suggested that he was expecting a complaining riposte. I was delighted—but no more so than my long-suffering family. They are not surprised however, that skis and sticks are going to Africa with us nor that a pair of roller skis are on the shopping list for double poling or even skating around the boulevards of Harare. They know only too well that opportunities appear out of thin air. They had helped me pack my kit and equipment in April 1982 when I was despatched to South Georgia at the rush. Skis and sticks went together with all the other implements for a military operation. They too had seen the telgram sent by Nick Vaux, a Commanding Officer to his Second in Command, which read:

FROM: S.S. CANBERRA
TO: H.M.S. ANTRIM
FOR SHERIDAN FROM VAUX

VERY MANY THANKS FOR YOUR WELCOME SIGNAL THAT WE WERE SO PROUD TO RECEIVE. ALL RANKS HERE SEND CONGRATULATIONS ON YOUR SUCCESS ACHIEVED IN DAUNTING CIRCUMSTANCES. WHEN WE HAVE SORTED OUT THE REST OF THE SOUTH ATLANTIC WE LOOK FORWARD TO A SPECTACULAR 42 COMMANDO REUNION. DID YOU HAVE THE RIGHT WAX?

Nick Vaux knew that skis were with us but was not to know we did not use them to recapture the island from Argentina. However, had the opportunity been there, their use was certainly an option even if only for garrison duties and relaxation thereafter.

I started this final chapter suggesting that when opportunity knocks, answer it positively. Skis are going to Zimbabwe with me in pursuit of that maxim. It snows in the Drakensberg; Kilimanjaro is a stone's throw north and it would be fun to go up there to try and unearth the pair of skis Odd used to keep up by the summit crater. Anyway, without a pair, a positive response to a half-expected telegram from my Norwegian friends to join them in Turkey, Afghanistan, Baffin Island, Spiti or wherever would not be possible.